T0316066

CONSTRUCTIVE
FEMINISM

CONSTRUCTIVE FEMINISM

Women's Spaces and Women's Rights in the American City

DAPHNE SPAIN

CORNELL UNIVERSITY PRESS

Ithaca and London

First published 2016 by Cornell University Press
First printing, Cornell Paperbacks, 2016

Printed in the United States of America

Library of Congress Cataloging-in-Publication Data

Names: Spain, Daphne, author.
Title: Constructive feminism : women's spaces and
    women's rights in the American city / Daphne Spain.
Description: Ithaca : Cornell University Press, 2016. |
    Includes bibliographical references and index.
Identifiers: LCCN 2015038567 | ISBN 9780801453199
    (cloth : alk. paper) | ISBN 9781501703201 (pbk. : alk.
    paper)
Subjects: LCSH: Feminism—United States—History—
    20th century. | Women's rights—United States—
    History—20th century. | Public spaces—United
    States—History—20th century. | Urban women—
    United States—History—20th century. | Women
    and city planning—United States—History—20th
    century. | Feminism and architecture—United States. |
    Feminist geography—United States.
Classification: LCC HQ1421 .S6753 2016 | DDC
    305.42097309/04—dc23
LC record available at http://lccn.loc.gov/2015038567

Cornell University Press strives to use environmentally responsible suppliers and materials to the fullest extent possible in the publishing of its books. Such materials include vegetable-based, low-VOC inks and acid-free papers that are recycled, totally chlorine-free, or partly composed of nonwood fibers. For further information, visit our website at www.cornellpress.cornell.edu.

Cloth printing   10 9 8 7 6 5 4 3 2 1
Paperback printing   10 9 8 7 6 5 4 3 2 1

For Steven

Proposed Equal Rights Amendment to the US Constitution

"Equality of rights under the law shall not be denied or abridged by the United States or by any State on account of sex."

1923: First introduced in Congress by Alice Paul of the National Woman's Party
1972: Passed both houses of Congress; sent to states for ratification
1982: Ratification failed, three states short of the required thirty-eight states

"If you pick up any constitution written since 1950, any place in the world, there will be a provision on the equal citizenship stature of men and women. It's not in our constitution. I would like to see a statement of women's full citizenship in the constitution on par with our freedom of speech, freedom of religion. It's a basic tenet of our society."

—Supreme Court Justice Ruth Bader Ginsburg, September 12, 2014, presentation at George Washington University, Washington, DC

Contents

Preface

               In 1975 the filmmaker Sheila Ruth directed and coproduced a video titled *Constructive Feminism*. In it she documented the renovation of a three-story abandoned warehouse on Spring Street in Los Angeles that was to become the second home of the Woman's Building.[1] (See figure 1.) The organization's first home, and the organization itself, came about as a result of the Los Angeles County Museum of Art's 1970 exhibition *Art and Technology*, which included only male artists. The artist Judy Chicago, the graphic designer Sheila Levrant de Bretteville, and the architectural historian Arlene Raven were outraged. They fought back by establishing, three years later, the first Woman's Building on Grandview Avenue. Its purpose was to serve as "a public center for women's culture"; the name was chosen to honor the Woman's Building at the 1893 World's Columbian Exposition in Chicago. Aware that much of women's contribution to the arts had been lost to history, the founders, intent on nurturing women's "insurgent muse," were determined to resurrect it.[2]

The renovated building on Spring Street housed the Feminist Studio Workshop, galleries for women's art, a print shop, a branch of Sisterhood Bookstore, offices, and a restaurant. The entire third floor was an open space where hundreds of lesbians once held a Dyke of Your Dreams Day dance to celebrate Valentine's Day. In 1978 members of the Feminist Studio Workshop hoisted a thirteen-foot-high papier-mâché-and-concrete model of a nude woman to the roof as one of a series of sculptures created by the author Kate Millett while she was an artist in residence. Before the Building closed in 1991, Adrienne Rich, Rita Mae Brown, Ntozake Shange, and many other emerging artists had read their new works to enthusiastic audiences.[3]

The Woman's Building and the title of the documentary capture the spirit of this book. I wanted to find ways in which the mid-twentieth century feminist movement known as the Second Wave created new uses for urban space in order to nurture women's growing autonomy. Art spaces were one example, but more common were the women's centers, bookstores, health clinics, and domestic violence shelters that appeared for the first time in the early 1970s. In remembering her days as a staff member at the Woman's Building, the performance artist Terry Wolverton acknowledged that she

FIGURE 1. The Woman's Building, 1727 North Spring Street, Los Angeles (2010). Drawing by Reed Gyovai Muehlman based on a photo by the author.

once thought "the physical architecture was of no consequence . . . that the walls, scarred floors, the girders connecting one story to the next . . . were just square footage, a pile of red bricks." But she came to understand that the first building, the physical one made of bricks, was "intrinsically the foundation for the second—that grander, gleaming manse of your imagination—their visions dependent on one another, joined at the heart."[4] This book is about how feminists transformed the walls and scarred floors of ordinary buildings into extraordinary material embodiments of women's rights.

When I was in Los Angeles in early 2010, I watched *Constructive Feminism* with Adele Wallace, the cofounder of Sisterhood Bookstore; Kit Kollenberg, the cofounder of the Silver Lake People's Playgroup; and their longtime friend Mary Tyler. My companions mentioned the time that Angela Davis attracted hundreds of women to a reading, and that the comedian Lily Tomlin and the authors Anaïs Nin and Alice Walker had made appearances. But what they remembered with the greatest delight was the New Miss Alice Stone Ladies Society Orchestra that played on the top floor while hundreds of women danced all night. Adele, Kit, and Mary brought the Woman's Building to life for me. In this book I have tried, through their stories and those of other pioneering feminists, to convey that same vitality.

During all that feminist activity on the West Coast, I was in college on the East Coast. There, the goal of the women's movement seemed simple: to create a society in which women and men had equal rights. I read Betty

Friedan's *The Feminine Mystique* (published in 1963), joined a campus consciousness-raising group, and became a certified feminist. When I arrived
at graduate school in 1972, I immediately found a women's support group.
Our Bodies, Ourselves (1971), created by members of the Boston Bread and
Roses collective, was our Bible. Although I did not realize it at the time, I was
destined to become part of Friedan's reform branch of the movement rather
than part of the radical activist branch represented by Bread and Roses.

All of us were white, and while we lamented that lack of racial diversity, we spent more time talking about the emerging rifts in the movement
between straight and lesbian women. Day care was a problem for only one
member, a single mother; the rest of us were childless and intended to stay
that way for the immediate future. Thus we had endless debates about the
safest and most reliable forms of contraception. We celebrated the passage
of *Roe v. Wade*. We were angered by statistics about the scarcity of women
among professionals (including college faculty). We all wore the National
Organization for Women's "59 cents" button symbolizing the prevailing
ratio of women's to men's earnings.

Not once in all those years do I remember talking about the spatial effects
of the women's movement. Abortion clinics did not exist pre–*Roe v. Wade*;
finding doctors who would perform illegal abortions conjured back alleys.
As women's health clinics and shelters for victims of domestic violence began
to appear, we were more interested in the services they provided than in the
actual spaces. I realize now, after more than two decades spent studying the
relationship between space and gender, how women's rights were tied inex-
tricably to the places created by Second Wave feminists.[5] They were made
by and for women, and autonomy from men was central to their identity.

Feminist places were voluntary. This distinguishes them from the spatial
segregation described in *Gendered Spaces* (University of North Carolina Press,
1992), where I argued that the mandatory segregation of men from women
in homes, schools, and workplaces lowered women's status by reducing their
access to knowledge. The key word here is *mandatory*. When women have no
choice—when their separation from men is involuntary—their status suffers.
I focused on sex segregation at the scale of the building and discussed women's
historical exclusion from "masculine" schools and workplaces.

In *How Women Saved the City* (University of Minnesota Press, 2001),
I moved my focus to the urban scale to examine new spaces created by
women's voluntary associations in the late nineteenth century. Based on religious ideologies, the YWCA, the Salvation Army, the College Settlements
Association, and the National Association of Colored Women's Clubs created places on behalf of others. Hundreds of settlement houses, vocational

schools, and boarding homes became what I termed "redemptive places" that protected single women, African Americans, and European immigrants from the dangers of the industrializing city. They also saved the city from the chaos accompanying the onslaught of so many newcomers.

With this book, my emphasis is on *voluntarily* gendered spaces, also at the urban scale, that were established by US feminists in the mid-twentieth century to meet women's needs. Unlike redemptive places fueled by the Social Gospel or evangelical zeal, feminist places created by radical activists were decidedly secular. Women's centers were among the first; they served as incubators of autonomy that strengthened women's resolve to demand political and social change. Centers, in turn, spun off feminist bookstores, feminist health clinics, and domestic violence shelters. Second Wave feminists enhanced women's rights to full citizenship by adapting existing urban spaces to new uses. They differed from Dolores Hayden's "material feminists" of the nineteenth century, who led a "grand domestic revolution" to collectivize unpaid household labor.[6] Material feminists created spaces to simplify routine housework; Second Wave radical activists constructed places that promoted women's engagement in the public sphere.

Numerous historians have revealed the role of women as city builders during the late nineteenth century,[7] while others have focused on women's participation in the public sphere.[8] Scholars have also reassessed the organization and accomplishments of the Second Wave.[9] The historian Anne Enke's study of the origins of the women's movement includes some of the same places I discuss, but she emphasizes their importance for expanding the feminist movement and celebrating its lesbian activism.[10] In contrast, this book is about the Second Wave as a social movement with spatial consequences for all women and for the city. Social movements generate unintentional as well as deliberate change, however, and the women's movement has been no exception. Repurposed buildings that helped women enter the workplace have given way to vast landscapes of franchises that deliver services women once provided. Meals and child care have been steadily shifted from the privacy of the home to the public realm of purpose-built facilities.

I write as much about radical activists as about the buildings they transformed. The buildings already existed; the founders imbued them with new meaning. As the architectural historian Abigail Van Slyck points out, buildings are the sum of social processes occurring in specific cultural settings.[11] Feminist places were exactly that: products of the multiple urban movements for social justice that took place during the 1960s and 1970s. The activists who created them had roots in the New Left and Black Power movements and embraced a feminist consciousness in addition to their other political identities. A hallmark of this ideology was the rejection of a hierarchical power structure in favor of collective decision-making. Thus the modifications that transformed the buildings were based on consensus among founders rather than on negotiations with professional designers.

Throughout the book, I have relied on interviews, organizational documents, newspaper archives, and secondary sources.[12] Some sources, like Robin Morgan's *Sisterhood Is Powerful* (1970), were products of the time, and I have treated them as primary material. Kirsten Grimstad's and Susan Rennie's *The New Woman's Survival Catalog* (1973) and *The New Woman's Survival Sourcebook* (1975) were valuable guides.[13] When possible I supplemented historical records by interviewing pioneering activists in Boston and Los Angeles, many of whom are included in Barbara Love's *Feminists Who Changed America, 1963–1975.*[14]

The information I gathered came from the founders, not clients. Most founders disliked the concept of "clients" and tried to minimize the distance between themselves and the women they served. Women who attended meetings at women's centers, for example, could join the core governing committee simply by volunteering for more work. Students attending liberation schools could become teachers once they learned the material. My focus is on the grassroots radicals who created feminist places. After reading this book, critics may charge that I have been too celebratory, too uncritical of their achievements. So be it. My research has led me to admire the women whose contributions to the Second Wave never generated the headlines accorded to Betty Friedan and Gloria Steinem. This book will not make these activists comparably famous, but it will validate their centrality to achieving rights for women.[15]

I began my interviews in the summer of 2009 with the founding members of Somerville's RESPOND domestic violence shelter. RESPOND's executive director, Jessica Brayden, introduced us and granted me access to the organization's uncatalogued archives. I spent January through March of 2010 in Los Angeles, talking with Carol Downer, the cofounder of the Los Angeles Feminist Women's Health Center; Simone and Adele Wallace, the founders of Sisterhood Bookstore; and Sherna Berger Gluck, of the Westside Women's Center. In the fall of 2013 I spoke with Carol Seajay, who started the Old Wives' Tales Bookstore in San Francisco and the *Feminist Bookstore Newsletter*, and Gilda Bruckman, an original partner at New Words Bookstore in Boston.[16]

I chose Boston and Los Angeles for maximum contrast. Boston is an older city, where feminist activities were centered in the urban core around Cambridge and Somerville. Los Angeles is younger with a more diffuse form of development; its feminist places were scattered across the metropolitan area. Although New York City and Chicago were among the earliest hotbeds of feminism, Boston and Los Angeles also had national reputations. *Sisterhood Is Powerful* listed the Bread and Roses collective in Boston and the Women's Center in Los Angeles as sources of information for women's liberation.[17] And in a study about the women's movement for the Russell Sage Foundation, Maren Carden identified Boston and Los Angeles as the cities where feminists were publishing newsletters with significant national circulation: Boston's *No More Fun and Games* and *Female Liberation*, and the Los Angeles Women's Center newsletter, *Sister*, which reached nearly three thousand readers in January 1972.[18]

In August 1968 feminists from both cities attended the first national women's liberation conference in Sandy Spring, Maryland.[19] According to Susan Brownmiller's *In Our Time: Memoir of a Revolution* (1999), "Boston was seething with small liberation groups in 1969." Cell 16, named after a member's house at 16 Lexington Avenue in Cambridge, was the face of Boston in the national movement. Founded by Roxanne Dunbar, Dana Densmore, and Betsy Warrior, Cell 16 inspired the formation of the socialist-feminist collective Bread and Roses. Dunbar had been a doctoral student at UCLA before moving to Boston, laying the groundwork for future connections between the two cities.[20]

Activists from these cities had numerous contacts with each other. Jeanne Córdova, who founded the Los Angeles magazine *Lesbian Tide* in 1971, remembered Boston as the "core feminist hub" responsible for the "birth of feminism." *Lesbian Tide* regularly published news from the Cambridge Women's Center. In Córdova's opinion, theory came from the East Coast, where feminists read and wrote more, while physical place-making occurred in Los Angeles. In addition, Los Angeles feminists, or at least lesbian feminists, had significant financial backing from the movie industry. The influence of a large Jewish population's support of the counterculture was another factor that allowed Los Angeles to "buil[d] whole maps' worth of institutions not possible elsewhere."[21] Figure 2, a reproduction of the graphic artist Shirl Buss's drawing for the January 1976 issue of *Sister* newsletter, illustrates Córdova's point.

My method for studying feminist places involves what the American studies scholar Thomas Schlereth calls "above-ground archaeology." Like their colleagues who work below ground, those who study existing buildings use material objects and physical sites as primary evidence of human behavior. Ordinary buildings are particularly amenable to above-ground archaeology. To interpret

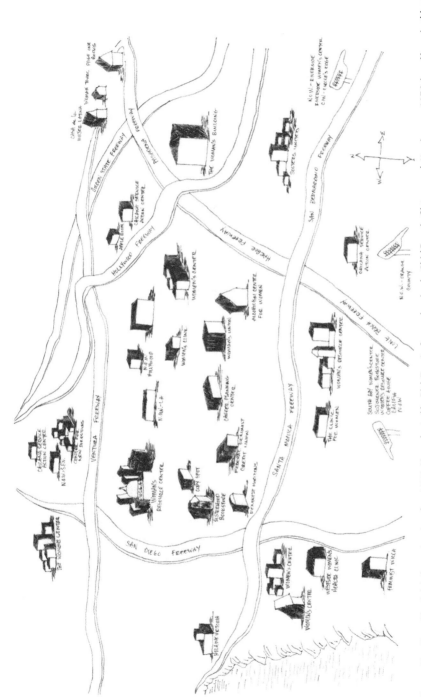

FIGURE 2. Map of feminist places, Los Angeles, 1976. Map adapted by Bich Tran Le from a drawing by Shirl Buss in *Sister* newsletter, January 1976. June Mazer Lesbian Archives, Los Angeles, CA. Redrawn by Reed Gyovai Muehlman.

them properly, one must pay attention to what has been added, removed, or never completed.[22] I traveled to all of the places I have written about here with the exception of domestic violence shelters in Boston. Trips to Boston and Los Angeles enabled me to gain a sense of the energy of the Cambridge Women's Center, which is still operating, and of the desolate interior space of Sisterhood Bookstore, which is not. The first feminist health clinic in Los Angeles, now defunct, is the office for a used-car lot in what has become Koreatown. Relying on photographs, floor plans, interviews, and archives, I have attempted to reconstruct what those buildings were originally like and how they fit into the surrounding cultural landscape.

Much of this place-making is more than fifty years old. Betty Friedan's *The Feminine Mystique* was published in 1963, and 2013 marked the fortieth anniversary of *Roe v. Wade*; *Our Bodies, Ourselves* turned forty in 2011. The year 2015 was the fiftieth anniversary of *Griswold v. Connecticut*, the Supreme Court decision that legalized contraception for married couples on the ground of a married couple's right to privacy. Battles over women's reproductive rights are still raging. In June 2014 the Supreme Court decision *Burwell v. Hobby Lobby* ruled that privately held companies have the right to deny contraceptive coverage to women if it violates the owners' religious beliefs.[23]

In August 2014 Supreme Court Justice Ruth Bader Ginsburg observed that the Court has been more supportive of gay rights than of rights for women. She cited as evidence its rulings protecting private sexual behavior for gays, while undermining equal pay, medical leave, and access to abortion and contraception for women.[24] On June 26, 2015, the Supreme Court confirmed Justice Ginsburg's assessment with its decision to legalize same-sex marriage. The Harvard historian Jill Lepore, observing that gay marriage was legalized on the fiftieth anniversary of *Griswold v. Connecticut*, points out a troubling difference between the two decisions: "When the fight for equal rights for women narrowed to a fight for reproductive rights, defended on the ground of privacy, it weakened. But when the fight for gay rights became a right for same-sex marriage, asserted on the ground of equality, it got stronger and stronger."[25] Women are still fighting for equality.

This book resurrects early feminist victories, both the famous and the forgotten, by highlighting the importance of space in feminists' struggles to establish their rights. Supreme Court Justices Ginsburg, Elena Kagan, and Sonia Sotomayor—and Sandra Day O'Connor before them—gained entry to the Court's chambers thanks to First and Second Wave feminists' demands to occupy previously all-male spaces. The radical New York City collective Redstockings has an apt slogan for this project: "Building on what's been won by knowing what's been done."[26]

Acknowledgments

Writing the acknowledgments provides an opportunity to ponder just how many people, in addition to the author, are involved in producing a book, and just how long it takes to accomplish the finished product. The first phase of my fieldwork began in 2009 in Boston. I wanted to find out more about places created by feminists during the Second Wave, but I had not yet defined which ones, or how they fit into my career-long interest in space and women's status. So I started with the Schlesinger Library at the Radcliffe Institute for Advanced Study. There, the librarians Sarah M. Hutcheon and Lynda Leahy introduced me to archives of local chapters of the National Organization for Women (NOW), Betty Friedan's papers, and the radical collective Bread and Roses, which had occupied a Harvard building in 1971 to form the first women's center. The library's collection included records for the Cambridge Women's Community Health Center and information on Boston's first domestic violence shelters, Transition House and RESPOND. I also learned that Boston was home to New Words, one of the earliest and most long-lived feminist bookstores. I now had my places: women's centers, bookstores, health clinics, and domestic violence shelters. These gave material presence to women's growing rights.

As I was reaching the end of my stay, one of the librarians mentioned that she knew the Executive Director of RESPOND, Jessica Brayden. Jessica was more than cooperative and ready to talk about the history of her organization; she also introduced me to the original members: Mary Ann Gallo, Deborah Gavin, Jean Marie Luce, Marie Siraco, and Maureen Varney. I was transfixed by their recollections, realizing that I was listening to women who had made history. A paper I wrote based on that initial research was published in *Frontiers: A Journal of Women Studies*.[27] In *How Women Saved the City* (University of Minnesota Press, 2001), I had written about places created by women in the nineteenth century. Everything I knew about them I had learned from archives and secondary sources. Now I was talking to the women I was writing about. It was a heady experience.

In preparation for the next phase of fieldwork in Los Angeles in 2010, I looked up feminist places similar to those in Boston; I arrived in the city expecting to conduct archival research at UCLA on West Coast feminism. However, I spent more time outside libraries than within them. Three pioneering feminists led me in that direction. One was Adele Wallace, whom I traced through the (now defunct) website for Sisterhood Bookstore; her sister-in-law and cofounder Simone Wallace; and Carol Downer, whom I called after reading about her work with the first feminist health clinic. Carol's assistant, Aracely Hernandez, was consistently helpful throughout my time in Los Angeles, and beyond.

While in Los Angeles, I lived for three months with my friend and former coauthor Suzanne Bianchi, who had recently joined the sociology faculty at UCLA. Suzanne listened to my stories of the feminists I interviewed and encouraged my pursuit of qualitative research methods despite her own grounding in quantitative demographic methods. When Suzanne died of pancreatic cancer in 2013, I was even more grateful for those months we had together.

My office in Los Angeles was provided by Kathleen McHugh, director of the Center for the Study of Women at UCLA. Kathleen arranged my position as visiting scholar and introduced me to students who had conducted research on Second Wave feminism in the city. Through them I learned of Michelle Moravec's UCLA undergraduate honors thesis, "In Their Own Time: Voices from the Los Angeles Feminist Movement, 1967–1976." I depended on her thesis, and on Michelle, for insights into early activists and their accomplishments. The footnotes reveal my debts to her scholarship.

Los Angeles was flush with archival resources. Jeanne Roberts of the Getty Research Institute told me about the video that provided the title of this book. Carol Wells and Joy Novak at the Center for the Study of Political Graphics gave me full access to their holdings; Joy also regularly forwarded information on the local lesbian and gay communities of the era, including some of her own work. Angela Brinskele, the director of communications for the June Mazer Lesbian Archives, led me to back issues of *Sister* magazine, one of which contained the 1976 map of feminist places in Los Angeles. The Mazer's shelves were full of periodicals and memorabilia from the 1970s. Angela helped me navigate the collection while telling great stories from the heyday of activism. Sue Maberry, director of the library and instructional design at Otis College of Art and Design, helped me find materials on the Woman's Building.

Numerous other people in Los Angeles contributed directly or indirectly to this project. Kit Kollenberg drove me around town to see many of the places I was studying, and some I wasn't, like the Silver Lake People's Playgroup she and others founded; she showed me the original two-car garage where they started their free day-care program. I spoke at length with Marie Kennedy, who had been one of only a few female architecture students in the Harvard Graduate School of Design when the building take-over occurred in Cambridge in 1971. She referred me to Marsha Steinberg, with whom I had several conversations about her memories of the take-over. Jeanne Córdova, founder of *Lesbian Tide*, invited me to her home for an extensive interview. I also talked with Sherna Berger Gluck, of the Westside Women's Center; and Sondra Hale and Ronni Sanlo, who shared information about UCLA's sponsorship of the first women's center. Joanne Parrent, the founder of the Feminist Federal Credit Union in Detroit (and a private investigator in Los Angeles when I interviewed her), gave me the background on a spatial institution I ultimately decided against including in the project. Feminist credit unions were scarce compared with the number of other types of places.

Everyone I have mentioned was instrumental in helping me develop the ideas at the core of this book. As I rewrote the first draft, I had the opportunity to talk with Gilda Bruckman and Rochelle Ruthchild, who opened New Words Bookstore in Boston. Gilda and Rochelle directed me to Carol Seajay, the founder and editor of the *Feminist Bookstore Newsletter*. I also spoke with Demita Frazier, an original member of the African American Combahee River Collective in Boston. Kathie Crivelli of the University of Massachusetts Amherst's Center for Women and Community sent me a history of that organization.

I conducted research and had time to write thanks to a sabbatical from the University of Virginia. Barbie Selby, research manager and documents librarian at the University of Virginia, helped from start to finish with city directories and maps. Sonia Gibson Lyons checked the citations. Students who assisted me over the years include Elisa Cooper, Dominique Lockhart, Bich Tran Le, Andrew Pompeii, Elizabeth van der Els, Cindy Xin, and Chelsea Zhou. Former students produced the images: Reed Gyovai Muehlman rendered the exquisite drawings that illustrate the feminist places, Lucas Lyons created the geographic information systems maps identifying the location of places nation-wide, and Bich Tran Le modified the 1976 map of feminist places in Los Angeles.

I am indebted to several people for reading various drafts of the work and encouraging me to complete the book. Bob Beauregard takes writing seriously and helped improve my prose considerably. My editor, Michael McGandy, had faith in the project from its earliest stages until its completion. Thanks to Michael and two anonymous reviewers, the book is much improved from its original version. Colleagues who invited me to present my work at Columbia University, Washington University in St. Louis, the University of Cincinnati, and in Rome provided useful feedback along the way.

Two other people deserve mention, although their important contributions are missing from the final product. Joan E. Biren (JEB), the professional photographer and original member of Washington, DC's, The Furies, searched her extensive collection of images of feminist events from the 1970s on my behalf. My sister, the photographer Marsha Spain Fuller, took pictures of the places in Los Angeles that were the basis for Reed's drawings. I owe them apologies for not being able to include their excellent work. My eyes were bigger than my production budget.

Finally, this book would have been impossible without continued contact with and support from Carol Downer and Simone Wallace. They have been involved since we first met in Los Angeles in 2010. We have seen each other several times since and have talked and e-mailed frequently. I greatly admire their accomplishments and continued commitment to feminist issues. If I had to name the most valuable consequence of this project, it would be their friendship.

Introduction
Spatial Consequences of the Second Wave

Anyone driving in the American suburbs soon encounters regional shopping malls, commercial strips, office parks, and endless franchises offering food, clothing, exercise, and auto parts. The contemporary suburbs are dotted with retail establishments that each provide parking and serve the car-dependent public. And while we might lament the sprawl and traffic congestion, we seldom view this landscape as gendered. What we are seeing, though, is a reflection of the different roles and identities of women and men. McDonald's and Kentucky Fried Chicken are not gender neutral. Because they sell meals once prepared by women at home, fast-food restaurants essentially function as surrogates for women now in the labor force. KinderCare and La Petite Academy mind the children, while adult day services tend to the elderly. These facilities proliferated during the 1970s and 1980s as more and more women joined the labor force. As the world of paid jobs was expanding due to women's presence, the sphere of unpaid care work was contracting due to their absence.

Observing the city through a gendered lens also reveals buildings associated with traditional masculine work. Jiffy Lube, Meineke Car Care Centers, and AutoZone relieve men of responsibility for keeping the car running; Lowe's sells lumber, tools, and paint for repairs. In the hierarchy of needs, though, transportation and home maintenance rank rather low. If every auto repair shop disappeared tomorrow, the consequences for daily life would be less dramatic than if all fast-food restaurants suddenly vanished. Besides, the majority of men have always been employed. The story for women is much different. Most of them entered the labor force after World War II.[1] Thus women's employment is intertwined with post–World War II metropolitan development.

In this chapter, I lay out the central argument of the book: The Second Wave, a social movement dedicated to reconfiguring power relations between women and men, had both deliberate and unintended spatial consequences. I briefly review the unanticipated consequences visible today as sites of women's work: fast-food restaurants and day-care facilities for children and the elderly. I then return to the main story of the 1970s, when feminists intentionally changed the use of urban space in two ways. Reform feminists used the legal system to end the mandatory segregation of women and men in public institutions, while radical activists created small-scale places that gave women the confidence to claim their rights to the public sphere. Women's centers, bookstores, health clinics, and domestic violence shelters established feminist places for women's liberation. Both gender-integrated and women-only spaces were necessary to improve women's rights but insufficient to maintain them. For that, spaces that provide substitutes for domestic labor are critical.

An emphasis on social movements, and gender, challenges standard explanations for decentralized patterns of urban development. Typically, these latter accounts focus on the shift from industrial production located in the central city to consumption of services distributed throughout the metropolitan area. Restructuring of the formal economy did more than move jobs out of the city and into the suburbs, though; it was accompanied by the spatial restructuring of women's care work. Economic restructuring transformed women's unpaid labor by taking it out of the home and moving it into the public realm of freestanding buildings.

In the US city, the government typically creates the legal and physical infrastructure, while the private sector produces most of the capital necessary for development. Yet social relations also shape cities. For much of history, gender relations that relegated women to the private spaces of the home and men to the public spaces of political and economic activity were ubiquitous. Just as zoning laws separated land uses, gender relations established separate spheres for women and men. For the two decades following World War II, the majority of middle-class white women stayed at home in the feminine suburbs to take care of their children, while their husbands went to work in the masculine city.[2]

This pattern became the norm despite the fact that women had begun to enter formerly all-male jobs during World War II. In 1940 only about one-quarter of US women were in the labor force; by 1950, one-third of women were working for pay. It was the largest percentage-point increase in women's labor force history. Women took jobs previously performed by men because the war effort demanded it, making Rosie the Riveter the symbol of women's physical and economic strength. But once the soldiers returned, men reclaimed their jobs and most women went back home. Some women sought clerical or teaching jobs, of course, and their labor force participation rates rose slightly, but the next decade in which women's employment increased significantly was the 1970s. By 1980 the majority of women were in the labor force.[3]

This other uptick in women's paid work was accelerated not by a war but by the women's movement of the 1960s and 1970s.[4] Although Second Wave feminism did not cause women to seek employment, it facilitated the development of an educated workforce ready to take the clerical and administrative jobs for which women were in increasingly high demand. Women were able to move into the labor force because, for the first time, motherhood was optional. Prior to the 1960s, due to lack of both information about and access to birth control, women had little control over their own fertility. When The Pill arrived on the market in 1960 it was greeted with great fanfare, but it did not become legally available until the 1965 Supreme Court decision *Griswold v. Connecticut* overturned laws in thirty states that prohibited the sale and advertisement of contraceptives to married couples; another Supreme Court decision in 1972 extended the right to contraceptive use to the unmarried.[5] The fact that so many women used The Pill before it was legal speaks to their determination to plan their pregnancies. And before *Roe v. Wade* in 1973, abortion was illegal or extremely difficult to obtain. Legal contraception and abortion allowed women to decide when, or if, they wanted to become mothers. For the first time, women had the freedom to pursue college degrees or full-time employment without the risk of interruptions due to unwanted pregnancies.

Early feminists recognized the inextricable relationship between women's equality and employment outside the home. According to the economist Margaret Benston's 1969 article, "The Political Economy of Women's Liberation," the enormous amount of unpaid household labor performed by women is devalued because society is organized to reward only paid employment: "In a society in which money determines value, women are a group who work outside the money economy. Their work is not worth money, is therefore valueless, and is therefore not even real work. . . . In structural terms, the closest thing to the condition of women is the condition of others who are or were also outside of commodity production, i.e., serfs and peasants."[6]

Benston predicted that working outside the home would fail to establish equality for women as long as household work remained a matter of private production and primarily the woman's responsibility. A precondition for women's liberation, she argued, required transferring private production into the paid economy. When child care, food preparation, and laundry were publicly provided, discrimination against women would evaporate. But prevailing conditions would be difficult to change: "true equality in job opportunity is probably impossible without freedom from housework, and the industrialization of housework is unlikely unless women are leaving the home for jobs."[7] Less than one-half of women were in the labor force when Benston's radical analysis was published.[8] Yet she anticipated a Catch-22 that would vex families and policy makers for decades.

Socialist-feminists like Benston expected that, after the revolution in sex roles, the government would industrialize housework. That never happened. Instead, the nearly three-quarters of wives and mothers in the labor force in the early twenty-first century depend on a mix of private, nonprofit, and government providers to cover domestic responsibilities.[9] Part of the sexual revolution depended on men taking over a share of domestic work, but men's behavior has changed too slowly to meet the daily needs of employed women.[10] Women's higher labor force participation therefore contributed to the increasing demand for outsourced services, and women's ability to earn more depended in part on their ability to pay for services they once performed. For every meal preparation or child-care task taken out of the home, a new business has emerged to provide it. Feminists could never have anticipated the staggering number of new buildings these businesses spawned. But they have become a crucial link in a self-reinforcing loop for middle-class employed women. Working-class women, in contrast, are filling the low-wage service jobs on which the middle class depends. The majority of employees performing domestic tasks are still women. Many of them are immigrants and/or women of color, and their work is still undervalued.[11]

Twenty-First Century Sites of Women's Work

Food is the most basic of all needs. Everyone has to eat, but the manner in which people in the United States take their meals has changed considerably since the 1950s. Families ate at home when husbands earned the only income. Once women entered the labor force, they had less time to cook. Meal preparation, in fact, is the most time-consuming task that women perform, followed by shopping for meals and cleaning up after them.[12] The invention of prepackaged and frozen convenience foods could go only so far toward reducing the number of hours women spent making breakfast, lunch, and dinner. Women still had to buy the food at a supermarket, put it away when they got home, set the table, cook, and clean up. The time spent preparing meals, like the time spent on every other household chore, was seldom reduced by "labor-saving" devices.[13] But eating out really could save time. Fast-food restaurants became the answer for busy parents trying to balance work and family. McDonald's to the rescue!

The McDonald's Corporation owns more property than any other fast-food business in the United States. With its McDonaldlands and Playlands, it also owns more playgrounds than any other US company.[14] These amenities lure parents through the door day and night. The rate of growth in sales at fast-food restaurants has far exceeded growth in any other category of the restaurant industry. In 1967 restaurant sales accounted for 20 percent of all food expenditures; by 1988 they equaled 28 percent. Working women contributed to their success. By the mid-1980s employed women ate out almost twice as often as women who did not work outside the home.[15] And families with children eat out far more often than singles, the elderly, and childless couples.[16]

The legendary Ray Kroc gets much of the credit, or blame, for transforming eating habits in the United States. In 1955 Kroc bought the McDonald brothers' successful California drive-in; Kroc especially liked their new design for a red-and-white building with oversized windows and a pair of yellow arches that cut through the roof.[17] When Kroc discovered that children determined where three-quarters of all families ate out, he wooed kids with special meals and television advertising, helped by a clown named Ronald McDonald.[18] Appearing for the first time in 1966 national television commercials, Ronald McDonald soon came in second only to Santa Claus in name recognition among schoolchildren.[19] *Esquire* magazine considered Ronald McDonald one of the top newsmakers of the 1960s, crediting McDonald's with the "biggest impact on the eating out habits of Americans in the decade."[20] Its December 1983 issue included Ray Kroc in its list of the fifty people who had made the greatest contribution to the US way of life in the twentieth century, an honor he shared with the psychologist Abraham Maslow, the theologian Reinhold Niebuhr, and the civil rights activist Martin Luther King Jr.[21]

In the 1950s and 1960s Kroc and his real estate team aggressively acquired suburban sites—they were plentiful and relatively inexpensive. Commercial development had lagged behind the construction of homes and the only competition for land came from oil companies building gas stations on every corner. McDonald's could take the cheaper midblock locations because its design included parking on two sides.[22] Using a company plane to take aerial photos, the team would fly over communities looking for schools, church steeples, and new houses. Kroc wanted to target "young families in the tricycle and bicycle neighborhoods—the station wagon set, or one car going on two."[23]

In the mid-1950s McDonald's formed the Franchise Realty Corporation to buy the land on which McDonald's restaurants were built. The corporation bought property and financed it with bank mortgages, avoiding use of its own money and leveraging its real estate holdings for future loans. Kroc's financial partner Harry Sonneborn told Wall Street investors that McDonald's was not in the food business; it was in the real estate business: "The only reason we sell fifteen cent hamburgers is because they are the greatest producer of revenue from which our tenants can pay us our rent."[24] This strategy allowed McDonald's to buy sites at depressed prices during the recessions of 1970–71 and 1974–75, accelerating its growth and establishing an insurmountable lead over its major competitors (Burger King and Kentucky Fried Chicken, both founded in 1954). In 1968 McDonald's owned 15 percent of its restaurants, and one-third by 1976.[25] In 1988, four years after Ray Kroc's death, McDonald's owned two-thirds of its sites, more than any other company in the fast-food industry.[26]

The Ray Kroc of the child care business was Perry Mendel, a real estate developer from Montgomery, Alabama. In the late 1960s Mendel predicted that the rising number of women entering the labor force would create a demand for preschool day-care facilities. Mendel bought a local day-care center and embarked on research to figure out what he needed to do to succeed. He sought advice from nutrition experts and education specialists before opening his first center and found that parents wanted food, exercise, and education for their children as well as babysitting. In July 1969, the KinderCare Nursery School opened and accepted its first 70 children. The building exterior was decorated with a Humpty Dumpty motif and a red bell tower that eventually became part of the company's logo. The name was changed to KinderCare Learning Centers when the company opened its second facility in 1970. Nearly twenty centers were in operation by the time the company went public in 1972. Through an ambitious building program and a series of acquisitions, KinderCare had three hundred centers by its tenth anniversary.[27]

Mendel's hunch was correct. The rise in mothers' labor force participation rates between 1955 and 1980, from one-quarter to one-half of all mothers, was matched by an equally dramatic change in the employment patterns of those with preschoolers. In 1955 just 16 percent of women with children under age six were in the labor force; by 1980 it was 45 percent, and it reached 50 percent in 1983.[28] With the exception of government-funded Head Start for low-income children, working women had few options for child care. Census data for 1965, the same year Head Start was established, show that more than 80 percent of children with mothers working full time were cared for in their own homes or in someone else's home. Only 8 percent attended group-care centers.[29] By 2010 one-third of children with working mothers spent large parts of their days in an organized facility.[30]

In 1969 KinderCare and three companies—La Petite Academy, Gerber Children's Centers, and Children's World Learning Centers—dominated the market and would for the next two decades. A *McCall's* magazine article in 1970 lamented the rush to open private day-care centers, asking, "Can you serve children the same way you serve Kentucky Fried Chicken?" Apparently the answer was yes. By 1985 KinderCare alone was operating 1,000 centers. The other three companies had an additional 747 locations.[31]

The industry analyst Bob Benson attributed the rapid growth of Kinder-Care and La Petite Academy to their "all-consuming focus on getting buildings built and the real estate financing contacts to make that happen." According to Benson, both companies were more dedicated to establishing market dominance and impressing Wall Street than to finding the perfect location or hiring expert teachers. The stronger their market position, the less expensive it was to borrow money to build more centers. Most of their facilities were constructed before the high inflation of the late 1970s and were subsequently inexpensive to operate. Benson predicted that huge increases in real estate development costs would limit the ability of other companies to compete.[32] He was correct, but the same market forces affected Kinder Care. In 2011 the company was operating 1,600 centers, only 600 more than in 1985.[33]

The private sector can profit from child care because the US government is alone among industrialized nations in refusing to provide day care for all families regardless of income. But it once came close. In 1971 the

House and Senate passed the Comprehensive Child Development Act, which would have established federally subsidized preschools with fees determined on a sliding scale. But President Richard Nixon vetoed the act. The John Birch Society and various conservative religious denominations mobilized a last-minute assault on the legislation, convincing Nixon that the national government should not side with "communal approaches to childrearing over against the family-centered approach." Child care experts believe that the lack of federal backing prevented the development of an efficient network of providers that would have benefited families and the private sector.[34] Despite heavy lobbying from feminists, the act may also have failed because employed women were still in the minority.

In addition to their primary responsibility for children, women are also more likely than men to attend to the needs of older family members. Having at least one daughter, in fact, is the key to receiving help among the elderly.[35] Adult day services (ADS) for the frail elderly have become the institutional alternative to home care, partially compensating for women's greater labor force involvement. ADS centers were designed to provide health and social programs for people with functional impairments in a protected setting for some portion of the day. Groups eligible for ADS enrollment include people with developmental disabilities, wheelchair users, people with cognitive disabilities living with a spouse, and those living alone who have dementia or mobility limitations. The goal in each case is to maximize independence for as long as possible.[36]

The National Institute on Adult Daycare (NIAD) was organized in 1979 and changed its name to the National Adult Day Services Association (NADSA) in 1995 to include centers providing health and respite care. In 1978 an official federal directory identified three hundred ADS centers in forty states, serving approximately five thousand clients. In 2012 there were more than forty-eight hundred centers.[37]

Approximately one-third of ADS centers are stand-alone 1,000- to 5,000-square-foot facilities, unaffiliated with a parent organization and licensed or state certified to operate. Between 2002 and 2010 the proportion of freestanding centers rose from 30 to 39 percent of all ADS facilities, with the remaining two-thirds affiliated with a hospital or clinic. Professionals project the need for additional space with the aging baby boom generation. ADS centers serve two main purposes: to keep the frail elderly out of nursing homes and to provide respite for their caregivers. Nearly one-half of the patients in ADS centers suffer from dementia and cannot be left alone.[38] In an attempt to address caregivers' needs, most centers operate Monday through Friday, opening between 6:30 and 8:30 a.m. and closing between 4:00 and 6:00 p.m. The typical patient is an elderly white woman with dementia and difficulties completing activities like bathing and medication management. She is in the company of about three dozen other participants, all of whom attend the center's full-day program five days a week. She most often lives with an adult child who is her primary caretaker.[39]

In the early 1980s nearly three-quarters of all caregivers of the elderly were women, mainly adult daughters or wives. Care providers experience conflict between job and family responsibilities and miss more days of work than employees without elder-care tasks.[40] Among the one-half of employed adult daughters interviewed in the 1980s, many rearranged their schedules, cut back on work hours, or took time off without pay to fulfill caregiving responsibilities; 12 percent left their jobs to become full-time caregivers. In every instance, women were more likely than men to make such accommodations.[41]

Sound economic reasons explain why women, who typically earn less than men, would reduce their employment hours. But even when they remain in the labor force, surveys show that women still feel more responsible than men for caretaking. During the 1980s employment reduced sons' level of caretaking by twenty-three hours a month, but had no effect on the number of hours daughters devoted to caretaking. The addition of caretaking without the subtraction of employment hours simply lengthens women's work week.[42] Caring for older adults can result in depression, health problems, social isolation, and financial difficulties for the caregivers; caregivers of patients with dementia experience the greatest emotional stress.[43] Multiple studies have shown that ADS centers reduce stress for caregivers and improve their quality of life.[44]

A significant proportion of adult day centers are run for profit, but the industry is dominated by the nonprofit and public sectors. Approximately three-quarters of all ADS centers are nonprofit or affiliated with the government, although the proportion of for-profit centers increased between 2002 and 2010. The growth of for-profits may reflect both the financial health of the industry and the expectation for further expansion as the baby boom ages. Both nonprofit and profit-making ADS centers accept more than one-half of their funding from public sources, a proportion that has risen since 2002. In 2002 Medicaid and state and local funding were the two main revenue streams, but by 2010 the Veteran's Administration had become the second-most important source of government funding.[45] The growth in the for-profit sector suggests that the public is becoming more familiar with ADS and will be more likely to use them, especially people who are able to pay. Passage of President Barack Obama's 2010 Patient Protection and Affordable Care Act, which provides increased coverage for ADS through its Community First Choice program, may spur that growth.

When an ADS center is no longer sufficient and home care is unavailable, a terminally ill patient may enter a hospice. The hospice movement in the United States developed out of the same commitment to collective action that fueled the civil rights and women's movements; it was part of a liberal effort to improve the quality of life until its end. Elisabeth Kübler-Ross's *On Death and Dying* (1969), in which she argued for noninstitutional settings for "death with dignity," became an internationally known best seller and was a catalyst for the movement.[46] Advances in medical technology that prolonged life and the rising cost of health care made the hospice option appealing to policymakers.[47] The National Hospice and Palliative Care Organization was founded in 1978 as the National Hospice Organization; palliative care was added to its concerns and its name in 2000 in recognition of the wider range of support services available for the management of physical, emotional, and spiritual pain.[48] The organization recorded only one hospice provider in 1974. There were 1,500 by 1985 and 3,700 providers by 2012.[49]

While Ray Kroc's goal of feeding hamburgers to the masses preceded the rise in women's labor force participation, both day-care and elder-care facilities were responses to women's employment; McDonald's simply took full advantage after it happened. The graph in figure 3 illustrates how new buildings rose apace with women's employment. These substitute care facilities would probably still exist without the women's movement, of course, but in much smaller numbers. If the majority of wives and mothers were at home, the demand for the facilities would drop significantly, perhaps enough to slow their galloping growth.

At this point some readers may think that I am blaming the women's movement for suburban sprawl. Not at all. First, suburban sprawl was well established before the 1970s. Second, metropolitan form depends on a large array of economic, political, cultural, and technological factors. I am merely pointing out that feminists' insistence on women's independence brought changes that were compatible, and concurrent, with other factors shaping metropolitan space after World War II.

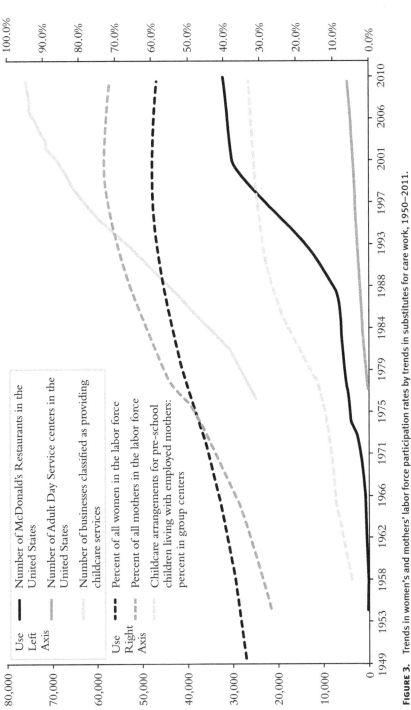

FIGURE 3. Trends in women's and mothers' labor force participation rates by trends in substitutes for care work, 1950–2011.
Source: See Appendix A

Feminist Places of the 1970s

Until the 1970s women had few places outside the home to gather separately from men unless they joined the YWCA, belonged to a women's club (the General Federation of Women's Clubs for whites and the National Association of Colored Women's Clubs for blacks),[50] or attended a single-sex college. These female-only spaces seldom promoted a feminist agenda, although they encouraged women's independence and intellectual growth. To gain political power, the Second Wave needed places in which women could share common concerns and mobilize for action. Jo Freeman of the Chicago Women's Liberation Union (CWLU) believed that "natural structures" were the key to the success of any social movement. She cited the factory for the labor movement, the church for civil rights, the campus for students, and the ghetto for blacks. Freeman lamented the loss of nineteenth-century women's clubs that had served as social and political bases, teaching women political skills and serving as a communications network for the Suffrage campaign. The equivalent space for the Second Wave, she believed, was the rap or consciousness-raising (C-R) group.[51] These all-female groups met in women's homes, then increasingly in women's centers.

Women's centers, bookstores, clinics, and domestic violence shelters were natural structures that I call "feminist places." They fostered a sense of solidarity among women. Founders spoke of self-determination, changed lives, and economic independence. The sites were politically charged, promoting power for women while celebrating their liberation from norms governing acceptable behavior for wives and mothers. According to Simone Wallace, the cofounder of Sisterhood Bookstore in Los Angeles, one of the best-selling posters at the store was the image of a long-haired avenging goddess, holding two parts of a broken broom, urging women to "Fuck Housework."[52] Feminist places gave women a new voice that was far from nice.

In their struggles for liberation, radical grassroots activists would spend the 1970s establishing places that reinforced women's autonomy. The most important of these was the women's center.[53] Women's centers provided safe havens for women to explore their sexuality, express solidarity with the feminist movement, or vent their anger against men. There was plenty to be angry about. Lack of access to effective contraceptives, equal pay, and equal credit were just the beginning in a litany of complaints. Centers also helped women enter or return to paid employment through General Educational Development (GED) classes and workshops on marketable skills. Women's centers contributed to women's autonomy through C-R, liberation schools, and lesbian support groups. They launched numerous independent organizations. Bookstores connected women to local resources and to ideas from the larger women's movement. Health clinics provided information about contraception and abortion, giving women the confidence to wrest control of their bodies from the male-dominated medical profession. Shelters for victims of domestic violence declared that women would not be beaten. None of these places existed before 1970; it took a powerful social movement to produce them. They flourished because feminists poured thousands of hours, and considerable personal savings, into ensuring that women's voices were heard and their needs were met.

Women in feminist places could respond to, or withdraw from, gender discrimination and interaction with men in order to form their own identities.[54] Such places were created primarily by radical feminists, but they emerged in the context of major legal victories won by feminist reformers. Both equality and liberation would become cornerstones of Second Wave feminism.

Feminist places were "free spaces," environments in which women learned a new self-respect and asserted a group identity based on the values of democratic cooperation. According to the historian Sara Evans, voluntarily established free spaces are "settings between private lives and large-scale institutions where ordinary citizens can act with dignity, independence, and vision."[55] The political scientist Margaret Kohn calls them "radical democratic spaces," political sites where marginalized groups can claim their rights. Radical spaces are essential if social movements are to expand the meaning of citizenship to include the previously disenfranchised.[56]

Feminist places included features of natural structures, free spaces, and radical democratic spaces: they were spaces in which women mobilized for political action to claim their rights through democratic cooperation. They also combined elements of both exclusion and care.[57] They typically excluded men *and* they created environments in which women could take refuge from the psychological, physical, or emotional stresses imposed by a patriarchal society. These places increased public awareness of discrimination against women, defining what was morally good and clarifying for members what they needed to do to achieve equal rights.[58]

Rarely possessing the resources to buy property or construct new buildings, activists rented existing buildings and modified them to serve their needs. Consequently, feminist places are often lost to history because they were neither designed by architects nor identified with famous figures or events, although some have been noted by feminist scholars trying to restore women's history through historic preservation.[59] Because such places transformed the ideals of the women's movement into material form, they are worth recognizing. Activists adapted houses, storefronts, and offices so that women could gather and assert their rights to contraception, experience intellectual growth, and ensure their personal health. Such feminist places were examples of the French sociologist Henri Lefebvre's theory that the real citizens of a city are those who produce and use its spaces in their daily lives.[60]

Space is an abstract concept lacking materiality or meaning. Space becomes a place only when it is filled with people, cultural practices, objects, representations, and interpretations. Place can be described as space that is politicized, culturally relevant, and historically specific.[61] I use the terms *place* and *space* interchangeably. Although scholars distinguish between the two, few of the women I interviewed made such a distinction. Sometimes they referred to the same building as a space and as a place. Social, economic, and gender relations shape places, and places, in turn, influence relationships within their boundaries. Three features of place apply to feminists' creations: a geographic location; a physical form; and investment with cultural meaning. The meaning and value of places can vary over time and across cultures.[62]

Feminist places are always contested—none more so than clinics that provide abortions. To pro-choice feminists, they are a guarantee of reproductive rights; to pro-life activists (many of whom are women), they are places where doctors commit murder. Between 1977 and 1989, arson and bombings accounted for 74 of the 686 recorded incidents of violence against clinics in the United States.[63] In 1988 Operation Rescue, founded in 1986 by Randall Terry, orchestrated three months of protests in front of an Atlanta abortion clinic in which more than one thousand demonstrators were arrested.[64] Terry liked to claim that Operation Rescue's clinic blockades had led to more than forty thousand arrests by 1990. That year, his national office was forced to close due to bankruptcy resulting from lawsuits filed by the National Organization for Women (NOW).[65] In June 2009 the abortion provider Dr. George R. Tiller was slain at his church in Wichita, Kansas, the fourth abortion doctor to be murdered since 1993.[66] Dr. Tiller's Women's Health Care Services, the last remaining abortion clinic in Kansas outside Kansas City, was closed ten days later.[67]

Legislative attacks on abortion rights have proliferated in the twenty-first century. More abortion restrictions were enacted in the three years after the 2010 midterm elections than in the previous decade, almost all at the state level.[68] In the first half of 2011, states enacted eighty laws restricting access to abortion, quadruple the number enacted in 1985.[69] Restrictions include mandatory ultrasounds and waiting periods, prohibiting insurance carriers from covering abortions, imposing burdensome regulations on abortion providers, restricting funds to Planned Parenthood, and requiring parental consent for minors.[70] In the first quarter of 2012, legislators in forty-five of the forty-six states in which legislatures convened introduced nearly five hundred provisions restricting abortion access.[71] The latest weapon in the assault on reproductive rights is the "personhood" initiative. Although it has failed to pass in the seven states in which it has been introduced, it would grant fertilized human eggs the same legal rights that apply to people.[72] Women seeking abortions, and doctors performing them, could be prosecuted for murder.

Abortion is a lightning rod for partisan politics. On August 19, 2012, when asked in a television interview whether he thought abortion was justified in the case of rape, the Republican Representative Todd Akin of Missouri replied, "If it's a legitimate rape, the female body has ways to try to shut the whole thing down." Akin's profound ignorance of female anatomy, his implication that the crime of rape can be distinguished as "legitimate" or not, and his insensitivity to victims of rape unleashed an avalanche of criticism. Democrats touted Akin's remark as further evidence of the Republicans' war against women; Republicans tried to distance themselves from Akin by withholding endorsements and funding from his pivotal Senate race against the Democratic incumbent Claire McCaskill (who won the election).[73] Even as this controversy simmered, GOP leaders were adopting a party platform calling for a constitutional amendment to protect the lives of unborn children.[74]

The combination of intimidation and punitive legislation has greatly reduced access to abortion since it was legalized with *Roe v. Wade*. In 1980 approximately three thousand hospitals and clinics provided abortions in the United States. By 2011 that number had declined to 1,720, only slightly higher than the number operating in 1973 when the Supreme Court legalized abortion with the passage of *Roe v. Wade*.[75]

More than reproductive rights are under fire. The following headlines which appeared in the major news media between 2012 and 2015 reflect the contentious battles surrounding women's rights:

"House Passes Violence Against Women Act, Grudgingly" (*The Christian Science Monitor*, May 16, 2012)

"The Military's Sexual Assault Crisis" (*New York Times*, May 7, 2013)

"Protestors Urge Sacramento Landlord to Break Lease with Abortion Provider" (News10/KXTV, Sacramento, August 5, 2013)

"Contraception as a Test of Equality" (*Washington Post*, March 24, 2014)

"Senate Republicans Block Bill on Equal Pay" (*New York Times*, April 9, 2014)

"Court Upholds Texas Limits on Abortion" (*New York Times*,
    June 9, 2015)
"GOP White House Hopefuls Scramble for Anti-Abortion Vote" (*New
    York Times*, July 10, 2015)

The rights that feminists fought so hard to win in the 1970s were resisted initially and are still under attack. Sexual harassment is a significant problem in the military, as is rape, despite decades of attempts to control both. Women's rights to protection against domestic violence have been at risk. Even equal pay is controversial. These threats signal a return to an era most Second Wave feminists thought was over, one in which women are at risk of having fewer opportunities to be active members of, and influence, the public. The most critical places—abortion clinics, rape crisis centers, and domestic violence shelters—have all been subject to budget cuts due to political pressures and neoliberal policies from the federal all the way down to the local level. Closing feminist places will close a door on women's rights.

Citizenship, Rights, and the Public Sphere

Lefebvre argues that inhabitants of a city must constantly struggle to assert their "right to the city." Those who use space daily, or take it for their purposes, and sometimes produce it, are the true citizens of that place.[76] The geographer Don Mitchell echoes Lefebvre when he argues that the struggle for rights *produces* space; rights remain symbolic until they are given material form and public visibility.[77] Some of the ways citizens assert these rights are by creating, claiming, or appropriating urban space; another is by fully participating in urban life.[78] Men have the capital to invest in real estate development, for example, and to wage expensive political campaigns that elect them to public office. Women, though, have few formal ways to appropriate urban space, and their participation in public is often restricted by fear of crime, cultural practices, or lack of mobility. Their participation can be increased by a sense of comfort, belonging, and commitment to the places they occupy.[79] Many feminist places, designed to combine an informal atmosphere with a political purpose, provided the sense of safety women sought.

According to the historian Thomas Bender, cities provide a "vital platform for men and women to think themselves into politics, to make themselves into citizens, to initiate a social politics."[80] Women "thought themselves into politics" through the feminist movement. They constructed places to highlight issues that assumed national importance. Feminist places were sites of identity formation and radical action. They enabled women to establish solidarity, independence, and bodily integrity. In the sociologist Gerda Wekerle's terms, feminists were "invoking the language of rights and citizenship in making a multiplicity of collective claims on the city for the fulfillment of basic needs, space, and inclusion."[81]

It is difficult to understand citizenship rights without invoking the controversial dichotomy between public and private spheres. Feminists have challenged the merits of this distinction, pointing out that men have traditionally defined the characteristics of and boundaries between them.[82] Yet much political debate is shaped by notions of public and private. Citizenship rights are established in public and a lack of those rights characterizes the private. Since historically much of women's lives have been spent on time-consuming domestic and child-rearing duties in the home, they have struggled to achieve full citizenship outside it. They have been less than full members of their communities.[83]

Feminist places straddle the divide between private and public. Their founders designed the interiors to be as different from their formal counterparts as possible. New Words bookstore in Boston provided chairs so its customers could sit and read as long as they liked. The founders' decision to encourage women to stay was a radical departure from the prevailing practice among large bookstores that discouraged loitering and hustled customers to the checkout counter.[84] Although feminist bookstores were intended to serve women and children, men occasionally walked in, a reminder that they were open to the general public. In this sense feminist places were similar to late-nineteenth-century settlement houses that served as neighborhood centers for poor immigrants. Furnished to evoke a domestic environment and serving primarily women and children, settlement houses also opened their doors to men. Feminist places and settlement houses were neither completely private nor public; they were "quasi-public."[85]

Most people in the United States understand what it means to be a citizen in a democracy. Beyond the right to vote, citizens have the right to bodily integrity, or the ability to control what happens to them.[86] For women, reproductive rights are the core of bodily integrity. Women's ability to shape their own lives depends on whether they can control their own fertility. Safety from violence is also a prerequisite for autonomy and empowerment. Citizenship includes the ability to speak and move about freely in public, which can be inhibited by the threat of male violence outside or inside the home.[87] Women who fear for their physical safety might avoid certain parts of the city or stay away from events after dark. Battered wives, even if their physical injuries are too minor to require medical attention, may be ashamed of visible bruises and avoid leaving home. Without the ability to move freely in public or to halt battering at home, women cannot be full citizens.[88]

Oppressed groups who are denied full citizenship due to their race, ethnicity, age, sex, or disabilities can practice a "politics of difference" by joining social movements to protest their exclusion. An initial period of separatism helps marginalized groups develop independent identities and mobilize for political action. Separatism in the feminist movement, according to the philosopher Iris Marion Young, "promoted the empowerment of women through self-organization, the creation of safe spaces where women could share and analyze their experiences, voice their anger, play with and create bonds with one another, and develop new and better institutions and practices."[89] Young identified health clinics, rape crisis centers, emergency shelters, and bookstores as such places. There, women formed alternative publics, or what Nancy Fraser calls "subaltern counterpublics." Subaltern counterpublics function as spaces of withdrawal and regrouping, and they are training grounds for political activities directed toward wider publics.[90]

Women's employment in the public realm is crucial to their claim on rights; having a paid job signals economic independence and productivity.[91] Legitimate access to social rights depends on whether one has been employed or acted as a caregiver inside the home. Unemployment benefits, worker's compensation for disabilities incurred on the job, Social Security, and pensions are all honorable ways to receive income subsidies. Men are the primary beneficiary of such entitlements. Women who receive welfare for taking care of a family, however, are suspected of fraud, and their benefits are subjected to government oversight. Welfare is more vulnerable to budget cuts than employment-based benefits.[92] As a result, women and their children have higher poverty rates than men, and poverty is incompatible with the full rights of citizenship.[93]

As the example of welfare illustrates, it is difficult to achieve full rights to citizenship through care work. This is an issue because always and everywhere women perform, and are expected to perform, care work. Care work is different from other types of work: it requires women to constantly organize and arrange their lives to meet the needs of others.[94] Being on call for others, whether by choice or necessity, interrupts women's lives in ways that men seldom experience.

Care work is doubly devalued, first, because it is women's work, and women's work typically garners less respect than men's. Second, care work is done by people marginalized by their gender, race, class, or immigrant status, which reinforces the view that caring is low-skilled labor. This dual devaluation of the work and its providers rationalizes their weak market position.[95]

The political theorist Joan Tronto reveals how gendered assumptions underlying paid employment and unpaid care work influence the rights of citizenship. Police and firefighters who save lives are *not* considered caregivers, while women who nurse family members through illness and crises are. "Recipients of 'masculine' care," Tronto points out, "are perceived, by their nature, to be citizens who, for one reason or another, find themselves *in extremis*. Recipients of 'feminine' care, on the other hand, are people who are somehow dependent: children, the disabled, the ill and infirm, the elderly."[96]

As long as people in the United States believe they do not, and never will, need care, they can exclude caregivers from full citizenship. Tronto's solution is simple: care work should be grounds for conferring citizenship. Caregivers would then be entitled to the same benefits as individuals who contribute through employment or military service.[97] According to the philosopher Deborah Stone, "caring for each other is the most basic form of civic participation. Caring is the essential democratic act, the prerequisite to voting, joining associations, attending meetings, holding office, and all the other ways we sustain democracy."[98] In an ideal society that values caring, care would be both an obligation and a right for all citizens, but given how little currency caring as a basis for citizenship has gained over the years, it is logical that women find more rights in the labor force.

The concept of rights can be envisioned as a series of circles that reach farther and farther outward from a small center. In the United States, citizenship rights were first assigned only to white male property owners, then to all white males, eventually to African American males, and finally to women. As each barrier was breached, the circles of inclusion expanded farther from the original center.[99] Social movements like the Second Wave played a crucial role in widening those circles.

Social Movements and the Power of Place

Places in which people can gather voluntarily are central to the formation of movements for social justice. One example is the Occupy Wall Street movement for "retribution against the financial elite," as its website proclaims.[100] On September 17, 2011, thousands of protestors encamped at Zuccotti Park in New York City's Wall Street district to challenge the vast social and economic inequalities generated by globalization. They clashed with police and, in the chaos, people were injured. Within a month the movement had spread across the country and the world. Taking their cue from the Arab Spring uprisings in Cairo's Tahrir Square and the M-15 demonstrations in Madrid's Puerta del Sol Square, the occupants of Zuccotti Park raged against the "1%" of wealthy Americans and proclaimed themselves the "other 99%." According to the scholar Cornel West, the movement was "a democratic awakening."[101]

The group's tactical committee chose Zuccotti Park over seven other locations in the city. The protest needed a highly visible space near Wall Street and Broadway that could hold two thousand people. It also had to be a privately owned public space exempt from city park curfews and required by law to be open twenty-four hours a day. Zuccotti Park and One Chase Manhattan Plaza were the only sites that fit the criteria. The plaza was closed to pedestrians by September 17, so Zuccotti Park became the destination. Out of concern that the police might track social media, organizers distributed paper maps to advertise the location about thirty minutes before the event. Word of mouth generated the critical mass needed to attract television crews.[102]

Occupy Wall Street is only one in a long line of social movements that have appropriated space for marginalized groups. The most significant US social movements resulted in the abolition of slavery, the vote for women, the assimilation of immigrants, civil rights for African Americans, and greater equality for women. None of these moral crusades achieved its goals quickly. The campaigns for social justice that began with the founding of the country are still being waged today. Most important for my argument, each has been identified with a particular type of place.

Consider Quakers, among the first white people in the United States to promote the abolition of slavery. Many of their discussions occurred in Friends meetinghouses. These were square or rectangular structures without a steeple. The interiors lacked religious symbols, and Friends sat in rows of benches facing each other. Simplicity in all things was the guiding principle in design and construction. Their buildings, and Quakers' opposition to slavery, reflected their values of equality and community.[103] Among African Americans, ministers and congregations of black churches sheltered slaves fleeing the South through the Underground Railroad.[104]

A place of worship was also the staging ground for the beginnings of the woman suffrage movement. In 1840 Lucretia Mott and Elizabeth Cady Stanton were prevented from speaking at the all-male World Anti-Slavery Convention at the imposing Exeter Hall in London. Incensed, Mott and Stanton vowed to fight for women's rights when they returned to the United States. After much correspondence and numerous visits, they agreed to hold "A Convention to discuss the social, civil, and religious condition and rights of woman." In 1848 they created their own space to begin the struggle at the Methodist Wesleyan Chapel in Seneca Falls, New York. They chose the

chapel, built by a congregation of abolitionists, because it was the only location that would allow an assembly for women's rights.[105] The Declaration
of Sentiments written by participants at that convention has ever since been
identified with Seneca Falls.

Like abolition and suffrage, the temperance movement also depended on
the church for its moral justification. One of the earliest instances of wom-
en's mobilization against alcohol use by men began in 1873 as an ecumenical
event organized by women in the Presbyterian and Methodist Episcopal
churches in Hillsboro, Ohio. After Christmas that year, women gathered at
the Presbyterian church and marched toward saloons in town, singing and
praying. Their campaign successfully closed the majority of saloons before
the New Year. Temperance crusaders recruited other women through their
churches, and the Woman's Christian Temperance Union (WCTU), formed
in 1879, became the largest organization of women in its time.[106]

Although the settlement house movement at the turn of the twentieth
century did not begin in a church, it was based on the philosophy of the
Social Gospel, the belief that poverty was due to structural injustices and
not to the moral failure of individuals. As a young adult, Jane Addams of
Chicago's Hull-House settlement became a Presbyterian;[107] members of the
College Settlements Association were Protestants of several denominations.
They were all united in their determination to practice a pragmatic the-
ology in the poor neighborhoods where they lived and worked, although
as the movement matured, settlements became increasingly secular. White
middle-class settlement house residents created spaces to teach immigrants
how to read and speak English and how to demand municipal services for
their neighborhoods. Typically located in old homes, settlement houses provided temporary relief from squalid living and working conditions for thousands of immigrants.[108]

By the mid-twentieth century, political and institutional instability gave
rise to numerous urban protest movements, of which the civil rights movement was the most significant.[109] Responding to the institutionalized racism
that pervaded US society, blacks declared they would no longer settle for
second-class citizenship. The battle for the vote and for racial integration
of public facilities gained momentum in racially segregated churches where
African Americans of all classes worshiped. The leader of the civil rights
movement, the Reverend Martin Luther King Jr., invoked Christian principles to fight racial prejudice.

All of these social movements used houses of worship and/or religious
ideology to battle marginalization and oppression. The Second Wave is alone
in its secular origins. Although the radical branch of the feminist movement

held its first conference in a Friends meetinghouse in Sandy Spring, Maryland[110] (echoing the first meeting of suffragists in Seneca Falls), religion was anathema to many feminists; they blamed the male-dominated institution for promoting women's submission to men. Secular feminist places were to the women's movement what churches were to the civil rights movement: safe havens that fostered political action among people who had experienced lifetimes of discrimination.[111] The difference is that churches already existed, whereas feminist places were new.

Feminist places were most like settlement houses. There were differences, of course. Settlement houses welcomed men, while feminist places typically excluded them. And women lived in settlement houses while that was atypical for feminist places. Yet they shared a common goal: turn-of-the-twentieth-century settlement houses created new Americans. Mid-twentieth-century feminist places created new American women.

Organization of the Book

Chapter 1 reviews the Second Wave as one among many social movements that altered the use of urban space. Throughout US history, for example, the rights of women and the rights of blacks have been closely linked. The suffrage movement had roots in nineteenth-century abolitionism similar to those that the mid-twentieth-century Second Wave shared with the civil rights movement.[112] Turn-of-the-twentieth-century suffrage, settlement house, and temperance movements, all connected by women's activism (or volunteerism, as it was called then), had symbolic and spatial implications.[113]

Chapters 2 through 5 address how women's rights took material form during the 1970s. Feminist places produced small-scale changes in the built environment but were no less significant in opening up the city to women. For these chapters I relied on archival data for selected organizations in Boston and Los Angeles, and on interviews with founders. Chapter 2 identifies women's centers as the first and most important feminist places that launched the places I analyze in chapters 3, 4, and 5: bookstores, health clinics, and domestic violence shelters. I should note that I have excluded feminist art spaces and feminist credit unions. Although both existed, as the Los Angeles Woman's Building illustrates, there were fewer of them—about a dozen of each—than the more ubiquitous places I describe.[114]

In chapter 6 I propose that feminist places like those created by the Second Wave are still important, in the United States and abroad. I summarize the significance of both desegregated male spaces and feminist places in promoting women's rights to the city, arguing that these rights can only be maintained to the extent that women have access to substitutes for their previously unpaid labor. Desegregated places, feminist places, and care substitutes form a triad of "necessary spaces." The chapter concludes with commentary on current threats to women's rights and speculation about what lies ahead.

The "E" Word

Essentialism, the "E" word of feminist politics, has been both a boon and a bane to women's rights. Essentialism is the belief that all women (or African Americans or any other population group) are alike in significant ways because of their biology. Suffragists used essentialism to their advantage in the nineteenth century when they argued that they were more morally fit than men to care for the city through municipal housekeeping and holding elected office.[115] Feminists of the Second Wave rejected essentialism, believing it was a concept used by men to justify the oppression of women. Now, with new research on genetics, lesbians and gay men are arguing that their sexual preferences are biologically determined. Adding to the confusion is "egalitarian essentialism," a cultural construct that emerged in the 1990s that recognizes a woman's right to choose to stay home with her children rather than seek full-time employment. In this scenario, women are not being ground down by a patriarchal society but are committing to "intensive motherhood" and their own sanity by stepping away from job demands.[116]

Some risk is associated with "deconstructing the unitary woman."[117] In an attempt to reject essentialism, feminists have obscured the very real consequences of being a woman independent of other identities. Only women, *because* of their biology, share the ability to become pregnant by choice, mistake, or force, and only women are subject to the uncertainties and health risks that accompany a pregnancy. Feminists who created self-help clinics to educate women about their bodies recognized this reality. Addressing the importance of alliances across class lines (and implicitly across race, ethnicity, and sexual preference), they reminded their members that "professional women and [working-class] laywomen alike will ultimately be a lone naked patient of the medical profession in danger of victimization."[118]

One thing that feminist scholars do agree on, though, is that no single voice captures all women's experiences. Race, social class, ethnicity, and sexual preference are major sources of difference. Race, especially, has had profound effects on women's rights.[119] During the 1970s, unlike today, blacks were the largest minority group in the United States. For this reason I write more about African American organizations than those of other women of color.

Nevertheless, it is important to acknowledge the multiracial and ethnic origins of the Second Wave. The Chicana Hijas de Cuauhtémoc and Asian Sisters were both formed in 1971 in California, and Women of All Red Nations (WARN) was formed by Native American women in 1974. Unlike white radical feminists, however, members of these groups often cooperated with men to achieve their goals. Women in these groups faced criticism from their male colleagues who were engaged in "more important" (from the men's perspective) liberation struggles for their race or ethnicity.[120] In 1972 the Los Angeles chapter of the Comisión Femenil Mexicana Nacional (CFMN) opened Centro de Niños to provide child care for about eighty women learning carpentry and plumbing at two Chicana Service Action Centers. The CFMN, though, was less a feminist organization than a community action group that supported bread-and-butter issues like fair wages for farmworkers and green cards for working women.[121]

Women of color were less likely than whites to find feminism through antiwar activism, but many African American women shared whites' membership in the civil rights movement. The Black Women's Liberation Group of Mount Vernon/New Rochelle in New York was formed by women who had been active in the civil rights movement. The Mount Vernon group was sometimes known by its founder's name, the Pat Robinson Group, and sometimes as "The Damned." The Third World Women's Alliance (TWWA) was started by the Student Nonviolent Coordinating Committee (SNCC) member Frances Beal and others. The National Black Feminist Organization (NBFO) was founded in 1973. Its offshoot, the Combahee River Collective, formed a year later and drew from feminist, civil rights, and Black Power movements.[122]

The only feminist places that transcended the historical moment to become institutionalized are domestic violence shelters, now supported by municipal funding, and abortion clinics, increasingly stripped of financial and public support. Of all the rights women have won since the 1970s, bodily integrity is still elusive, not just in the United States but around the world.[123]

CHAPTER 1

Feminist Practice

Social Movements and Urban Space

Social movements on behalf of marginalized people in the United States have been the engines for significant progress toward a just society. They take shape when one or more highly visible advocates (Betty Friedan and Gloria Steinem, in the case of postwar feminism) identifies an injustice and brings it to public attention; they gain strength when grassroots activists engage in collective action.[1] New spatial institutions became a hallmark of the Second Wave; creating them was a practice feminists inherited from US social movements that preceded them. Meaningful spaces, both religious and secular, sheltered disenfranchised groups while they gained the momentum to fight for their rights.

A long-standing scholarly emphasis on ideology has been augmented by the recognition that social movements also depend on a common identity as a basis for action. This distinction differentiates "old" from "new" social movements. "Old movements" are based on economic and class interests that mobilize participants to address injustices through a shared *ideology*, while "new movements" emphasize a common *identity*.[2] Second Wave feminism incorporated both. On the one hand, radical feminists proposed that women were a class, thereby centering them squarely in a Marxist ideology.[3] Other feminists underscored formerly weak dimensions of identity, such as sexual preference, as a common bond. Developing positive identities requires members to reject the dominant, oppressive society and create their own values and structures.[4] At its extreme, this leads to lesbians creating male-free communities. Some feminists used disruptive tactics to refute old identities.[5] In 1968 the New York Radical Women staged guerilla theater actions at the Miss America beauty pageant in Atlantic City. To protest women's being judged only by their looks, about 150 demonstrators crowned a sheep as Miss America, then tossed their bras, high-heeled shoes, girdles, and hair curlers into a "freedom trash can." They never burned the contents, but the media gleefully portrayed feminists as "bra burners" ever after.[6]

According to the sociologists Frances Fox Piven and Richard Cloward, mass defiance is most disruptive when protesters withdraw a crucial contribution from the institution that depends on it; they have their greatest political impact when powerful groups have large stakes in the disrupted institution. Those in power must also possess resources to grant if the protesters are to be satisfied.[7] This theory was translated into practice when Second Wave feminists challenged the very institution of marriage, urging wives to demand that their husbands help with housekeeping and child care. Release from sole responsibility for domestic tasks, the thinking went, would enable women to establish full public citizenship. Men were less enthusiastic; it would be hard to overstate their investment in traditional marriage. Their ability to earn a living depended heavily on women's unpaid work at home. And in the late 1970s most people in the United States supported that arrangement. National opinion polls revealed that approximately two-thirds of men *and* women agreed that it was "much better for everyone involved if the man is the achiever outside the home and the woman takes care of the home and family."[8] Feminists thus faced a skeptical audience when they tried to convince women that there were alternatives to marriage and the typical division of household labor. Eventually, though, feminists' attitudes began to permeate society. By 1986 about one-half of women and men believed that wives should care for the home while men earned a living outside it.[9]

Such significant social change required feminists to create places where women could learn to demand it. A long line of social movements set the example. The abolition, suffrage, temperance, settlement house, and civil rights movements all changed the use of urban space. The Second Wave was next in line.

Historical Precedents

Social movements almost always alter the use of space, inevitably producing conflict in the process. Changes may be deliberate or unintentional, and they include both the destruction of existing places and the creation of new ones. Abolition is a prime example.

From the mid-eighteenth century until the Civil War, slave markets were central features in southern cities like New Orleans, Louisiana; Richmond, Virginia; and Washington, DC. Richmond's flourishing slave trade between the 1830s and the 1860s spawned a dense network of auction houses, slave jails, and auxiliary businesses in the downtown commercial district.[10] During the same era, abolitionists and African American ministers created safe havens in churches and homes along the Underground Railroad for slaves escaping the South. The black church was central to the "geography of resistance" developed by African Americans in search of freedom; it served as the black community's political and social gathering place as well as its spiritual center.[11]

Bishop Richard Allen, the founder of the African Methodist Episcopal (AME) denomination, was known as the "Apostle of Freedom" because he and his wife, Sarah, used the basement of their Philadelphia AME church to shelter escaped slaves; they also opened their home to fugitives. In 1822 the minister William Paul Quinn was inspired by Allen to found the Bethel AME Church in the heart of Pittsburgh, which soon became a station on the Underground Railroad, as did the Cincinnati AME church. Across the country, black congregations operated way stations, with ministers as their active agents. Many destinations in Illinois, Indiana, and Ohio eventually became free black communities for those who could make it that far.[12] When the Emancipation Proclamation abolished slavery in 1863, slave markets were demolished, and the stops on the Underground Railroad were returned to their original uses.

A significant geographic change also occurred, over many years, as a result of abolition. The vast majority of former slaves lived in the rural South and had inadequate resources to leave immediately after being freed. By the turn of the twentieth century, though, African Americans began an exodus to Northern and Midwestern cities. They were encouraged to move by the nation's best-selling black newspaper, the *Chicago Defender*, which called for a "Great Northern Drive" to begin on May 15, 1917. Within a few decades, the majority of African Americans lived outside the South.[13] If one counts migration as spatial redistribution, the exodus of such an enormous number of blacks from one part of the country to another is indeed a significant spatial change wrought by a social movement.

Abolition laid the political groundwork for the suffrage movement.[14] Since suffragists could demonstrate for their rights in ways that slaves could not, white women had more power to appropriate public space.

Known as the First Wave by today's scholars, the suffrage movement began with the 1848 Seneca Falls Convention. The abolitionists Elizabeth Cady Stanton and Lucretia Mott met in 1840 at the World Anti-Slavery Convention in London. Each had accompanied her husband, and both were prevented from speaking at the all-male convention. Angered, Stanton and Mott vowed to hold a women's rights conference when they returned home.[15] Exclusion from the all-male space in London motivated Stanton and Mott to create the all-female space of the Seneca Falls Convention at the Wesleyan Church, where they participated in the writing of the convention's Declaration of Sentiments, which included the demand for woman suffrage.[16]

The First Wave encouraged women to appear together in public. Suffragists gathered at conventions and paraded in the streets as forms of political activity. Stanton remembered, "I could not see what to do or where to begin—my only thought was a public meeting for protest and discussion."[17] Stanton, Mott, Angelina and Sarah Grimké, Susan B. Anthony, Lucy Stone, and Antoinette Brown mobilized other women with their lyceum lectures, conventions, and legislative committee hearings.[18] On March 3, 1913, the day before President Woodrow Wilson's inauguration, more than five thousand suffragists took to the streets of Washington, DC, on behalf of their cause. Mobs heckled, tripped, and shoved the women, sending more than one hundred to the hospital and injuring hundreds more. Media outrage over the violence was so great that the Senate convened hearings the following week. One of the senators reminded the protesters that "there would be nothing like this happen [sic] if you would stay at home," but the march earned public sympathy that would eventually translate into support for the Nineteenth Amendment guaranteeing women the right to vote.[19] Women understood the power of their unprecedented visibility in the city.

Suffrage was controversial because it demanded rights for women. Temperance, though, was a respectable endeavor for women because it revolved around church and home. By the end of the nineteenth century most suffragists were supporters of temperance, and most temperance advocates were in favor of suffrage.[20]

The temperance movement had a specific spatial agenda—to close saloons. This was the means to save the family from the moral perils of alcoholism. Temperance was also an indirect avenue for improving women's rights. Since wives had no control over their husband's wages, men could drink away their paychecks at the corner bar. The loss of family income meant mothers and children went hungry and unclothed. Drunken men might also beat their wives and children. It was easy to make the connections between alcohol, poverty, and violence. Eliminating alcohol would go a long way, the thinking went, toward ensuring women the rights to food, shelter, and physi-cal safety.[21]

To this end, the American Temperance Society, including both women and men, was formed in 1826.[22] In 1879 women formed their own organi-zation, the Woman's Christian Temperance Union (WCTU). With Frances Willard as its president for nearly two decades, the WCTU was the largest women's organization of its day.[23] Across the nation, members of the WCTU marched from their churches to saloons, singing and praying for barkeepers to shutter their doors.[24] Closing a bar did more than eliminate a source of alcohol. The nineteenth-century saloon was a social center where men could play cards or pool, talk about politics and sports, find a job, or spend time while unemployed. The saloon also filled more basic needs. It had a public bathroom, was often the only place to get a drink of water, and served "free lunches" for the price of a beer.[25] Most women, of course, never entered a saloon; it was a male-only space. The shock of seeing women kneeling and praying in a barroom was one of the WCTU's most effective strategies in its crusade to banish alcohol.[26]

While saloons were being closed, members of the WCTU were opening new places in the city. Willard issued guidelines about how to set up local headquarters, temperance coffee rooms, Friendly Inns (a type of settlement house), and homes for inebriate women. Spaces that already existed were put to new uses. The coffee rooms were to include reading areas, and the Friendly Inns established manufacturing shops in which men could trade their labor for food and lodging.[27] Temperance women gained victory when Prohibi-tion became national law in 1920—the same year women won the right to vote. Although Prohibition was repealed in 1933, women had proved they could exert political pressure and modify the urban landscape, even without the vote.[28]

The settlement house movement was a similar effort, not only fighting for the rights of women and children, but also adapting existing urban space for its purposes. Drawing inspiration from London's male-only Toynbee Hall, Jane Addams and other college-educated white women feminized the US version of the settlement house movement at the turn of the twentieth century. In 1889 Addams and Ellen Gates Starr established Hull-House settlement on Halsted Street in Chicago in a home originally built in 1856 for Charles J. Hull. The house had been used as a secondhand furniture store and as an old-age home before Addams and Starr rented it from Hull's niece, Helen Culver. In the next twenty years Hull-House expanded from one building to thirteen.[29] It became the most famous in a network of set-tlement houses, including Hiram House in Cleveland and Denison House in Boston, which eventually numbered more than four hundred across the country.[30]

The social settlement was a new use of space in the city. Residents appropriated existing places, most often in a converted home or row house, to serve as a "neighborhood living room" where immigrants could escape their dingy and overcrowded quarters. Its agenda included the educational purposes of a school, the social role of a club, the recreational functions of a gym, and the cultural goals of a museum. It was a distinctly secular place. Although Addams invoked the Social Gospel when founding Hull-House, she later discontinued its interdenominational services because she believed residents came together over their common goals rather than a shared faith.[31] For the volunteers who lived there, it was a site of work, leisure, and cooperative housekeeping. By entering the new profession of settlement house worker, middle-class women could justifiably live apart from their families, and in lower-income neighborhoods at that—a radical choice. The settlement house was thus a refuge for independent women in an era before women could vote and when they had few occupational choices.

The settlement house movement harnessed the energies of hundreds of educated women and men to assimilate European immigrants into the industrializing city. Residents were concerned about citizenship rights for immigrants when the rest of the country was consumed by xenophobia. Hull-House, in fact, was the first settlement house in the United States to offer citizenship preparation classes.[32] Addams recognized the importance of the building itself when she wrote that it "clothed in brick and mortar and made visible to the world that which we were trying to do; they [the buildings] stated to Chicago that education and recreation ought to be extended to immigrants."[33] Women who lived in the house and those who volunteered daily saved newcomers from the worst conditions of urban life, and in the process they saved the city from the social unrest inherent in such an enormous influx of strangers. The public baths, libraries, kindergartens, and clinics under the settlement house roof were eventually spun off into independent facilities paid for by municipalities.[34]

In terms of spatial consequences, the Second Wave is most similar to the settlement house movement. Feminists saw the need for rape counseling, contraceptive information, and help for victims of domestic abuse before localities acknowledged the problems. The intensity of activists' efforts to create spaces where these services could be delivered is reminiscent of the passion with which volunteers opened the settlement house to improve the lives of immigrants. Both volunteers and activists of the Second Wave successfully adapted existing spaces for a different use. Just as settlement residents invented an occupation for themselves, feminists shaped new jobs in their own health-care clinics and bookstores. And the spatial institutions each built were considered radical for their era.[35]

The social movement historically and ideologically closest to the Second Wave was the mid-twentieth-century civil rights movement. At its heart lay the black church, made up of Baptists, Presbyterians, and members of AME congregations and numerous smaller denominations. The church was the only institution blacks could own and control, and it played a critical role in more than religious life: it was also the center of social and political activities. African American ministers had the power to mobilize the entire black community from the pulpit, and clergymen sanctioned protests as a Christian response to oppression. The people originally in charge of the Southern Christian Leadership Conference (SCLC), in fact, were overwhelmingly black ministers. One of its founders, the Reverend Joseph Lowery, described the SCLC as "the black church coming alive . . . across denominational and geographical lines."[36] Most important, the church was a free space in which members could plan tactics and strategies for, and collectively commit themselves to, the struggle for equal rights.[37]

The civil rights movement was a fight for the vote and for access to spaces of the city from which African Americans were historically barred. Segregated from whites in public facilities since the Jim Crow era, African Americans realized the penalties associated with confinement to black spaces. Civil rights protesters fought to integrate white institutions in order to benefit from their significant resources. They demanded equal access to white schools, neighborhoods, restaurants, public transit, and workplaces. Places of leisure like municipal swimming pools and movie theaters were also targeted.[38] Fortified by sermons on racial justice, African Americans fought in the courts and through demonstrations to integrate the city under the auspices of the National Association for the Advancement of Colored People (NAACP, founded in 1910), the Congress of Racial Equality (CORE, founded in 1942), the SCLC (founded in 1957), and the Student Nonviolent Coordinating Committee (SNCC, founded in 1960).[39]

Although these groups were dedicated to non-violence, nearly every civil rights protest triggered vicious retaliation from whites. Black students integrating Little Rock High School in Arkansas were spit on by white students and their parents. The infamous Sheriff Eugene "Bull" Connor turned police dogs and fire hoses on demonstrators in Birmingham, Alabama. A bomb planted by the Ku Klux Klan at Birmingham's Sixteenth Street Baptist Church killed four young black girls in 1963.[40] To say that white schools and neighborhoods were contested terrain would be an understatement.

Racially restrictive covenants prevented African Americans from buying property in white neighborhoods and real estate agents would show African Americans property only in black neighborhoods (a practice known as racial steering). If those legal options failed, bombings and shootings ensured that blacks who had the courage to integrate would soon want to leave.[41]

Events in "Bombingham" influenced President John F. Kennedy to sign the Civil Rights Act of 1964, which prohibited discrimination in employment and public accommodations. That same year, Congress passed the Twenty-Fourth Amendment to the Constitution, which outlawed fees African Americans had to pay in order to vote (the poll tax) in federal elections. The Voting Rights Act of 1965 made state poll taxes and literacy tests illegal and authorized federal supervision of voter registration. The successes of the civil rights movement may not have changed the way whites thought, but it did change the way they were expected and required to act. No longer could restaurants legally refuse service to African Americans; nor could movie theaters have a separate "colored" entrance.[42]

Legal changes came too slowly for younger blacks, and they eventually fought back using the violent tactics directed for so long toward them. More than one hundred riots occurred in cities across the country in 1967. The Kerner Commission, quickly assembled by President Lyndon B. Johnson to assess the damage, reported that nearly one hundred people were killed and millions of dollars in property destroyed, primarily in black business districts. The commission's report concluded that "our nation is moving toward two societies, one black and one white—separate and unequal."[43] More riots ensued after King was assassinated in April 1968. Burned-out commercial corridors in the riot cities discouraged reinvestment for decades, an unintended consequence of blacks' anger over their second-class citizenship.

Similarities between blacks' and women's experiences (excepting the role of the church) were not lost on white feminists, many of whom gained political skills in the civil rights movement.[44] NOW was modeled on the NAACP, as were its strategies for action. The overlap between the feminist and civil rights movements was symbolically sealed when King delivered his "I Have a Dream" speech at the March on Washington in 1963, the same year *The Feminine Mystique* gave voice to the Second Wave.[45]

Second Wave Feminism

The sense of inequality that sparked the Second Wave was, in a way, a product of World War II. Returning veterans could enroll in college courtesy of the GI Bill, and, if white, buy a house in the suburbs. Women who had worked for the war effort at home were accorded no such benefits. Displaced from the labor force to make way for men, women got married and started families. Both babies and suburbs were booming between the late 1940s and early 1960s. The birth rate soared in the midst of unprecedented prosperity. Large families demanded time, and few women were employed. In 1955 only one-third of all women, and about one-quarter of mothers, were in the labor force (see figure 3).[46]

One early feminist was particularly rankled by women's relegation to the home. Betty Friedan detected a "strange stirring" among US women in the 1950s. That stirring was the dissatisfaction that suburban housewives experienced when they realized that being only a wife and mother was insufficient for a fulfilling life. Friedan's *The Feminine Mystique* identified the "problem that has no name" as the assumption, accepted by both women and men, that women were destined for domestic tasks while men engaged in intellectual and economic pursuits.

It is difficult in 2016 to imagine the society in which such stereotypes prevailed. Assuming that women would become only wives and mothers was as common then as presuming that blacks were fit only to be janitors and maids. African Americans recognized the source of their oppression and fought white privileges through the civil rights movement, but women were slower to perceive men's vested interests in maintaining a (largely invisible) dominance. *The Feminine Mystique* changed that. It gave women the language with which to identify common interests and alter power relations between the sexes. According to the sociologist Stephanie Coontz, "*The Feminine Mystique* has been credited—or blamed—for destroying, single-handedly and almost overnight, the 1950s consensus that women's place was in the home."[47]

In addition to *The Feminine Mystique*, another significant publication in 1963 marked the arrival of the Second Wave: the final report of the President's Commission on the Status of Women. It became the catalyst for Friedan and other feminists to form NOW in 1966. The President's Commission stimulated the formation of women's commissions in every state. The network of representatives from state commissions, in turn, produced the leaders and core members of the reform branch of the women's movement.

Second Wave feminism consisted of two major camps, the reformers and the radical activists. Members of NOW, the Women's Equity Action League (WEAL), and the National Women's Political Caucus (NWPC) were liberals known as "rights" or "reform" feminists for their commitment to women's equality with men. These women, many of whom were professionals, sued for enforcement of the Equal Pay Act of 1963, for example, which had languished unenforced before NOW made employment discrimination an issue for national attention. Intense lobbying by members of all three organizations pushed the Equal Rights Amendment (ERA) through Congress in 1972 (although it was never ratified by the requisite number of states).

Both NOW and WEAL lobbied ceaselessly for passage of Title IX of the Educational Amendments Act of 1972 and for subsequent lawsuits to ensure its implementation. Title IX is most often associated with increasing girls' and women's access to sports. Before its passage, intercollegiate athletics existed for women, but their teams had to supply their own uniforms, practice in inferior conditions, and pay for food and lodging when on the road for competitions. Title IX required schools to ensure greater resources for women's sports. In 1970 colleges had an average of 2.5 women's sports teams each; by 2008 the average was 8.6. Basketball and softball are in the top five most frequently offered sports in women's intercollegiate programs, the same ranking as the top five high school programs.[48] Sports for women do what they have always done for men: build teamwork and leadership skills along with self-confidence. Title IX meant more than equal opportunities for women in sports, though. It also prevented discrimination against women in any educational program receiving federal funding.[49] By 2015 feminists were using Title IX to force colleges to protect women from sexual harassment and assault.[50]

In contrast to the "rights" branch of the Second Wave, radical feminists were dedicated to overthrowing the entire patriarchal system in their quest to abolish male dominance.[51] While NOW became the largest and most important of the reform groups, there was never a comparable organization for radicals. Nor could there have been, according to the activist Jo Freeman: the thousands of women's liberation groups around the country relished their independence, making it virtually impossible to coordinate a national action, had they even been able to agree on the specific issues around which to organize.[52]

Reformers for Equality

On June 6, 1966, at the Hilton in Washington, DC, Friedan, the African American lawyer Pauli Murray, and about twenty members of state Commissions on the Status of Women met at the national conference of commission members. Dissatisfied with progress since publication of the President's report, these women decided to form NOW. Open to both men and women, NOW was patterned after the NAACP with the goal of lobbying for legislation on behalf of women's rights. NOW's founders were angry about the Equal Employment Opportunity Commission's (EEOC) failure to enforce the sex discrimination clause of the Civil Rights Act of 1964. Unless they marched like blacks in the civil rights movement, they decided, their demands would be ignored.[53]

In October 1966 three hundred women and men attended the first meeting of NOW in Washington, DC, where they adopted bylaws, elected officers (including Friedan as president and Richard Graham as vice president), and approved a lengthy Statement of Purpose.[54] The statement proposed to bring women into the "mainstream of American society" and into a "truly equal partnership with men." Noting that there was no civil rights movement for women comparable to that for African Americans, the statement's first declaration was:

> WE BELIEVE that the power of American law, and the protection guaranteed by the U.S. Constitution to the civil rights of all individuals, must be effectively applied and enforced to isolate and remove patterns of sex discrimination, to ensure equality of opportunity in employment and education, and equality of civil and political rights and responsibilities on behalf of women, as well as for Negroes and other deprived groups.[55]

The first task forces NOW established were on education, women in poverty, legal and political rights, images of women in the mass media, equal opportunity in employment, and the family. The task force on the family recommended an expansion of child care services to be available all day, year round, for children from preschool to early adolescence. The centers could be provided by private- or public-sector employers at places of work or by local governments as part of the educational system. The task force also recommended a tax deduction for child care expenses. They were unsuccessful on the issue of child care centers, but the tax deductions were eventually written into law.[56]

In 1967 NOW issued a Bill of Rights that included the following eight demands:[57]

1. Passage of the Equal Rights constitutional amendment
2. Enforcement of the law banning sex discrimination in employment
3. Maternity leave rights in employment and in Social Security benefits
4. Tax deduction for home and child care expenses for working parents
5. Child day care centers (established by law on the same basis as parks, libraries, and public schools)
6. Equal and unsegregated education

7. Equal job training opportunities and allowances for women in poverty
8. The right of women to control their reproductive lives

The ERA was at the heart of feminists' demands: "Equality of rights under the law shall not be denied or abridged by the United States or by any state on account of sex." The amendment passed in both houses of Congress in 1972 but failed to become a constitutional amendment—only thirty-five of the required thirty-eight states ratified it before the June 1982 deadline.[58]

Two of NOW's eight demands had spatial implications: day care centers and desegregated education. About one-quarter of universities and colleges were still single sex in the late 1950s, while almost all were coeducational by the 1970s. Integrated educational opportunities were to have the same effect of reducing demand for women's colleges that racial integration had on historically black colleges. Inattentive to issues of place, NOW's Bill of Rights focused on how the federal government should establish equality for women in education, employment, and earnings.[59]

Reformers did, however, understand the power of space. They resented their exclusion from commercial establishments in the late 1960s, when male-only bars and restaurants routinely refused entry to women. The Oak Room of New York's Plaza Hotel, Schroder's Café in San Francisco, and The Retreat in Washington, DC, along with hundreds of working-class neighborhood pubs, considered unaccompanied women a threat to public morals. Members of NOW and WEAL waged many legal battles to stop those practices. They also successfully fought against sex-segregated newspaper employment ads that steered women toward lower-paying jobs than men and took on cases of discrimination against women in the workplace. Laws were only the first step; enforcement was the key to change. Doors may have been opened, but vigilance on the part of feminist lawyers and organizations was, and still is, crucial to maintaining integrated urban spaces.[60]

Enforcing laws banning sex discrimination in employment was high on NOW's agenda. Its first formal action was to challenge the EEOC. In 1967 President Johnson issued an executive order prohibiting sex discrimination by federal contractors. At the same time, NOW forced the EEOC to acknowledge that sex-segregated newspaper want ads were discriminatory. Enforcement of these victories, though, was lax for many years.[61] Not until 1973, when NOW filed suit against the *Pittsburgh Press*, were sex-segregated want ads abolished. The *Press* fought the case all the way to the Supreme Court, arguing that eliminating separate job categories by sex would "choke off the economic life blood of newspapers and . . . destroy the press."[62] That same year AT&T, the country's largest employer of women, was forced by the EEOC to pay $50 million in damages to thousands of women and minority employees against whom it had discriminated.[63]

The original members of NOW recognized the need for local chapters if they were to increase their influence. Within a year of its founding NOW had 14 local chapters; by 1973 there were 365. The earliest chapters were formed by women in Los Angeles (1967) and Boston (1969).[64]

The first meeting of the Southern California chapter of NOW was held on April 1, 1967, at 6:30 p.m. at Clifton's Restaurant in the Century City district of Los Angeles. The requisite ten members of NOW necessary to form a local chapter were there, eight of whom were immediately elected as officers. The home addresses of the members suggest a prosperous group drawn from Beverly Hills, Hollywood, and Santa Monica, in addition to the city of Los Angeles. The chapter's mission was to urge the passage of State Bill 564 to extend the Commission on the Status of Women, and to lobby for passage of State Bill A.B. 109 to add the word *sex* to the Fair Employment Practices Commission law. The national organization was still so new that the typed notes from the meeting listed affiliation with the National Organization of (not for) Women.[65]

Although the elected board met at a member's home the first time, subsequent general membership meetings were held at expensive restaurants. More than the setting was formal. At the December 1967 meeting at the Century House Restaurant in Century Plaza, the president called the meeting to order, minutes from the previous meeting were read and approved, and reports from the treasurer and various task force chairs followed. Friedan had written to the chapter to ask for its participation in a protest against the EEOC, but the members declined on the basis that the chapter was still too new to take such a political risk. Members did, however, vote to endorse NOW's resolution to support the ERA. And by April 1969 the chapter was planning a demonstration at the *Los Angeles Times* to protest its sex-segregated want ads. It still had some conflict with national NOW, however. Members voted to send a letter to the national organization explaining that they could not afford the requested $1,500 to $2,000 in dues. The treasurer had reported a balance of $161, with some outstanding bills remaining; members agreed to use their Blue Chip Stamp books to purchase a television that could be raffled off to raise money.[66]

The Boston chapter of NOW, founded in 1969, quickly established a record of success in acquiring legal rights for women. Within the first several years, the chapter ensured that Massachusetts passed its own ERA, enforced equality in sports for public school students (before Title IX was enacted nationally), and guaranteed that banks were required to grant equal credit to women. Members published an annual guide to women's services, including a survey of the quality of abortion and gynecological services in the Boston area. The chapter's top priorities were reproductive rights, child care, and help for battered women.[67]

The Boston chapter's solution to its financial obligations to the national organization was to spell out for members how their $10 annual dues were spent: $7.50 went to national NOW and $2.50 to the local chapter. An appeal for funds mailed in August 1970 listed, among the national actions, a campaign to desegregate want ads in the *New York Times*, effective lawsuits against Southern Bell and Proctor and Gamble to secure job opportunities for women, and the successful challenge to California's abortion law that gave doctors sole authority to approve abortions. In 1970 California allowed abortion if a physician considered the pregnancy a risk to the physical or mental health of the mother, if the child would be born with a serious physical or mental defect, or the pregnancy was a result of rape, incest, or "other felonious intercourse."[68] The Boston chapter counted among its victories setting up a day care center, convincing the Civil Liberties Union of Massachusetts to form a committee on the rights of women, and forcing an abortion-law repeal bill out of committee for the first time in the history of the state legislature.[69]

Carrying out NOW's initial intent to march like blacks, Friedan called for a Women's Strike for Equality day on August 26, 1970, to commemorate the fiftieth anniversary of the Nineteenth Amendment granting women the right to vote. Tens of thousands of women went on strike, the largest protest on behalf of women in US history. In New York City, thousands of women marched down Fifth Avenue carrying signs that read, for example, "Don't cook dinner—starve a rat today!" and "Eve was framed." This was the point at which the women's movement, and NOW, gained serious attention from the media and politicians. During the 1960s Congress passed only ten bills related to women's issues. By 1980 seventy-one bills improving women's rights had been passed.[70] Public opinion polls showed increased awareness of, and support for, women's issues. The media coverage thus established feminism's public identity.

In adopting the civil rights "master protest frame,"[71] members of NOW identified women as a group experiencing overt systematic discrimination in education, employment, credit, and politics. Members lobbied for legislation and sued to overturn discriminatory practices, using marches and demonstrations to publicize their struggles.

Holding its first meeting in the nation's capital symbolized NOW's mission to attack inequalities through the legal system. Electing officers and passing bylaws signaled its hierarchical structure and top-down style. And admitting men as members, even electing one to office, marked a significant difference from the radical feminists' policy of excluding men.[72]

Radicals for Liberation

A younger branch of the women's movement that developed during the same years as NOW emphasized liberation rather than rights. Baby boomers were coming of age and demonstrating in large numbers for civil rights and against the Vietnam War. This group of feminists was also mostly white and middle class, but members came from a confrontational tradition of protest politics associated with the New Left. One activist of the time remembers the moment when New Left women mobilized on their own behalf: it was June 1968, when "young female activists were hissed and thrown out of the SDS [Students for a Democratic Society] national convention by their male comrades for demanding that women's liberation become part of the platform."[73] C-R groups and collectives were the organizing vehicles for this branch of the movement, and their names conveyed their anger: Society for Cutting Up Men (SCUM); Women's International Terrorist Conspiracy from Hell (WITCH); and the Furies (a lesbian separatist group in Washington, DC).[74]

Grassroots activists thought only a revolution could change women's status. Boston's radical collective Bread and Roses, formed in 1969 by women with experience in the male-dominated Left, was among the most notable. The group took its name from the 1912 Bread and Roses textile strike in Lawrence, Massachusetts, in which women strikers demanded fair wages (bread) and decent working conditions (roses). As more women joined Bread and Roses, they formed approximately two dozen small autonomous subgroups that met once a week. In 1970 the collective introduced itself in a letter to other radical women's liberation organizations in the United States. The letter listed projects that organized clerical workers, discussed socialist feminism with working-class high school women, and conducted research on local health facilities. In closing, the letter summarized the collective's politics: "We feel that only an autonomous women's movement can stage a successful fight against male supremacy. We also believe that the success of that fight depends upon radical change in the whole of society, and the defeat of other forms of institutionalized human suffering, like racism and class oppression."[75]

Members of Bread and Roses rejected liberal reformers' desire to work within the system. Changing state and federal legislation to enact rights for women, they believed, only let women into a man's world. The Collective distributed a leaflet at a march in 1970 that asked "DO WE WANT EQUALITY IN THE MAN'S WORLD, OR DO WE WANT TO MAKE IT A NEW WORLD? . . . Women finding the strength to live how we feel, *powerful* women, can lead the way to create a new kind of politics, a new life."[76] With this statement the collective was distancing itself from NOW and other formal organizations in the Second Wave.

Every member of Bread and Roses was expected to belong to a small group of five to sixteen women who met for weekly C-R. By sharing their personal histories, women would connect with other women and recognize their common bond. This exercise was meant to lead to a critical analysis of sexism, classism, and imperialism. With a fluid membership base, the smaller subgroups continuously formed and dissolved; in January 1970 there were about two hundred members of Bread and Roses in twenty-three groups. Mass meetings were called to convey information about feminist activities in the Boston area and to mobilize political actions. There women would learn about projects they might want to join, like the "doctor's project" which evolved into the Women and Their Bodies group, and, eventually, the Boston Women's Health Book Collective.[77]

Bread and Roses was instrumental in creating dozens of women-centered projects in the Boston area: the Boston Women's Health Book Collective published *Our Bodies, Ourselves* (still in print in 2016) and formed the Somerville Women's Health Project and the Somerville Mental Health Collective. Members also established a Women's School that offered classes in the history of the women's movement and the New Left. New Words Bookstore, Bread and Roses Women's Restaurant, and the Women's Community Health Project in Cambridge made a "feminist heaven" out of Inman Square.[78] But their most visible accomplishment was seizing a Harvard University building at 888 Memorial Drive as a temporary women's center. The take-over lasted more than a week and succeeded in establishing a permanent women's center in Cambridge (see chapter 2).[79]

Radical feminists wanted to liberate women from the grip of the patriarchal system which was the root of women's oppression. Their organizations were democratic to a fault. Ideology dictated that everyone should participate in decision-making because hierarchy was anathema and consensus was the ideal. But there was a gap between theory and practice. Reflecting on the early days of Bread and Roses, member Ann Popkin noted that a group with forty or more women could rarely give everyone a chance to talk, much less reach consensus. Members rejected the concept of leaders because it meant some women were more powerful than others. In fact, women with leadership skills who were suspected of trying to dominate the group might be harshly criticized through a practice known as "trashing"; some were expelled.[80] As a result the group was never able to develop effective leadership styles. Popkin speculated that the resulting lack of institutionalization may have contributed to the relatively brief existence of Bread and Roses, which disbanded after a few years.[81]

Jo Freeman, a CWLU member and the editor of the national feminist newsletter *The Second Wave*, addressed this problem in 1972 with her soon-to-be classic article "The Tyranny of Structurelessness." Freeman recognized that a lack of structure and officers could actually hinder the democratic process. When leadership is informal or completely absent, no one is responsible or accountable to members. Too little structure can also impede political action. Freeman concluded that "unstructured groups may be very effective in getting women to talk about their lives; they aren't very good for getting things done."[82]

The First National Conference of the Gynecological Self Help Clinics of America in 1972 illustrated Freeman's point. Those attending the meeting celebrated their decision-making style in the following newsletter account, making one marvel that activists ever accomplished anything. "The conference did NOT abide by the traditional parliamentary procedures of WESTERN MAN but used the traditional commonsense methods of WESTERN WOMAN of talking, arguing and exchanging views, making firm friendships and then on the fourth day going home with no unanimous decisions or majority votes, but the commitment to work until death for WOMEN."[83]

Reform and liberation feminists shared some common goals but used different tactics to achieve them. Their approach to child care is an example. NOW's 1967 Bill of Rights demanded that child care centers be publicly funded along with schools, parks, and libraries. In 1970 the president of NOW, Wilma Scott Heide, presented a position paper titled "Why Feminists Want Child Care" at the White House Conference on Children. The statement read, in part, that "women will never have full opportunities to participate in our economic, political, and cultural life as long as they bear this [child-rearing] responsibility almost entirely alone and isolated from the larger world. . . . We reject the idea that mothers have a special child care role that is not to be shared equally by fathers."[84] At the beginning of the Second Wave, feminists were optimistic about men's willingness, perhaps under duress, to cross gender boundaries and assume childrearing tasks. Yet the reality was that in the 1970s husbands earned significantly more than wives could, making the mother's decision to stay at home in part an economically rational one. And few could have predicted the dramatic increases in divorce and out-of-wedlock births that would reduce many fathers' daily contact with their children.

While NOW was focusing on public opinion and legislation, radical groups were establishing cooperative day-care centers. New York City's Women's Action Alliance published *How to Organize a Child Care Center* in 1973.[85] The Women's Union Child Care Collective in New York City believed that "child care is a right and not a privilege; that centers must be controlled by the men, women, and children directly affected and must be available wherever we work, live, or study." Once women were freed from childrearing, feminists thought, the nuclear family would become a relic. Cooptation of child care by corporations and official regulations was to be avoided at all costs. The liberation child care centers in New York City refused state and city funding, existing instead as parent cooperatives or as voluntary endeavors. Several centers banded together to stage a demonstration on Columbus Avenue in which children took their toys into the street under banners proclaiming "Power to the People" and "Power to the Children."[86]

In an article titled "On Day Care" from the Winter 1970 issue of *Women: A Journal of Liberation*, the authors Louise Gross and Phyllis MacEwan emphasized the positive effects of group care on children's development. Although the primary reason for demanding day care was the liberation of women, it could also be a liberating influence for children, especially if men were also involved in caretaking. Gross and MacEwan cautioned against letting the institutions from which they might solicit support exert any pressure on the project: "In order to develop a radically structured day care program we must not allow any control to be in the hands of the universities or corporations. Our demand to these institutions for day care must be a demand solely for space and money. Control must rest with those who struggle for and use the day care center."[87]

The Silver Lake People's Playgroup of the Silver Lake/Echo Park community in Los Angeles exemplified the battle for control of urban space. In 1970 Ruth Beaglehole, a teacher in a nursery school for wealthy children, decided to start a free preschool in her own less affluent neighborhood. She and a few parents met in a park several mornings a week. When the weather turned cold they rented a double garage, added teachers, and offered a full day care program between 6:00 a.m. and 7:00 p.m. Soon they had thirty children, with more on the waiting list, and began charging $15 per month. As soon as the center was successful they became embroiled in a major conflict with the city of Los Angeles. The fire marshal wanted to see their license (they had none), zoning prohibited day care centers in residential neighborhoods, and the Department of Building and Safety cited them for numerous violations which it refused to specify.[88]

The real catalyst for the City's reaction, according to parent Kit Kollenberg, was that Bobby Seale of the Black Panthers had come down from Oakland to learn how to set up similar community-controlled day care centers.[89] The Silver Lake People's Playgroup fought officials at every turn, appealing to their councilman, state assemblyman, and state senator. They demanded a new facility before they would close the garage. The city balked at providing space because they were afraid of setting a precedent, to which Beaglehole and her colleagues responded with "Right on! Since ultimately we want the state to provide day care for all who need it."[90] On the brink of closing, the playgroup was given temporary use of the Recreation Center in Elysian Park, at some distance from the community. The group was incorporated in 1974 as the nonprofit Echo Park–Silver Lake People's Child Care Center. It is now located at 1953 Lake Shore Avenue.[91]

Diversity and Disagreement within the Second Wave

The differences among feminists were numerous, and arguments were inevitable. Some were based on political theory that pitted Marxist, socialist, and radical feminists against each other. Some were based on sexual orientation that divided straight from lesbian women. Racial and ethnic differences were quite significant, and black, Chicana, Asian American, and Native American feminists formed their own organizations. Disagreements, misunderstandings, and sometimes anger between whites and blacks were unavoidable given the state of race relations at the time.[92] Although the women's movement has been portrayed primarily as white, a reassessment of the Second Wave has revealed substantial contributions made by black women and other women of color.[93]

Feminism and Women of Color

The Black Feminist Movement had roots in both the black liberation movement and women's liberation movement.[94] Black women confronted sexism from radical black men and racism from feminist white women. In 1964 the SNCC leader Stokely Carmichael infuriated black (and white) women with his infamous statement that "the only position for women in SNCC is prone."[95] Angered by his arrogance, the SNCC member Frances Beal formed the SNCC Black Women's Liberation Committee in 1968. The following year she wrote the essay "Double Jeopardy: To Be Black and Female," which attacked black men for their failure to recognize black women's oppression.[96] White women in the feminist movement were reluctant to admit their own racism. Such racism manifested itself, however, in their failure to include black women on conference panels, in women's studies curricula, and in feminist writings. Black women grew tired of educating black men about sexism and white women about racism.[97]

Shirley Chisholm, Florynce Kennedy, and Eleanor Holmes Norton were among the most prominent black feminists in the early 1970s. In 1968 Chisholm became the first African American woman elected to Congress. Kennedy, the second African American woman to graduate from Columbia University's School of Law, was an original member of NOW and helped form the National Women's Political Caucus (NWPC).[98] Norton received a law degree and a master's degree in American studies from Yale University. While in college she was an organizer for SNCC, and after graduation she traveled to Mississippi for the Freedom Summer civil rights protests.[99]

Few black women in the early 1970s were ready to identify themselves as feminists. Some thought racism was more damaging than sexism, others that white feminists were privileged man-hating lesbians, and still others that black men's need for dignity overruled women's problems. Nevertheless, in 1973 a dozen black women in New York City formed the National Black Feminist Organization (NBFO). The founders were Doris Wright, Margaret Sloan, Jane Galvin-Lewis, and Deborah Singletary. Chisholm, Kennedy, and Norton were all members of the board. Wright, the author of the 1970 militant essay "Angry Notes from a Black Feminist,"[100] attended Hunter College at night and worked during the day at Rockefeller University; she was also a member of the board of NOW. Sloan, from Chicago's South Side, was the first black editor-writer at *Ms.* Magazine. Wright and Sloan convened an all-day conference in 1973 called "Black Women and Their Relationship to the Women's Movement," and the NBFO was born. Sloan was elected Chair.[101] Affiliate chapters opened in Boston, Los Angeles, and other cities.[102]

Michele Wallace, the author of the controversial *Black Macho and the Myth of the Superwoman* (1979), was at that meeting. Wallace thought Sloan was a poor choice: "It was probably our first mistake because the only thing my grandmother and thousands of other black women knew about Margaret Sloan was that she had sung a love song to her white female lover locally on television, strumming her guitar, her child at her feet." The selection of Sloan, Wallace believed, ruled out the possibility of mass appeal for the NBFO. She was ultimately correct in predicting the organization's inability to recruit new members, although other factors also contributed to its demise.[103]

The NBFO's Statement of Purpose blamed the "male-dominated media" for obscuring the importance of the women's movement for black women:

> The Movement has been characterized as the exclusive property of so-called white middle-class women and any black women seen involved in this movement have been seen as "selling out," "dividing the race," and an assortment of nonsensical epithets. Black feminists resent these charges and have therefore established The National Black Feminist Organization, in order to address ourselves to the particular and specific needs of the larger, but almost cast-aside half of the black race in Amerikkka, the black woman.[104]

The NBFO had a brief life-span. Within a year or two Wright quit the group, Wallace criticized the organization, and Sloan left New York when she was let go by *Ms.* magazine. According to Wallace, like other feminist groups, the NBFO "simply could not work out a balance of power between lesbians and non-lesbians; non-lesbians spent most of their time being intimidated or feeling guilty for fear of some deeply buried anti-lesbian feeling."[105] In 1975 the national group disbanded when the New York board was ousted at the NBFO's convention. The organization's work continued in some cities, however. Under the leadership of the writer Barbara Smith, the Boston chapter became the Combahee River Collective, named after the site of Harriet Tubman's Civil War military raid in South Carolina. Smith eventually joined with the poet Audre Lorde to found Kitchen Table: Women of Color Press.[106]

In order to promote a radical agenda of social change, members of the Combahee River Collective made alliances with other women of color, and with women and men in progressive and leftist organizations. One of their early projects was a response to the daily stories of domestic abuse they heard. Partnering with Boricuas en Acción (IBA), a Latino group working for affordable housing in Boston's South End, they established the Casa Myrna Vazquez domestic violence shelter for women and children of all races (see chapter 5).[107]

Feminism and Lesbians

The Combahee River Collective was formed out of frustration with the NBFO's refusal to address sexual preference. The Collective's 1977 statement outlined its struggle against "racial, sexual, heterosexual, and class oppression";

members intended to develop an "integrated analysis and practice based upon the fact that the major systems of oppression are interlocking."[108] Barbara Smith's coedited *Home Girls: A Black Feminist Anthology*, published in 1982 by Kitchen Table, was meant to educate others about their issues.[109] Lorde identified lesbians as "strongly woman-identified women where love between women is open and possible, beyond physical in every way . . . the true feminist deals out of a lesbian consciousness whether or not she ever sleeps with women."[110]

Lorde tapped into a major debate in the feminist movement, black and white, about whether lesbians were the only true feminists because they rejected men sexually. Straight feminists worried that opponents would discredit the movement by calling all feminists lesbians. In 1970 Friedan expressed this concern when she proclaimed that the "lavender menace" would destroy the women's movement.[111] But lesbians refused to remain silent; for them lesbianism was a political as well as a personal choice. The group Radicalesbians, initially calling themselves the Lavender Menace after Friedan's statement, published a manifesto titled *The Woman-Identified Woman* (1970). It began "What is a lesbian? A lesbian is the rage of all women condensed to the point of explosion" who has lived all her life in a patriarchal, heterosexual society. Radicalesbians emphasized political anger over sexual preference.[112]

Soon after the article appeared, a group calling itself "Anonymous Realesbians" attacked the Radicalesbians for appropriating the lesbian label without accepting its sexual practices. A rift developed over who held the moral high ground. Radicalesbians, some of whom were straight, declared themselves lesbians in all but sexual practices, or experimented with lesbian sex. "Realesbians," however, chose other women as a manifestation of their rights to control their own bodies with "erotic liberation."[113] Their motto was "feminism is the theory and lesbianism is the practice."[114] Then there were the extremists, who saw complete separation from men as a critical tool to fight male supremacy.[115]

The first group to advocate separatism was formed in Washington, DC, in 1971 by Charlotte Bunch, Rita Mae Brown, Coletta Reid, and Joan E. Biren.[116] Together with eight other women, the Furies lived collectively in a rowhouse at 219 11th Street SE, where they published *The Furies: Lesbian/ Feminist Monthly*. The first issue, in January 1972, announced the group's stance:

> The development of Lesbian-feminist politics as the basis for the liberation of women is our top priority. . . . To be a Lesbian is to love

oneself, woman, in a culture that denegrates [*sic*] and despises women. The Lesbian rejects male sexual/political domination; she defies his world, his social organization, his ideology, and his definition of her as inferior. Lesbianism puts women first while the society declares the male supreme. Lesbianism threatens male supremacy at its core. When politically conscious and organized, it is central to destroying our sexist, racist, capitalist, imperialist system.[117]

The group was united by sexual preference and their political identity as lesbians but riven by ideological and class divisions. Biren was the first to be trashed and eventually expelled, followed soon after by Brown. The Furies disbanded completely in the spring of 1972.[118] In 2009 the *New Yorker* journalist Ariel Levy described the Furies and other separatist groups (Gutter Dykes, Gorgons, and Radicalesbians) as having created a "shadow society devoted to living in an alternate, penisless reality." Levy profiled the Van Dykes, a "roving band of van-driving vegans who shaved their heads" and avoided talking to men. They drove around North America, staying only in "womyn's lands" owned and inhabited by women. The Van Dykes were in quest of a "dyke heaven" to save them from a world suffering from "testosterone poisoning."[119]

In Los Angeles during the early 1970s, lesbians gathered in a variety of places where they felt safe and comfortable. One of the earliest was at the Crenshaw Women's Center for the Tuesday night lesbian feminist meetings. Another was Jeanne Córdova's house on Ogden Street, which served both as a place of business for publishing the *Lesbian Tide* magazine and as a political meeting space. In 1971 Del Whan opened the Gay Women's Service Center on Glendale Boulevard in Echo Park, believed to be the first lesbian services center in the country. Z. Budapest's Wicca shop, the L.A. Women's Saloon, and the Alcoholism Center for Women were part of a network of more than two dozen lesbian spaces across the metropolitan area.[120]

Lesbians played a pivotal role in establishing and maintaining feminist places. The first "free spaces" where women asserted their newly-discovered sexual identities mushroomed into sites at which feminists organized politically, socialized, and developed new skills and authority.[121] Such places became "islands of resistance against patriarchy."[122] The historian Anne Enke argues that the Second Wave gained strength through commercial spaces (bars, bookstores, and cafes), civic spaces (public parks and softball fields), and feminist institutions (shelters, clinics, and coffee shops) that politicized private sexuality through public display. According to Enke, between 1967 and 1977 "women's spaces" increasingly became "lesbian spaces."[123]

The Second Wave and Urban Space

Both reform and radical feminists built women's rights into the city, the former by integrating male-only spaces and the latter by creating female-only places. Reformers lobbied for amendments to Title VI of the Civil Rights Act of 1964 that would protect women, not just minorities, from discrimination in education and employment. They filed federal lawsuits against colleges and universities for sex discrimination, which resulted in significant increases in the number of women in undergraduate and graduate programs. Successful lawsuits for violations of Title IX of the 1972 Educational Amendments Act tapped into an enormous demand: high school girls' participation in sports increased by more than 800 percent, and college women accounted for approximately 40 percent of varsity athletes at the beginning of the twenty-first century.[124] Before the 1970s higher education and sports had been almost exclusively masculine realms.

Radical feminists, for their part, rejected the male world. The women's centers they established included libraries that documented women's accomplishments and liberation schools that taught new skills. Feminist bookstores provided an alternative to the "dead white male canon," as it came to be known. Grassroots activists formed their own health clinics to escape the male medical establishment's control of their bodies, and they founded domestic violence shelters to protect themselves against male aggression. All of these places had street addresses; they were sites of discourse about women's lack of power and the ways they could capture it.

While reformers were suing for women's rights, radical activists were enshrining women's rights into material form. Both types of struggle contributed to the contemporary city. Women are now highly visible in sex-integrated colleges, offices, and commercial establishments thanks to NOW and WEAL. Many were able to take advantage of those opportunities because of the confidence and freedom they gained in feminist places. Women's significant presence in public has generated the demand for thousands of buildings that compensate for their lost services in the home. These substitutes for their unpaid labor are critical to the maintenance of women's rights. All three types of spaces are necessary for women to attain and retain full citizenship.

As this chapter demonstrates, social movements have the power to alter the use of space. Some, like abolition and civil rights, were mobilized on behalf of a small minority of the population. The settlement house movement spoke for immigrants who made up large proportions of cities at the turn of the twentieth century, while temperance battles were waged by the few against the many so successfully that, for approximately one decade, Prohibition affected the entire US population. Suffrage and the Second Wave were alone among social movements in generating long-term benefits for fully one-half of all people in the United States. Women's ability to occupy public spaces, and to create feminist places, cemented their gains.

CHAPTER 2

Women's Centers

Nurturing Autonomy

The Everywoman's Center at the University of Massachusetts Amherst opened in September 1972, the same month I arrived for graduate studies in sociology. The center consisted of a small room in Munson Hall, a two-story brick building constructed in 1898. Architect Emory Ellsworth had incorporated a hodgepodge of design elements that made the building's style difficult to classify. A porch with classical columns was flanked by semicircular bays and ornamented with wood and brownstone trim. The exterior combined Queen Anne, Colonial Revival, and Gothic features that stood out among all the modernist buildings added to campus during the boom years of the 1960s.[1]

Its name proclaimed the center's intent to serve all women. When they walked in the door, women saw other like-minded women milling about one of the information tables or relaxing on the couch in the middle of the room. A telephone and a sign-up sheet for the mailing list were available at the table, and notices of local resources were posted on a bulletin board.[2] The center was where one could find C-R groups, and, like women's centers elsewhere, it was a safe place for lesbians to come out. Volunteers distributed a mimeographed newsletter with coverage of feminist events and causes. Women's music was especially important to the community. The all-female Deadly Nightshade was popular with feminist and lesbian groupies who showed up every time the band played at a local club.

The center occupied a niche in the cultural landscape of this large state university. It was "discourse materialized," a symbol of the theories and practices associated with the emerging feminist movement.[3] The center was connected—by newsletters, correspondence, and visits—to women's centers at other campuses and in other cities. In fact, its inspiration came from a founder's visit to the Berkeley Women's Center.[4]

Today we might classify the Everywoman's Center as a "third place," like bars or coffee shops: crucial settings for the informal public life that creates a sense of community. Neither home nor work, they are neutral ground where people can comfortably gather for conversation or just to enjoy seeing and being seen. According to the sociologist Ray Oldenburg, the best third places are in nondescript buildings that fade into the streetscape. They attract regulars who provide continuity throughout the week and year. With the exception of its high visibility, the Everywoman's Center met Oldenburg's criteria.[5]

Such places flourished in the feminist community during the 1970s. Since the majority of women had yet to enter the labor force, though, they were not "third" but "second places," an alternative to the home. Unlike the neutral ground of Oldenburg's third places, feminist places were politically charged. They promoted power for women while celebrating their liberation from traditional sex roles. The slogan "Sisterhood is Powerful" was apt: these places built the feminist movement.[6]

Of all feminist places, women's centers were the most important for both the women and the movement. A completely new use of space, they nurtured the formation of yet more places. Women went to centers to find out what a feminist was and figure out whether they qualified. They carried on serious conversations about sexism, racism, and homophobia with other women, or joined a C-R group to explore the relationship between their personal lives and the political economy in which they were enmeshed. Centers were also clearinghouses for finding a doctor, a roommate, a job, or other resources.

Women's centers' very structure was a political statement. Since masculine hierarchy was anathema to feminists, most centers were run collectively. In places as distant as Iowa City and San Diego, the same words appeared repeatedly in organizational documents: *collective spirit, collective responsibility, noncompetitiveness.*[7] Despite the attempt to avoid bureaucracy, though, informal structures inevitably developed; there was a constant tension between the desire to replace existing institutional models and the need to function as a group. Informality typically worked for small groups if participants wanted only to talk, but larger groups pursuing political action required greater organization.[8]

C-R groups, which began in individual's homes, became an integral part of every women's center. In 1972 the New York Radical Feminists issued instructions for organizing a small C-R group, recommending that the size be limited to eight to twelve women to allow everyone a chance to speak. A group would meet once a week for about three hours; including new members after the third or fourth meeting was discouraged, in order to preserve the bonds established among existing members. C-R was *not* therapy, but a "free space to talk about yourself as a woman." Groups talked about memories of childhood activities and toys that differed from those of boys. They shared experiences of puberty and physical development, or analyzed current issues of wage discrimination and sexual harassment. Interrupting was forbidden, as was challenging another woman's experience or offering advice about how to solve individual problems. The meeting would end with a summary of the issues women shared, through which members would "begin to discover the nature of our oppression."[9]

C-R was the cornerstone for all other political work in women's centers. C-R groups were designed to turn the personal into the political. That process allowed women to bond in sisterhood; it also taught them to recognize power inequalities both inside and outside the home. Women who had spent a lifetime as "nice girls" often learned for the first time how to express their legitimate anger. The C-R groups were transformative; few women left them with the same mind-set they had on joining.

By 1975 more than one hundred women's centers had sprung up independently across the country (see figure 4 and appendix B). That same year, New York City's Women's Action Alliance issued its guide "How to Organize a Multi-Service Women's Center." Section 1 of the sixty-page typewritten pamphlet included information on organizational structure, the legalities of incorporation, and how to raise money. It also advised readers to give serious consideration to the location of the center. The first step was to look for free space. As examples, the guide cited YWCAs in Honolulu, Minneapolis, and Lincoln, Nebraska, that donated space. Universities also provided free space, as did some churches. The most important considerations in choosing a location were access to public transportation, safety at night, parking, and proximity to the women who would visit the center. Section 2 described fourteen projects that women's centers had sponsored. Some, like rape crisis centers and women's health centers, would eventually spin off into their own organizations. Others, like C-R and information and referral, would remain core features of the women's centers themselves. Section 3 of the guide listed all the known women's centers at the time of publication. Thirty-nine states had at least one center; California, Massachusetts, and New York reported the highest numbers.[10]

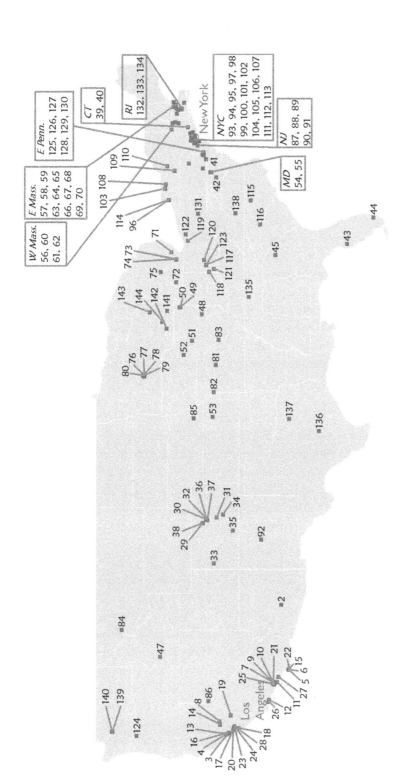

FIGURE 4. Women's centers in the continental United States, ca. 1973. Map created by Lucas Lyons. Source: Appendix B

W Mass.
56, 60
61, 62

E Mass.
57, 58, 59
63, 64, 65
66, 67, 68
69, 70

E Penn.
125, 126, 127
128, 129, 130

CT
39, 40

RI
132, 133, 134

New York

NYC
93, 94, 95, 97, 98
99, 100, 101, 102
104, 105, 106, 107
111, 112, 113

NJ
87, 88, 89
90, 91

MD
54, 55

Los Angeles

Two of the centers in the Alliance guide were in Los Angeles. The one on Crenshaw Boulevard, founded in 1970, was known variously as the Women's Center, the Women's Liberation Center, or the Crenshaw Women's Center. The second was Westside Women's Center, formed in 1972 as a spin-off from the Crenshaw Center. Members of the Crenshaw and Westside Centers often cooperated, and sometimes competed, in providing services.[11]

Los Angeles

Ann ForFreedom (née Herschfang) was a student at the University of California Los Angeles (UCLA) in 1968 when she attended a Women's Liberation conference in Chicago, making her the "Joanie Appleseed" who brought the feminist movement to Los Angeles.[12] There, she established a women's liberation group that met at the university. The self-identified anarchist/leftist Joan Robins, a freelance reporter for the alternative *Los Angeles Free Press*, learned about ForFreedom's group and started attending its meetings. Eventually dissatisfied with its academic focus, Robins and her friend Dorothy Bricker founded Women's Liberation One to promote an activist agenda.[13]

Robins came up with the idea for the first women's center in the fall of 1969 when she met with about twenty women to discuss the future of the local feminist movement. Robins had read about a women's center in New York City and thought the idea could work in Los Angeles. The New York center provided crisis counseling, abortion referrals, shelter, a place for women to socialize, and C-R groups.[14] The gathering Robins attended had been organized by radical Methodist women; other women from the political Left joined them to form the founding group that proposed L.A.'s first women's center.[15]

Robins envisioned the women's center as an umbrella organization for nine feminist groups already in existence: Haymarket Liberation, New Adult Community Women, National Organization for Women (NOW), Socialist Women's Organizing Project (SWOP), Union of Women's International Liberation (UWIL), Venice–Santa Monica Women's Liberation, Women's Liberation Front-UCLA (WLF), Women's Liberation One, and Working Women's Group.[16] A center would facilitate communication among the groups, provide services women needed, educate them about female liberation, and organize them for social change.[17] In her *Handbook of Women's Liberation* (1970), Robins proposed an organizational structure that included "External Radicalizing Activities Coordinators who would facilitate localized (block) organizing."[18] It is unclear how Robins thought coordinators would radicalize citizens, but her vision evokes an image of individual Wonder Women conquering territory block-by-block until the entire city is a feminist utopia.

The center would be set up as a nonprofit corporation with a board of directors composed of one representative from each of the nine original organizations and five at-large members from the community. An executive committee of officers would coordinate activities among divisions dedicated to education, services, communications, and operations. The social change division would coordinate activities of the original feminist organizations. Robins's plan was quite structured, although nonhierarchical. Each of the existing feminist groups would have an equal voice in running the center, as would community members. The inclusion of local women signaled the founders' intent to respond to community concerns and become good neighbors.[19]

Everyone in the founding group agreed on the concept of the women's center, but they disagreed on its implementation. Some wanted the center to have the informal atmosphere of a coffeehouse, some thought it should be an office, and some thought it should be a large mansion where staff lived (much like the Progressive Era settlement houses).[20] Whatever its form, they believed there was "a great need for a visible, concrete *place* for women to go to, a place where women could meet and talk—even late at night, a place where books and literature on women would be available to borrow and read, a place where sound, professional advice and counseling on *all* women's problems could be provided, a place of central communication—a kind of 'nerve center'—to serve and inform all persons in the Los Angeles area who are involved in woman's struggle to become full, human, and free."[21]

The building itself was also meant to have symbolic value. According to a proposal prepared by the Women's Liberation One member Sylvia Hartman, the center "would be visible evidence that 'something is being done' about women's problems and needs." Organizers believed that once they established an actual place, women would "start to crawl out from under the woodwork" to support something tangible, something more than abstract feminist goals. A building would add legitimacy to the movement. It might "have the effect of making women's problems *real* to society for once," making people see that "if there's a Women's Center there must be a real *need* for it.[22]

One of the Methodist group members, Sue Rodman, worked at UCLA, a connection that proved instrumental in the center's genesis. She convinced administrators to fund the center for six months, but the founders wanted the center to be off-campus in order to reach a larger audience. It also had to be easily accessible by public transit and large enough to partition into separate spaces for the main office, library, and counseling.[23] A duplex behind an ice machine on South Crenshaw Boulevard fit the bill.[24]

The Crenshaw Women's Center

The Crenshaw Women's Center was located in a twelve-hundred-square-foot brick duplex at 1027 South Crenshaw Boulevard in midtown Los Angeles (see figure 5). The area had good bus service and was near both the Santa Monica Freeway on the south and the upscale Wilshire Boulevard corridor on the north. Sue Rodman lived on one side of the duplex with her children; the other side became the Women's Center.[25] It had four newly painted rooms arranged in shotgun style: the living room was at the front, which led directly into the dining room, kitchen, and bathroom; one bedroom occupied the back. The front yard was paved over for parking, so staff fenced off part of the rear parking lot to build a playground. The small painted sign announcing the Crenshaw Women's Center was visible from the street. All of this was theirs for one hundred fifty dollars a month.[26]

The Crenshaw Center was a feminist place in a particular cultural landscape, which the geographer Pierce Lewis defines as "nearly everything that we can see when we go outdoors," an "unwitting autobiography" that reveals our tastes, aspirations, and fears in tangible form.[27] When women at the center walked out the door, they saw a neighborhood in transition from lower

Figure 5. Crenshaw Women's Center, 1027 South Crenshaw Boulevard, Los Angeles. Drawing by Reed Gyovai Muehlman based on photograph by Marsha Spain Fuller

middle-class white and African American to middle-class Korean. Across the street was a supermarket, other retail establishments, and single-family detached housing that was being converted to apartments. It was a safe neighborhood, neither fancy nor run down, and women felt comfortable going to the center at all hours. The door remained unlocked when women were there, and several trusted regular volunteers had keys to open or close the center. Carol Downer, who started a health clinic at the center with Lorraine Rothman (see chapter 4), remembers taking cash to the night deposit slot at a nearby bank without any incidents.[28] The center contributed to the change in the South Crenshaw landscape, its constant process of "becoming."[29]

Founders wanted to be ready by mid-December 1969 for a formal opening in January 1970. They asked for donations of a wide range of items, including playground equipment and children's games. From the beginning, they expected that women staffers and clients would bring their children to the center. They needed office equipment like desks and typewriters, but they also wanted to make it a comfortable place to gather. So they asked for a couch, chairs, lamp, and area rugs in addition to a small refrigerator and large coffee pot. It took a while for gifts to arrive. (Women attending a counselor training session on December 13 were advised to bring their own pillows to sit on.[30]) Eventually the founders collected two rooms of hand-me-down furniture. The front meeting room had couches and chairs, while the larger former bedroom in the back had rugs and beanbag chairs. The back room also contained a wide wooden bookcase overflowing with pamphlets and books from around the country.[31]

According to the architectural historian Abigail Van Slyck, buildings are products of the people who use and modify the structure to fit their needs. Feminists did that with their side of the duplex. They set up a main office as a place to plan programs, and they appealed for household items to make the center welcoming. The playground was the biggest change to the landscape surrounding the building. The center was thus more than a nondescript building; it was a structure transformed into a symbol of women's liberation through the actions of its founders, the materials they assembled, and the women who visited.[32]

The Open House on January 11, 1970, drew about fifty women.[33] An ad in the *Los Angeles Times* for free abortion referrals, and a request for volunteers that ran in the UCLA *Daily Bruin*, attracted the crowd. C-R sessions, a film series, and a feminist theater group all started operating out of the center. In May 1970 Jean Murphy of the *Los Angeles Times* wrote a story about the center that ran on the front page of the View section. Under the headline "Clearing House for L.A. Women's Lib" with the subhead "Forum Attempts to Coordinate Splinter Groups," the article featured pictures of staff members helping "an unhappy housewife" and explaining "womlib [sic] purposes." A hand-drawn poster with the center's address and phone number was in the body of the article.[34]

Much of the center's activity occurred in the evenings; hours during the day were sporadic and dependent on the availability of volunteers from the nine groups participating in the center, in addition to Women's Lib UCLA and Cal State. By August 1970 more than fifteen hundred women were affiliated with the center through their feminist groups or subscriptions to the center's newsletter.[35] Despite the center's primary purpose, men sometimes visited. Simone Wallace remembers that many of the women active in progressive causes wanted the Left to recognize women's struggles, so they occasionally welcomed men to political meetings.[36]

One of the early volunteers was Zsuzsanna Budapest. Born in 1940 in Budapest, Z. (as she was known) immigrated to the United States in 1959 as a refugee from the Hungarian Revolution. After attending the University of Chicago, she moved to Los Angeles, found an affinity with radical feminist politics, and became a volunteer at the Crenshaw Women's Center. Budapest believed that "in 1971, the Women's Movement *was* the first women's centers. [They were] the first visible manifestation of a political movement that gave room to grow to many projects. [They were] a place to meet and plot the downfall of patriarchy. . . . When I staffed there, I felt I was sitting close to the heartbeat of history."[37]

Budapest was a flamboyant woman. A disciple of Paganism and Goddess worship and a practitioner of spiritual healing for victims of rape and abuse, she founded the Susan B. Anthony Coven Number 1 that became the model for thousands of other Wiccan (witches') covens around the country. Budapest opened a feminist Wicca store on Lincoln Boulevard in Venice that sold tarot cards and other psychic paraphernalia. In 1975 she was arrested after reading tarot cards for an undercover policewoman. Her crime? Practicing witchcraft without a license. Budapest lost her case, but it helped abolish state laws against psychics nine years later.[38]

Within a year of opening, the Crenshaw Center had generated immense energy. Abortion and contraceptive counseling were in greatest demand,[39] followed by personal and vocational counseling; there was also a suicide hotline for lesbians. The center's newsletter, the *Women's Center News*, had the largest circulation nationally of any feminist publication: twenty-seven hundred copies of the January 1972 issue were distributed. (A year later the newsletter became *Sister* newspaper.) The center's library offered mimeographed pamphlets and articles of key feminist writings, including Margaret Benston's "The Political Economy of Women's Liberation," Ann Koedt's "The Myth of the Vaginal Orgasm," and Pat Mainardi's "The Politics of Housework."[40] Its publications reflected the center's leftist politics. Members talked about revolution and some considered themselves Maoists or Trotskyites.[41]

Suspecting the media of bias against feminists, the center established a speaker's bureau to deliver its message directly. Committees researched issues of relevance to women's rights, such as child care, women in the labor force, and abortion law repeal. The center taught classes on self-defense and sponsored a "Women and the Law" lecture series.[42] Speakers in that series included attorneys who explained California's new divorce law, one who discussed welfare rights, and Barbara Schlei, the district counsel for the federal EEOC in Los Angeles. Schlei was there to recruit volunteers for paralegal training. She argued that employment discrimination against women had to be legally challenged; fourteen women signed up to learn how to initiate legal proceedings.[43]

Expanded programs and multiple successful events hid schisms that began to sap energy from the Crenshaw Center during its second year. First, the local chapter of NOW withdrew its support and opened its own Center for Women's Studies at 8864 West Pico Boulevard. Its open house was on December 5, 1970, less than a year after the Crenshaw Center opened. The first center in the country opened by a NOW chapter, it differed in two significant ways from the Crenshaw Center. First, its opening was limited to members and their guests, while the Crenshaw Center welcomed all women. Second, the NOW Center invited men to all its activities, while it was understood that the Crenshaw Center was predominantly a female-only space.[44]

The NOW center offered a set of services almost identical to those at Crenshaw.[45] The month it opened, a karate expert gave a self-defense demonstration, and the NOW newsletter for December 1970 promised members they could take a course with the instructor, who taught local police officers. UCLA contacted the center with an offer to hold a class on the psychology of women, and NOW members volunteered to teach seminars on debating techniques and women's legal issues. Sundays were reserved for shows featuring art by members of NOW.[46]

According to the Crenshaw Center founder Joan Robins and member Sherna Berger Gluck, NOW fled because its officers considered the Crenshaw Center too leftist. Robins and Gluck thought NOW was too eager to take credit for everything feminists accomplished. NOW had three core goals: equal pay and equal job opportunities, abortion on demand, and comprehensive child care programs. These changes would be good, Gluck admitted, but were too limited; the Crenshaw Center, she declared, wanted *total* change.[47]

A second crack in the Crenshaw Center's foundation appeared when disagreements erupted over organizational structure—or lack thereof—and leadership issues. Radical feminists rejected hierarchical structure, which they saw as a male concept, in favor of collective leadership. Positions would rotate and everyone would have an equal say in group decisions. While that model reflected democratic ideals, it was an organizational disaster. No one gained enough experience to establish institutional memory, nor did anyone accept responsibility for a particular function. The departments Robins proposed in her 1970 *Handbook* never materialized, and the clerical tasks necessary to keep an organization going were considered "shit work" by radical women who refused to do it. Internal dissent had become so overwhelming by March 1971 that a steering committee was formed to run the center. Carol Downer was a member of the steering committee; she remembered weekly meetings in which little was accomplished. The center was understaffed and disorganized just as demand for it was increasing dramatically.[48]

The third blow was delivered in February 1972, when a group of women from the Venice–Santa Monica area created the Westside Women's Center. Santa Monica was already a hotbed of feminism. By 1971 a large house on Third Street had become a women's collective where weekly C-R groups were attended by as many as sixty women. Residents were evicted at the end of the year but continued to hold C-R meetings at a nearby church in Ocean Park. This group formed the core of the Westside Women's Center, which offered services similar to those at Crenshaw and the NOW center.[49]

Cofounder Sherna Berger Gluck remembered the original Westside Center at 219 S. Venice Boulevard as a ground-floor apartment with two or three bedrooms and a front porch. Despite its location in a residential neighborhood, it experienced no challenges from the city regarding appropriate zoning.[50] In an April 1972 *Los Angeles Times* article announcing the center's opening, the member Debby Rosenfelt described the Westside Center as "affiliated with" the Crenshaw Center. According to Rosenfelt, feminists who had been traveling to Crenshaw believed they needed to address Westside women's special needs: welfare rights counseling, drug abuse, and self-defense. The Westside Center, she noted, was within walking distance of a bus stop so that welfare recipients could reach it easily.[51] Since the Crenshaw Center was also near a bus stop, this rationale was less convincing than the fact that many of the activists living near Santa Monica were tired of the long commute to the original center.[52]

The Crenshaw Center could not withstand the cumulative effects of the departure of NOW, internal organizational difficulties, and the loss of members to the Westside Center. The entire enterprise finally collapsed: the Crenshaw Center closed its doors on New Year's Eve, 1972. During its two years, it inspired five volunteers to establish their own places: Downer founded the first Feminist Women's Health Center (that would soon be replicated in other cities across the country); Simone Gold (who would soon return to her birth name, Wallace), Gahan Kelley, and Adele Wallace opened Sisterhood Bookstore; and Budapest opened her Wicca shop.[53]

The Westside Center closed in 1974. After a hiatus, it reopened on Hill Street with an explicitly radical feminist mission. But the Westside and Hill Street Centers, like the Crenshaw Center, were underfunded. The Hill Street Center survived on pledges, and as membership declined, so did revenues; it closed in 1975.[54]

Center Programs

During their brief existence, the Crenshaw and Westside Centers were home bases for a resilient network of activists who launched multiple programs to promote women's rights. The Women's Liberation School taught women to stand up for themselves, the Anti-Rape Squad mobilized women to take an active role in removing predators from the streets, and the Gay Women's Service Center provided a safe place for lesbians to express their sexuality.

The Women's Liberation School educated women about feminism and trained them in practical skills with which they could become self-sufficient. The school started at the Crenshaw Center in October 1971 with fifteen classes. The flyer announcing the school began with a passage describing the need for the school:

> In this society, women are taught that they are passive, illogical, impulsive, and emotionally unstable. They are taught that they are inferior and subordinate to men. Education, religion, law, the media, and other environmental influences cast them in roles as sex object, housewife and mother, servant and emotional comforter of men. Women are rarely directed toward skills and information which would help them recognize their capabilities and realize their potentials. They are rarely given the opportunity to develop the critical skills necessary for them to function autonomously.
>
> The Women's Liberation School is designed to correct some of the distortions of traditional education; and to help women understand

themselves, realize the nature of their oppression, and do what is necessary to achieve true liberation.[55]

Classes met at the center in the evenings and on weekends for eight weeks. The cost was two dollars per class or five dollars for an unlimited number of classes; those who could not afford to pay could donate their time to the center.[56] Half of the fees went to the center and the rest was distributed evenly among the teachers. Recruiting instructors was a time-consuming job. A guide titled *How to Start a Women's Liberation School* recommended contacting women who had spoken at the center, advertising in the feminist media, and approaching professors at UCLA's women's studies program. Arranging the timing and content of courses demanded the full-time attention of at least one person.[57]

Women were the vast majority of those asked to teach liberal arts courses, but two men were drafted to teach auto mechanics. Two skills courses, though, carpentry and "Electricity and You," were taught by women.[58] Courses were offered throughout 1972 and were advertised in the *Los Angeles Times* and the Los Angeles chapter's *NOW News*. The August 1972 issue of the *NOW News* explained that the school was "designed to enrich women to understand their position in society, recognize their capabilities and potentials, and develop the skills necessary for them to function autonomously."[59] The selection of courses varied slightly from term to term, sometimes including Tai Chi or money management, and almost always self-defense, women in history, and practical skills.[60] In October 1972 the *NOW News* listed classes being offered, for three dollars each, at both the Crenshaw and Westside Centers.[61]

By holding classes at the centers, feminists were infusing the spaces with knowledge produced and consumed by women. With the liberation school, women gained an appreciation for the accomplishments of women throughout history, which they may have been reading about for the first time. They also acquired the power to modify their surroundings through carpentry, or at the very least to rewire a lamp and fix their own cars.

The crime of rape was of the utmost importance to feminists in 1971. When Joan Robins learned that a friend had been raped while hitchhiking, she and others at the Crenshaw Center mobilized the Anti-Rape Squad. Their first action was to produce a bumper sticker proclaiming "Sisters give rides to sisters" to encourage women to pick up female hitchhikers. They also aired public service announcements on the radio to increase awareness of the political implications of rape and to encourage women who had been raped to call or visit the center. The squad used dramatic means to publicize the problem and protect women. If women who had been raped could describe the rapist, the squad would post his description on the Venice Beach Boardwalk. If they discovered the rapist's identity, they would spray-paint his name on the Pier. A member of the center once took a picture of a man who had been punching out women on the beach and posted it with the warning "THIS MAN ASSAULTS WOMEN."[62] In an era when neither the police nor many citizens took the crime of rape seriously, such guerrilla actions were meant to force the issue into the public consciousness.[63]

The Anti-Rape Squad moved to the Westside Center when the Crenshaw Center closed. It continued its vigilante approach until 1973, when it became formalized as the Los Angeles Commission on Assaults Against Women (LACAAW). The LACAAW got a financial boost when Councilwoman Pat Russell gave the Westside Women's Center fifty dollars a month to run the city's first rape crisis hotline. Counselors did more than take phone calls. They would also go with victims to the police station, the hospital, and sometimes to court.[64] The LACAAW was modeled on the Rape Crisis Center of Washington, DC. Opened in 1972, the Washington center is believed to be the first in the nation to take emergency calls from victims. Its publication *How to Start a Rape Crisis Center* helped establish groups in major cities and college towns.[65]

It is worth noting that the Washington and Los Angeles anti-rape movements gained momentum before Susan Brownmiller published the definitive feminist treatise on rape, *Against Our Will: Men, Women, and Rape* (1975). Brownmiller labeled rape a crime of power, not passion, and claimed that all men used its threat to subjugate all women. It was the beginning of efforts to change the public perception of rape from one in which the woman was complicit to one in which she was a victim of assault.

Both straight and gay women worked on anti-rape squads, but gay women (the term they used then) searched for places where they could focus on their emerging sexual identities as well. In 1971 Del Whan provided such a place when she founded the Gay Women's Service Center. Energized by the Stonewall Riots of 1969 and ready to come out of the closet, Whan became active in the (mostly male) Los Angeles Gay Liberation Front (GLF). In 1970 Whan and the one or two other women in GLF ran an ad in the *Los Angeles Free Press* announcing the formation of a "Women's Caucus." Soon five to fifteen women were attending Tuesday evening meetings. They learned of gay women at the Crenshaw Center, and the two groups began to socialize, engaging in intense discussion about the "male chauvinism" rampant in GLF.[66] The GLF member Brenda Weathers cited as an example the gay pride parade in 1971, when lesbians had to "march . . . together with the guys who were dragging a twenty-foot papier-mâché penis down Hollywood Boulevard."[67]

When the Crenshaw lesbians invited GLF women to join them, the two groups merged to become Gay Women's Liberation. Brenda and Carolyn Weathers and Sharon Lilly, also of GLF, chose to affiliate with the Crenshaw Center because they did not want to work with NOW; its membership was too blatantly heterosexual. Gay Women's Liberation changed its name to Lesbian Feminists in February 1971 when, as the story goes, a straight woman from NOW saw lesbians staging a kiss-in and said "Oh, you lesbian feminists!" They liked the name and it became a favorite term among radical lesbians.[68]

As a recovering alcoholic, Whan wanted to establish a place outside the bar scene where lesbians could gather without encountering drugs or alcohol. Toward the end of 1970 she found a storefront at 1542 Glendale Avenue in Echo Park for one hundred fifty dollars per month. On impulse, and without consulting members of the Lesbian Feminists, she rented the building. She had unwittingly committed a major feminist sin by taking a leadership role. She was accused of being "male identified," "elitist," and of "dividing the movement." Remembering her expulsion, Whan wrote that it was a "deeply shaming event to be trashed by my erstwhile 'sisters.'" She left the Lesbian Feminists, taking eighteen-year-old Virginia Hoeffding with her, and turned the empty building into the Gay Women's Service Center. They installed a pay phone, and Whan learned later that it may have been the first time the word *gay* appeared in the Los Angeles telephone book.[69]

The gay women who visited the center lacked a political agenda and did not call themselves feminists. Rather, they sought respite from the heterosexual world while they sorted out who they were. Some had been kicked out of their homes by their parents or had been in jail and needed a place to stay. Many had alcohol and drug abuse problems, and Whan and Hoeffding reasoned it was better for them to sleep on the floor at the center than on the street. Whan considered herself to be a feminist but believed that helping lesbians overcome their oppression was more important than helping them develop a feminist identity. "That was the whole purpose," she said, "of starting a service center as differentiated from a political action group."[70]

Throughout 1971 the center held meetings, dinners, and dances. Lesbians marched in the second gay pride Christopher Street West Parade in Los Angeles. Ads in the *Free Press* attracted plenty of volunteers. Always struggling to pay the bills, the center moved up the street to a place with cheaper rent. Whan was beginning to burn out. Her fatigue was compounded by the fact that GLF established its own Gay Community Service Center and challenged Whan's territory by scheduling women's events on the same nights as dinners at the Gay Women's Service Center. After Whan's departure in late 1971, Mina Robinson Meyer and Sharon Raphael took over management of the center. They organized free spaghetti dinners on Tuesday nights, discussion groups on Thursday nights, and dances on Friday nights.[71]

Soon after Whan left, the very group that had purged her showed up to instill some feminist consciousness at the center. The Lesbian Feminists, who had condemned Whan and the center for dividing the movement, taught women not to use the word *chick*, and to call themselves *lesbians*, not *gay*. As feminism became more widespread, so did places for lesbians to gather. Fewer women came to the center, and fewer still volunteered to help keep the doors open. By the end of 1972 Meyer and Raphael closed the center and joined the thriving Gay Community Services Center.[72]

The Gay Women's Service Center became the first lesbian space in Los Angeles established during the 1970s, but it was not the city's first. That designation belonged to the local chapter of Daughters of Bilitus (DOB), begun in 1955 by San Francisco middle-class lesbians searching for alternatives to lesbian bars. By the 1960s there were enough Los Angeles members to sponsor several social events.[73] Los Angeles became the epicenter of lesbian activism in the 1970s, and Jeanne Córdova supplied much of its energy. Córdova, the founder and editor of the news magazine *Lesbian Tide*, was serving as the president of DOB in 1971 when the organization opened a lesbian center at 1910 South Vermont Avenue with "lesbian" printed on the glass front door.[74] Córdova was not yet a feminist, but when members of the Crenshaw Center sent announcements of its activities to *Lesbian Tide*, Córdova visited the center in search of other lesbians. Her visits inspired her to join the women's movement.[75]

In 1971 Córdova organized the Gay Women's West Coast Conference, which attracted conservative, older "gay women" and radical, younger "lesbian feminists" (as they identified themselves) from the East Coast, South, and Midwest. Elated by the success of the first conference, Córdova staged the West Coast Lesbian Conference in 1973. This one drew nearly two thousand women from across the country and overseas to the UCLA campus. The "largest single gathering of lesbians known in history" generated camaraderie and conflict. A Lesbian Mothers' Union was formed, but there was also a raucous protest over whether Beth Elliot, a male-to-female transsexual musician, should be allowed to perform. This conference was a reminder that sexual politics could play out between women as intensely as between women and men.[76]

By 1973 Córdova and others had formed the Tide Collective to take over publication of the magazine. They felt that the former publishing group had become too bureaucratic and hierarchical, and they wanted to experiment with a more egalitarian structure. Acknowledging that money, time pressures, and feminism were difficult to integrate, they made an effort to listen to each other, seek and extend personal support, and do away with voting. They also fought the urge to compete with other feminist publications, struggling to be "sisterly and non-competitive." The Collective's decision to subtitle the magazine *A* [not *The*] *Voice of the Lesbian/Feminist Community* is indicative of their effort.[77]

A variety of spatial institutions emerged to serve lesbians in Los Angeles. The Woman's Building, one of whose founders (Arlene Raven) was a lesbian, had a distinctly "lesbian energy." This energy took its most visible form in the 1977 Lesbian Art Project (LAP), an attempt to rescue lesbian culture from an "oppression mentality." Members of LAP used performance art, dances, and collaborative projects to add glamour to lesbian identity.[78] The L.A. Women's Saloon and Parlour was another place popular among activists, although it was open for only about one year. Córdova remembers it as a big, cavernous space with about fifty tables that served meals and drinks. It was a de facto women's center for women looking for places to hang out; men were excluded, and it was acceptable to wear sloppy clothes.[79] The October 1973 issue of the *Lesbian Tide* listed ten bars in Los Angeles that served only women. One of them, Butterfly West at 5617½ Melrose Avenue, advertised itself as "A New Women's Bar" where food, drinks, and coffee were served. Dancing, chess, and pool were available, and the Last Woman's Rock and Roll Band often performed there.[80]

Created by radical activists, the Crenshaw and Westside Women's Centers took inspiration from women's liberation groups throughout the country. Just as UCLA was a crucible for feminist activism in Los Angeles, Harvard served a similar purpose in Boston. But whereas the Crenshaw Center was modeled on a women's center in New York City, the Women's Educational Center in Boston borrowed its structure from centers in London and Chicago.

Boston

The Cambridge Center, also known as the Cambridge Women's Educational Center, opened in 1972 after members of Bread and Roses collective and other feminist groups used unconventional methods to demand new space for women.[81]

The Cambridge Women's Educational Center

"Women's Group Seizes Harvard Building: Demand Low-Income Housing and Permanent Women's Center." This headline appeared in the March 8, 1971, issue of the *Harvard Crimson*, the student-run daily newspaper of Harvard University.[82] Two days earlier about one hundred fifty women had gathered at the Boston Common to celebrate International Women's Day. They marched past sites of women's oppression, including the Playboy Club, and headed across the Charles River on Massachusetts Avenue into Cambridge. The demonstrators took a left on Pearl Street to 888 Memorial Drive, where Harvard's Graduate School of Design held architectural technology workshops. Barely habitable, the building had been slated for demolition to prepare for construction of graduate student and faculty housing. When they arrived around 3:30 that afternoon, the women were let in by a prearranged "welcoming committee." There they stayed for ten days.[83]

The low-income housing to which the headline referred was for the nearby Riverside area. The community-led Riverside Planning Team had been negotiating with Harvard for two years about building low-income housing on the site, and members of the largely black neighborhood resented the occupiers' involvement. Saundra Graham, the president of the Riverside Planning Team, had initially denied any connection with the group that occupied the building. But after she met with them to explain her concern about losing leverage with Harvard, the occupiers modified their demands to emphasize that any talks about low-income housing should take place only between Harvard and the Riverside community.[84]

The occupation of the Harvard building had been well orchestrated. In the summer of 1970 Bread and Roses members decided to create a women's center where existing women's groups could get together and offer services for women. Throughout that year women in various organizations coalesced around the idea of seizing a building. In addition to Bread and Roses, others involved were Boston's Gay Women's Liberation, the Old Mole Women's Caucus, a group called Hysteria, the Women and Imperialism Group, and the Women's Law Commune. Occupier Marsha Steinberg remembered the actors as about evenly split between the socialist-feminist Bread and Roses with its mixed straight and lesbian membership and an "action faction" of radical activists (some former Weathermen[85]) skilled in street demonstrations and "getting into places."[86] About three weeks before the march they held a meeting to review their strategy. Not everyone knew each other, but they all shared the goal of taking over a building. They believed that the take-over would make the women's movement more unified and powerful.[87]

The planning group divided the tasks necessary for a successful take-over. Some women looked for eligible buildings and talked to people in the community about how they would feel about a take-over. Others organized medical, legal, and child care services. One group gathered supplies, one collected food, and another made banners. They also formed committees to deal with security, tactics, and negotiations. As the parade was forming on Boston Common, twenty women entered the building to prepare for the marchers.[88] When the demonstrators arrived, the planning group triumphantly declared "this liberated building a women's center where women from all over will be able to meet with each other, exchange ideas and feelings, and determine what we need to do together."[89]

The occupiers were excited about building a center, even though they had no model on which to base it.[90] Some women were straight, some were lesbian, and some were just coming out of the closet. "A million political discussions were going on all the time," remembered Steinberg. No men were allowed, although they could deliver food to the protestors. Everyone was jubilant, dancing and singing and painting murals on the walls. A "lavender lounge" was reserved for gay women. Women from the community were welcome to take classes in karate, auto mechanics, and silk-screening; child care was provided communally. There was even a children's party for kids from the neighborhood.[91]

Harvard officials were determined to evict the occupiers. When the university sent in an electrician to padlock the switch box controlling the electricity, women removed the padlock with a saw. Occupiers also fixed broken plumbing facilities. They lacked heat, though, and it was a cold month. But if Harvard officials thought they could freeze them out, they were wrong. On March 9 the university ordered the women to leave the building. The women refused.[92]

Negotiations continued throughout the week with Archibald Cox, a Harvard law professor and the designated contact with the occupiers. Harvard argued that the forcible take-over was unacceptable and that the building was unsafe for occupancy. The women kept reiterating their demands for a women's center. The very fact of their occupancy was already transforming the space into one. A group of Radcliffe students calling themselves the Ad Hoc Committee to Defend the Women's Center and the Right to Live issued a statement declaring, "They [the occupying women] are not just sitting, paralyzed by Harvard's attempts to remove them; they're building a women's center."[93] One of the occupiers shared that sentiment, observing that "Even while a women's center is being demanded, it is being created."[94] If, as Lefebvre argues, the people who appropriate urban spaces are the true citizens of the city, the occupiers were announcing their rights to the city by taking over the Harvard building. They imbued it with meanings it had never before held. It had never been a place where women belonged; only two women were in the architecture program at the time.[95]

Cox had the authority to order a police raid, but never used it. Instead, he worked with the women occupying the building to find new space. On March 15 he announced that a place had been found near Central Square. But the women rejected the single basement room, reminding Cox they were demanding a women's *center*, not a closet. They needed more space to continue offering classes, day care, and medical and legal counseling; they also wanted a lesbian lounge similar to what they already had.[96]

The occupation finally ended on March 15, 1971, when about sixty-five singing and chanting women left the building after rumors of an impending police raid. The organizers felt their energies would be better spent trying to find a new women's center than in bailing themselves out of jail.[97] The occupiers conducted a search of more than fifty sites, looking for a suitable location. They narrowed the choice to three properties and began the process of incorporating as the nonprofit Women's Educational Center, Inc.[98] On the same day the take-over ended, four members of Bread and Roses signed the articles of organization with the state in order to become recognized as a nonprofit organization. Because they did not yet have a permanent location, the address was given as 102 Trowbridge Street, the home of the member Winifred Breines.[99]

The center found a home in June 1971 when a group of wealthy Boston feminists donated five thousand dollars toward the purchase of a large Victorian house at 46 Pleasant Street in Cambridge. At twenty-eight thousand dollars, the house was in serious need of plumbing and electrical upgrades. But the location was excellent. It was near Central Square, making it accessible by transit, and far enough away from any of Boston's many universities to avoid its being identified with, or dominated by, an academic institution. The house was surrounded by dilapidated apartment buildings and large houses that had been converted to apartments. Arson had taken a toll on the area, and the rumor was that landlords had set the fires themselves so that they could sell their properties to Harvard or the Massachusetts Institute of Technology (MIT). It was a mixed-use, working-class neighborhood in transition from a Jewish to an Irish and African American population: the center was on the Irish working-class side of the street, while the African American community was on the other side. A large "Women's Center" sign placed above the door, and another one on the front wall, advertised that a new neighbor had arrived (see figure 6).[100]

FIGURE 6. Cambridge Women's Center, 46 Pleasant Street, Cambridge. Drawing by Reed Gyovai Muehlman based on photograph by the author

The Women's Center opened in January 1972. Within a year thirteen projects, both logistical and service oriented, were in place. On the logistics side were groups responsible for running introductory meetings, training staff, serving as an information clearinghouse, maintaining the building, and fund-raising. The staff project had the greatest need for volunteers. Staff members were the front line for information and referral services, answering the phone and greeting walk-ins. Sometimes staff members were alone in the building, which presented problems with security.[101]

On the services side were a women's school, a lesbian mothers' support group known as Boston Dykes and Tykes, psychological counseling, photography, and sports. Soon added were abortion, pregnancy, and birth control counseling; a rape crisis center; and GED preparation classes. A library collective and the newsletter *On Our Way* had begun in 1971 before the building was acquired. These were the activities directly sponsored by the Women's Center. Other organizations used the building for support groups dealing with incest, sobriety, and domestic violence.[102] Since the center was only open on weekdays from 1:00 to 6:00 p.m., it took significant management of time and space to keep women from overflowing onto the sidewalks. There was one sidewalk, however, that women were encouraged to occupy: the one in front of Cronin's Restaurant, where waitresses were on strike for higher wages and overtime pay. Members of the Women's Center were urged to join the picket line.[103]

The founders made every effort to avoid traditional hierarchical structures in which power operated from the top down. They drew inspiration from London's Women's Liberation Workshop. Jane de Long of the Boston group had visited and described how it worked in the January 17, 1972, issue of *On Our Way*. The workshop was an umbrella organization of thirty to forty small groups in the London area that subscribed to the English women's movement's Four Campaigns: 1) equal pay and opportunities; 2) equal education and training; 3) twenty-four-hour nurseries; and 4) free contraception and abortion on demand. A representative of a group existing for at least six months could vote in monthly Office Collective meetings to make decisions for the workshop. For important decisions, the Collective would work out the wording for ballots and send it to groups for individuals to vote.[104]

Day-to-day coordination of activities was handled by the Working Party. Open to anyone who wanted to participate, the Working Party consisted of eight women. They put out a weekly mimeographed newsletter announcing meetings, results of votes, and the formation of new groups. But efficiency had its price. Members of the Working Party were suspected of being an elite, the "heavies" who manipulated the organization. Eventually the Workshop recognized the limitations of an all-volunteer staff and hired a paid office worker. Here, too, lurked danger. An office worker would have disproportionate power because she would possess all the information, which she could use consciously or unconsciously to manipulate decisions. (To avoid this risk, de Long suggested that office workers' terms in Boston should be limited to three months.) De Long was impressed with her London experience and proposed something similar for Boston: an organization founded on "a real women's politics, based on trust and equality" that got things done.[105]

The founding members of the Cambridge center were also influenced by the Chicago Women's Liberation Union (CWLU), which they discussed at a retreat on the MIT campus in early February 1972. They knew that a coordinating committee would be necessary; the questions were who would be on the committee and how much power it would have. The Chicago Women's Center, much like the London Workshop, featured a Coordinating Committee made up of representatives of each group affiliated with the women's center. The Boston Committee would make all decisions by consensus. A separate group would be responsible for staffing the office, in which volunteers would rotate weekly to avoid forming a Center bureaucracy. Members of a permanent Welcoming Committee would greet women new to the center and inform them about activities and opportunities; they would also host a dinner for new members every two weeks. This idea was reported to have worked well in Toronto, matching more experienced women's movement members with newcomers and avoiding the formation of cliques.[106]

The February 22, 1972, newsletter announced the results of the organizational retreat. A Coordinating Committee would be formed with one representative from each of nine project areas: office, lesbian, health center, school, child care, welcoming committee, orientation, legal, and media. The term of each representative would be determined by their groups; terms were typically two or three months. Groups with a nonfeminist political agenda, such as SDS, were denied representation. Decision-making would be achieved through the Chicago model, with the proviso that consensus would rule if fewer than fifty women were present at a mass meeting, by four-fifths majority vote if more than fifty attended. Coordinating Committee meetings would be open to all, although only representatives could vote. Ever mindful of the dynamic processes of governance, members planned to review the organizational structure in May.[107]

The Coordinating Committee proved inadequate to the mundane tasks of running a center, so "after much struggle" the Boston group developed a Core Committee to oversee daily operations. The Core was composed of representatives from all the center's projects; decisions were made by consensus or majority vote. Group governance would provide women with "valuable experience in political decision-making . . . a skill not usually taught to women."[108] Each of the eight members made a commitment to remain in the Core for a year. They convened every Monday evening from 6:00 to 8:00 p.m. in a closed meeting, which violated feminist ideology, but they found that allowing everyone to vote made it difficult to reach consensus on necessary operating procedures.[109]

In October 1974 the Core Committee published a list of the center's goals and purposes. Its first priority was to overthrow male supremacy by providing services for women "so that they can be strong." They believed that services could change women's lives only if they were linked with political consciousness. The center would steep women in feminist concepts and ideologies and become a "breeding ground for political activities ranging from legislation to militant action." It would be the place where women of all races, ages, and sexual preferences gained the knowledge they would need to challenge patriarchal power and establish a new women's culture.[110] Did you want to know how to prevent pregnancy? Counselors provided the details. Did you need to finish high school? The center offered GED classes. Ashamed that you had been raped? Staff members educated you about the politics of rape and assured you that it was not your fault.

The center had to overcome significant obstacles to keep its doors open. Physical and verbal harassment began almost immediately. The April 10, 1972, issue of *On Our Way* reported several instances of boys aged seven to twelve hanging out on the front porch, breaking and entering through windows, and stealing money. Members tried a range of responses, from talking with the boys to "kicking their asses" (in unspecified ways). Treating the kids harshly backfired. One Friday night after a noisy performance at the center, teenagers harassed women leaving the concert. One of the women put out her cigarette on a boy's cheek, and from that night on the center was a target for mayhem.[111]

Linda, the author of a brief article in *On Our Way* titled "The Trouble with Kids," observed that women who expressed anger toward "the little pricks" had only complicated the problem with their own immaturity. She suggested several solutions, including advising women who could not deal constructively with the kids to keep their opinions to themselves. Women who thought they could solve the problem should meet, and in the meantime, boys were never to be allowed inside the building. Nor should women staff the center alone.[112]

On April 18 a staff member who must have missed Linda's article recorded in the log that she was the only woman in the building and "there is a gang of pricks outside hanging around and banging on the doors—yelling threats and shit." On the afternoon of May 15 the log showed that "5 or 6 younger kids have been in the building—access through already broken and newly broken windows."[113] Three days later, a fire in the basement destroyed the electrical and gas systems throughout the house; members of the center suspected the two teenage boys who lived next door of throwing a lighted cigarette through the basement window.[114]

After the fire, staff members worked without light for months. Repairs went slowly due to difficulties in settling the insurance claim. Staff members suspected they were being deceived because the insurance company thought they were a "bunch of silly, gullible women" and offered payment that would cover only half of the total damage. Two women volunteered to live at the house to prevent further vandalism.[115] On the positive side, the incident spawned the Tooth and Nail Collective, a group of female mechanics, electricians, and carpenters who brought the house back up to code.[116]

Judy Norris of the collective remembers finding a male contractor who would teach the women the skills they needed, since they were all complete novices.[117]

In response to the vandalism, the staff decided that someone should live at the center. They chose the newcomer Libby Bouvier. Prior to her arrival in September 1972, Bouvier had lived and worked as an antiwar activist at the Los Angeles Peace Center. She moved into the center on October 3, and two days later there was a contentious debate among members about whether the center should even stay open. Those in favor of closing argued that the neighborhood was unwelcoming, as demonstrated by the fire, and that neighbors resented the presence of so-called lesbian man-haters; it was also increasingly difficult to staff the center adequately. Neither did they trust the police, who often delivered battered women to their door. Center staff would take the women to the domestic violence shelter it sponsored, Transition House, rather than let police know the shelter's address.[118] Those who wanted the center to remain open cited the importance of keeping a women's space to meet and work on projects; besides, they owned the building. Bouvier thought that owning the house was key to the center's success: "Having a three-floor house (and basement) owned by a community of women—rather than rented—was essential for starting all types of projects and groups. It was a place for arguments and struggles about how to be a feminist. Groups can get started in women's homes, but are harder to continue [without a central place]."[119]

Trouble continued after the fire. On March 28, 1973, a volunteer named Pinto Beans reported on a "siege happening every nite [sic] by neighborhood young people. The situation is getting so bad that I am petrified to come here at night. Since September on three different occasions young men of the neighborhood have attempted to rape me. It has been really scary. I have tried to deal with my reactions to this in [such a] way that these men would not come and harm the center (to retaliate against me)."[120]

Pinto Beans observed that women would have to think carefully about their reactions to harassment, because the "Women's Center is vitally important to the survival and growth of all of us and we're going to have to put up with some shit in order to be part of the community." She reminded others reading the log that everyone had to make an effort to secure the building and defend it if necessary; it was a "physical necessity that this center stays [sic] alive." Everyone would also have to become more tolerant of verbal abuse—after all, they'd been called dykes, queers, and chicks for years. Pinto Beans must have been particularly frustrated and exhausted that day. She finished her log entry despairing that so few women made a commitment to the survival of 46 Pleasant Street, pleading "how can we be a powerful force in bringing women into the Women's Movement if we can't even get enough of us together at one time to keep the kids from busting into the house?"[121]

By the following week Pinto Beans had recovered her equanimity. She reported a peaceful morning at the center, and admitted that "when I get so frustrated that I want to quit the whole women's movement, good work and keeping busy gets me back into a feeling of wanting to continue the struggle."[122] It might also have helped that the two boys who lived next door joined the military, and things calmed down.[123]

Center Programs

The Cambridge Women's Center offered programs similar to those offered by the Los Angeles Centers and many other centers across the country. Women's problems were the same regardless of their location. Women needed to learn more about their own history and accomplishments through libraries and women's liberation schools, they demanded that rape be treated as a crime, and they wanted to explore their sexual identities. Members at the Cambridge center also opened Transition House for victims of domestic violence (see chapter 5).

In March 1972 two women taking the high school equivalency course at the center came up with the idea for a library to make women's literature and ideas accessible to other women. By October the feminist library had opened. Volunteers collected books that women were unable to find at the public library or afford to buy. One goal was to make out-of-print books by and about women available again; another was to stock the best of current literature about women. There was also a small collection of nonsexist children's books.[124] Women from all over the community used the facility. High school and college students came to do homework for classes, some visitors read for pleasure, and others conducted research for articles or bibliographies.[125]

A history of the library written a year after it opened acknowledged the challenges associated with building the collection. E. Sylvia Pankhurst's *The History of the [Women's Militant] Suffrage[tte] Movement* (originally published in 1911), for example, was "virtually unobtainable." But women pitched in to do what they could by donating books and volunteering to staff the facility. Their task became more difficult when the fire that broke out in the basement destroyed most of the books stored there. As they built up the collection again, they found that they could use only about half of the books they received; some were easily available at the public library and others were irrelevant to women's concerns. Discarded books were sold to used bookstores or exchanged for more relevant titles. Despite progress, volunteers feared that they would never be able to obtain some important titles. They wished to have more than one copy of the most popular books, and they wanted to subscribe to feminist periodicals. Financial constraints, though, limited their aspirations. The budget for 1973 listed $1,000 for books, two staff members at $2.50 per hour for a total of $6,000, and $250 for miscellaneous materials.[126]

The library continued to grow despite budget problems. From its original location on the first floor in shared space with the lounge, it eventually moved to a separate room on the third floor. In addition to literature by women, it included materials on rape, sexuality, job skills, and numerous national and international feminist newsletters, some of which were early papers no longer in print by the 1970s.[127]

The Women's Center School opened on March 5, 1972. Among its thirteen original courses were Women's History, Introduction to Women's Liberation Literature, Black History, Women and Their Bodies, Lesbian Liberation, and European Revolutionary Movements.[128] Once again the women in Cambridge borrowed from the CWLU, whose Liberation School for Women was already operating.[129] In Cambridge, fifteen women had been planning the school simultaneously with preparations for opening the women's center. Of those fifteen, six were teachers and the others had previous teaching experience. They set up the Women's School as an alternative to the traditional educational system that "perpetuates a mythology of passivity, dependence, and ultimately powerlessness" for women. The school would teach skills otherwise inaccessible, encourage women to think analytically, and provide support for developing leadership skills. Classes were open only to women and taught only by women, thereby eliminating men's tendency to dominate discussions and assume authority. Teachers tried to downplay the traditional distinctions between experts and passive students, encouraging students to actively engage in course content and even become teachers themselves.[130]

More than 300 women registered for the first term for a fee of three dollars per class. Over the next year, enrollment stabilized at between 200 and 250 women per term. Rising expenses forced the registration fee to increase to five dollars, but donations subsidized women who could not afford to pay. Most of those enrolling were new to the women's movement and wanted to learn new skills or to take classes more cheaply than at other educational facilities. The school offered three ten-week terms per year, with twenty to twenty-five night courses per term. Free child care was provided by a novel arrangement: each student without a child was required to provide one night of babysitting per term for a student with children. Some classes were offered in Somerville to the north and Jamaica Plain to the south to enhance their accessibility. A Women in America class was offered at a Catholic girls' high school in East Boston, and a nutrition course in the Cambridge Riverside neighborhood. Sunday afternoon forums featured speakers and films in an effort to reach women employed during the week.[131]

The school operated with a steering committee of about a dozen members who met regularly. Within a year, the school opened an administrative office near the center and hired two part-time staff members. The school paid $120 rent monthly for the office and $50 monthly to the center for the use of classrooms. The steering committee's early goals were modest: to increase paid staff, pay teachers, and buy a typewriter. They also saw a long-range need to develop a child care program and increase the number of classes, especially those at other locations that would reach a diverse audience.[132] Organizers struggled constantly with attempts to reach the community beyond the walls of the center. They tried to hold more classes outside the center, and they coordinated classes with community action projects and political work. In these efforts, as with others, they took their lead from the CWLU. The main reasons for decentralizing were to make transportation and child care easier for new participants and to offer classes in more familiar surroundings for working-class women. In June 1973 the Cambridge women attended a conference sponsored by the CWLU on how to start a liberation school. They found common ground in their efforts to balance service, direct action, and education.[133]

The Rape Crisis Center opened on March 25, 1973; it was the first in the Boston area and one of only a few in the country. It was created because women who had been raped started calling the women's center as soon as it opened. Victims of rape had few rights at the time. They were subject to humiliating treatment by the police if they reported the crime, so an estimated 90 percent of rapes in Boston were never reported. Neither police nor hospital personnel provided adequate information about the risks of venereal disease or psychological trauma. If the case went to trial, the victim's sexual history could be used against her in an attempt to save the rapist's reputation. Women were left wondering if they had "asked for it," why they hadn't resisted more forcefully, and what their husbands or boyfriends would think. In this context, about a dozen members of the center, some of whom had been rape victims, formed Women Against Rape (WAR).[134]

The committee's research led them, as it had the women in Los Angeles, to the Washington, DC, Center's paper *How to Start a Rape Crisis Center.*

Establishing the twenty-four-hour Rape Crisis Hotline was the first step. Their initial efforts to claim the number 492-RAPE were thwarted by the telephone company because another customer, a Mr. Sanchez, already had that number. When the organizers contacted Mr. Sanchez and explained their request, he immediately gave up his number so the hotline could use it. Mr. Sanchez's generosity demonstrated some community sympathy for the center's programs. It also validated the organizers' successful negotiation techniques with men from whom they needed cooperation.[135]

When a woman called the hotline, counselors were available to accompany her to the police station or to the hospital, and even to court if necessary. Individual or group psychological counseling was available to anyone who wanted it. The advantage of a discussion group was that it gave women the opportunity to speak and hear other women's experiences, through which they would "mobilize pain and guilt into constructive anger."[136] The center planned to sponsor community seminars and meet with the mayor of Cambridge to garner more police cooperation; they also printed brochures for distribution in hospital emergency rooms.[137]

Members of the Rape Crisis Center wanted to change public attitudes toward victims and rapists and develop programs aimed at rape prevention. To those ends, WAR became the education and action arm of the Rape Crisis Center. Members of the group spoke to high school and college students and to community service agencies. They appeared on numerous radio programs and were interviewed for articles in local newspapers. Members of its Self-Defense for Women group taught twenty Tae Kwon Do courses in the Boston area. A conference on self-defense techniques they offered at the YWCA drew two hundred women. Their biggest challenge remained educating the public, police, and medical providers about the frequency and seriousness of rape.[138] They strove to "make visible the dynamics of hostility as the motivation for rape in our society; to help women avoid and identify rape situations; and to show how we set ourselves up as victims."[139]

"Lesbian liberation" had been one of the initial demands in the takeover of 888 Memorial Drive. Part of the first floor of 46 Pleasant Street was a lounge for lesbians, and the center had a "lesbian phone" for information and referrals. Lesbian Liberation get-acquainted meetings at 6:00 p.m. were followed by 8:00 p.m. C-R sessions that included discussions of coming out, relations with straight women, and lesbian motherhood. After the meetings, women would sometimes adjourn to the Saints, a women's bar at 112 Broad Street in Boston.[140] A lesbian mothers' group covered topics such as working outside the home, dealing with the public school system, coming out to one's children, and raising nonsexist children.[141]

The gay-straight issues permeating the women's movement at the time were muted at the Cambridge center. Several meetings called to deal with perceptions that lesbians and nonlesbians had different ways of looking at women's issues failed to attract many participants. The small group that gathered had no tangible evidence of disagreements; they suggested perhaps a lesbian/nonlesbian label was being used to obscure other types of personality clashes. The women discontinued the meetings, citing a lack of perceptible tensions, but invited others to reconvene if they saw the need.[142]

In April 1973 members of Lesbian Liberation wrote an article "In Amerika they call us Dykes" that appeared in *Our Bodies, Ourselves*. Women outside of Boston knew about Lesbian Liberation and wrote to its members for advice, or to express gratitude for its members' courage. A letter from a lesbian couple in Corning, New York, illustrates how difficult it was to be gay in the early 1970s:

> After reading your chapter in *Our Bodies, Ourselves* many times, we decided to write you, and ask for your help. My friend and I have been together for 5 years, since our first year of college. We have not "come out" as gay . . . I'm sure many people might suspect that we are queer (hate that word—gay), but we have never been faced with any sort of confrontation.
>
> We always have felt that all we needed was each other, but now we are beginning to feel very alone and isolated. . . . What we would like to know is if there are any lesbian groups in this area [southern New York State, northern Penna] or if you know of any couples in this area that are in a situation similar to ours. . . .
>
> When you constantly live in a secret, you begin to feel as if you are not *real*. We *need* contact with other gays so we can say to someone— "look! We love each other and we *do* exist!" We admire your courage and openness. But we are not now in the position to stand up and announce our relationship. . . . We would feel much at ease if you could send your reply in the enclosed envelope.[143]

Sometimes women needed to affirm their new choices. J. L. W. from Los Angeles wrote in August 1973 that she had "had an experience that changed my thinking and changed my outlook on life tremendously. I felt emotions I had never felt before, and I want to explore it [*sic*]. How would I find out if there is a Lesbian Liberation Center in Los Angeles? . . . I don't know who else to ask. . . . I am suddenly becoming in love with being a woman."[144] This plea is especially poignant since Del Whan had opened the Gay Women's

Service Center in Los Angeles two years earlier. J. L. W.'s lack of knowledge of Whan's center indicates how isolated lesbians could be.

Others were still trying to sort out what it meant to be a lesbian. "M" from Beverly, Massachusetts, who had been in and out of love with several women, wondered whether she was a lesbian because she seemed to "prefer women to men in any kind of intimate relationship." She had told friends about her feelings but was afraid she would lose her job if she were "discovered." Therapy had helped M understand and accept herself; she did not consider herself to be sick.

> It's just that it is so hard to see all the straight people around me loving openly, raising families, and talking about their loved ones. Loving in silence is so straining on the soul, and it can tear at your heart like a knife. I really don't know how much longer I can go on like this. . . . I am not ready to face an organization like yours in person; so I have chosen to communicate to you by writing. There are not too many places that one can turn to when one is a lesbian; so when I heard about the Women's Educational Center in Cambridge, I figured that it would not hurt to at least write to you. I am not asking you to answer me. . . . Just knowing that there is a place to write to that can understand my situation is somewhat of a relief.[145]

It was inevitable, perhaps, that Lesbian Liberation would also become a target for homophobia. An April 1975 letter from Mrs. E. U. of Portland, Oregon, started out benignly enough, acknowledging that *Our Bodies, Ourselves* provided valuable information. But she did not think information on homosexuality belonged in a "book of anotomy" [sic]. She thought homosexuality was unnatural and the equivalent of incest. Lesbians, in her opinion, were "copping out" of bad relationships with men. Then she got vitriolic: "I believe that the mind of a homosexual is malfunctioning and should be treated. I am deeply concerned for all human beings, but I do not believe all people are human beings. I am sorry that persons who are not human beings can not [sic] be disposed of accordingly. Hitler had the right idea of a superior race, but restricted his belief to only Jews, which was wrong. I believe human beings should use the idea of a superior race and rid the Earth of people who are malfunctioning."[146]

A staff member wrote "Whew!" at the bottom of this letter. It was a reminder that, like the neighborhood boys who terrorized the occupants, there were people who hated the women at the center, especially if they were lesbians. For some people, of course, all feminists were lesbians, so everyone at the center was at risk.

Plotting the Downfall of Patriarchy

For many women, like Z. Budapest of Los Angeles, the first women's centers of the early 1970s were the heart of the feminist movement. They were radical new spaces where feminists tried to put their democratic ideals into practice. In 1963 *The Feminine Mystique* spoke to women individually, but it took almost a decade for women's centers to bring feminists together to "plot the downfall of patriarchy," in the words of Budapest. According to Budapest, Centers were the "visible manifestation of a political movement" that gave many projects room to grow.[147]

The 1968 Sandy Spring conference attracted feminists from several big cities and college towns, but the notes from that meeting lack any mention of women's centers. Groups reported instead on political actions, like disrupting the Miss America Pageant or protesting segregated want ads in the *New York Times*, and on highly popular classes they had taught on women's issues. The idea of centers was in the air, though. The New York Consciousness Awakening Women's Liberation Group reported future plans to open a storefront on the Lower East Side that "would serve both as our office and a place where neighborhood women could come and rap."[148]

The states with the greatest number of women's centers in 1973 were California, Massachusetts, and New York. Knowing which among them was first in the country, much less how many there were by the 1980s, is nearly impossible. Documentation of activities took a backseat to the actions themselves. And unlike NOW, which archived its history from the beginning, radical groups rarely had the time or money to do likewise. There was no central office in which to keep the records. Instead, women's liberation groups were like "little islands in the river of the movement."[149]

Centers were typically created when a critical mass of radical activists identified the need for a women's place. Bread and Roses member Rochelle Ruthchild remembered that the whole idea behind the Cambridge center was to demand, take, or create a safe space for women to meet. It would be a place where women of all races and ethnicities determined their own agenda through democratic processes. For Libby Bouvier, the center was a place for discussions about how to be a feminist. Both agreed that having such a large house, owned by a community of women, was essential for starting so many successful new projects.[150]

The Crenshaw (1970–72) and Westside (1972–74) Women's Centers in Los Angeles had fairly short lives. Z. Budapest thought their closing was a natural part of the life cycle of the movement. Instead of being depressed about their inability to keep the Crenshaw Center going, feminists should have been delighted that so many projects "grew out of the greenhouse like flowers, or rather trees, taking root elsewhere." She cited Sisterhood Bookstore, the health clinic, and the Commission against Assaults on Women as examples. In 1974 Budapest claimed, "The Women's Movement has no walls."[151]

The founder Joan Robins agreed with Budapest about why the centers closed. Robins thought the centers were simply a place for new organizations to start and that they had served their purpose once they launched new endeavors. But Robins also thought the centers failed because they were too dependent on voluntarism instead of developing fund-raising mechanisms. Garage sales were never enough to remove the worry about how to pay the next month's rent. Sherna Berger Gluck had a different analysis. She thought that members of the centers were expending all their energy implementing the center's role as a referral agency and not putting enough into political actions. Gluck also blamed the way C-R groups functioned. Women might identify their problems, but instead of arriving at collective solutions, she complained, they would solve their problems individually, sapping strength from the movement.[152]

Neither Robins nor Gluck mentioned problems within the centers or between the Los Angeles centers and their neighbors. Gluck was especially sensitive to the split between straight and lesbian feminists but did not indicate that it was the cause of either center's demise.

By contrast, the Cambridge Women's Center, which opened in 1972 and is still operating, experienced a great deal of conflict with its neighbors. It represented a node at the intersection of feminist female and working-class male worlds. If ever there were a clash of cultural landscapes, the area surrounding 46 Pleasant Street was it. The "independent discourses" of teenage boys proving their manhood and women just discovering feminism made for a volatile mix.[153] The disagreements were so intense that they led to an acrimonious debate among members about whether to keep the center open. Those in favor of staying open prevailed, Ruthchild thought, because they owned the house.[154]

As "second places" to socialize outside the home, women's centers shared some characteristics with the turn-of-the-twentieth-century settlement house. They were both modifications of buildings that had once been homes, so their public spaces were quasi-domestic. And they were places where women created new identities for themselves in the process of helping others achieve their potential. Both also spun off a number of other endeavors. Women in settlement houses led investigations into labor and housing conditions before governments provided those services, while Second Wave feminists offered abortion and rape counseling that women could obtain nowhere else.

The greatest difference is that settlement houses allowed, and often encouraged, men within their walls, while women's centers typically excluded them. Settlement houses were "neighborhood living rooms" where immigrants of all ages and both sexes learned about democracy. Although men often attended evening classes or social events, during the day the settlement house was a feminized space of women and children reading, playing, and taking classes. Bastions of Progressive Era politics, settlement houses were considered radical because they supported labor rights and woman's suffrage.

Neither settlement houses nor women's centers are as numerous today as in their prime. Part of the reason is that other opportunities arose for their founders and users. Just as radical Progressive Era women won the vote and set the stage for greater rights enjoyed by their daughters and granddaughters, Second Wave feminists, while volunteering in women's centers, learned skills that opened new jobs and better pay for themselves and their daughters. Today there are fewer women-only places in the city and more sex-integrated spaces.

Women's centers never destroyed patriarchy in the United States, but they did significantly challenge its underpinnings. The safe spaces women's centers provided for lesbians, for example, were the first places women could publicly reject their dependence on men. Marginalized by gay men and by straight women, lesbians in the early 1970s gained the confidence to demand their rights. Differences in perspective between straight and lesbian women often created schisms within centers, but those internal struggles prepared lesbians to fight with gay men for equality in the gay rights movement.

By occupying 888 Memorial Drive, Boston activists aggressively asserted their rights to take urban space for their own use. Marsha Steinberg remembers the take-over as a result of women's need for "space controlled by women." Steinberg saw the center as a place where women could build an alternative culture and create new identities by exploring gender roles. The center fostered a woman's right to define herself, and it enhanced her power to change society.[155] Women's centers were incubators of autonomy for everyone who participated in them. As the following chapters demonstrate, they were especially important in launching other feminist projects. The Crenshaw Center gave birth to Sisterhood Bookstore and the Feminist Women's Health Center and the Cambridge Women's Center were the starting point for the domestic violence shelter Transition House.

CHAPTER 3

Feminist Bookstores

Building Identity

Feminist bookstores were often an outgrowth of women's center libraries. The libraries' collections grew as mimeographed copies of movement articles were brought back from conferences, and through subscriptions to national newsletters like *No More Fun and Games* and *off our backs*. Eventually women's centers sold these materials to pay the rent. An independent bookstore might follow, which would carry with it the mission to serve the women's community.[1] This was the case with Sisterhood Bookstore in Los Angeles. Its founders spent time at the Crenshaw Women's Center and were drawn to the literature accumulating in the back room. If women wanted to take an article or book, they would leave money in a metal box on the bottom shelf of a large bookcase. When the center closed in 1972, Simone Gold (her married name), Gahan Kelley, and Adele Wallace stepped in to fill the void by opening Sisterhood in a small shop set back from the street at 1915 Westwood Boulevard.[2]

On the East Coast, four Boston feminists had a similar idea. Rita Arditti, Gilda Bruckman, Mary Lowry, and Jean MacRae joined forces in 1974 for the explicit purpose of creating a women's bookstore. They met through radical theologian Mary Daly. On November 14, 1971, Daly became the first woman to preach at Harvard's Memorial Church. Instead of delivering a sermon, however, Daly descended from the pulpit and invited other women to walk out of the church to protest its patriarchal ideology.[3] Daly was teaching

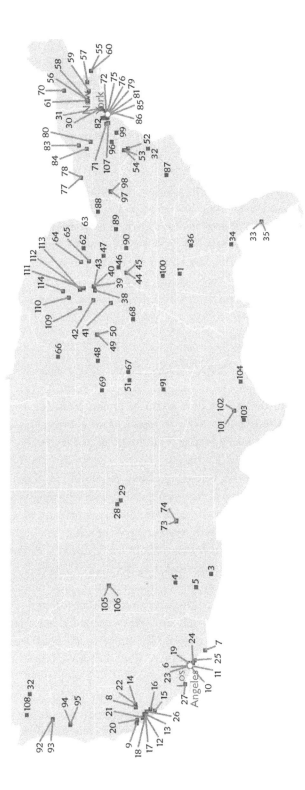

FIGURE 7. Feminist bookstores in the continental United States, ca. 1980. Map by Lucas Lyons. Source: Appendix C.

at Boston College and had become an influential figure in the local feminist community. In her 1973 book *Beyond God the Father*, Daly wrote, "Women are hearing each other and ourselves for the first time and out of this supportive hearing will emerge new words." This quotation appeared in New Words Bookstore's first flyer.[4]

In the early 1970s the future of feminist bookstores looked promising. The first ones were established by 1973 in Denver, Eugene (Oregon), Los Angeles, Minneapolis, New York City, Oakland (California), Seattle, and Washington, DC.[5] Within a decade there were sixty-five feminist bookstores in twenty-nine states. They had great names: Amazon, Old Wives' Tales, A Woman's Place, A Room of One's Own, and Women and Children First (see figure 7 and appendix C). Few survived intact into the twenty-first century, however, meeting the same fate as other independent bookstores. But during the crucial first decades of the women's movement, feminist bookstores played a significant role in disseminating its ideals.[6]

The Feminist Shelf

Feminist bookstores collected, in one place, a diverse array of publications that spoke to multiple and overlapping groups. Just one or two books were insufficient for the task; it took stacks of books, what the scholar Kristen Hogan calls "the feminist shelf," to represent the relationships among race, gender, ethnicity, sexual preference, motherhood, and the myriad other ways in which women define themselves. The space devoted to the collections was as important as the sheer volume of books. According to Hogan, that space was both shaped by, and in turn produced, feminist ideologies and ways of reading. A variety of texts revealed multidimensional and complex female identities that could transform women's sense of self.[7]

In 1975 the Common Woman Bookstore Collective of Austin, Texas, opened its store with the statement that "works by women . . . define their own context by being brought together in one place." New York City's Womanbooks used identical language in a 1976 newsletter. The concentration of multiple authors and disciplines created a sense of belonging for readers and a sense of purpose for the owners. Gilda Bruckman of New Words remembered that "there was something inherently exciting about putting books together in collections, and everybody who walked in here had that response . . . the sense of 'Wow, I didn't realize there was so much.'"[8]

Collectives that created bookstores adhered to consensus decision-making. Collective ownership was also an effective way to pool finances and share the labor necessary for opening a store. According to the *Feminist Bookstore News* (*FBN*) editor Carol Seajay, collectives were a conscious attempt to minimize the gap between the theory and the practice of feminism. In avoiding what they saw as male-model capitalism based on hierarchical relations, collectives tried to create a non-exploitive way to operate, one that emphasized participatory democracy, equality, and community.[9]

The Amazon Bookstore in Minneapolis lived longer than any other. Opened in 1970 by Julie Morse and Rosina Richter and run by a collective, it closed in 2012.[10] Amazon began in the Brown House Commune, a center for draft resistance, where Morse and Richter lived. The two women started selling feminist and lesbian literature from cartons on the front porch. When Morse and Richter left Brown House in 1972, they sold their boxes of books to Cindy Hanson and Karen Browne, who formed their own collective and moved the stock to a house with a large sign announcing it as "Amazon Bookstore Feminist Literature." After several more moves, Amazon opened a store on Hennepin Avenue in 1974; by 1975 they were breaking even. Most important, the bookstore served as a central meeting place for local and visiting feminist lesbians.[11]

Some of the least expensive acquisitions a new bookstore could stock were mimeographed newsletters and movement publications. These were already plentiful by 1970. Among the most famous were the *Female Liberation Newsletter* produced in Cambridge, Massachusetts; *It Ain't Me, Babe* from Berkeley; and *off our backs* from Washington, DC. Thirty-two others were listed in Robin Morgan's anthology *Sisterhood Is Powerful*, along with a bibliography of recommended titles.[12] By the end of the 1970s there were an estimated five hundred publications with a readership of more than three hundred thousand people.[13] *Off our backs* was in print the longest, from 1970 to 2008. It was begun by a Washington, DC, grassroots collective dedicated to publishing articles about the international feminist movement.[14]

Many of these periodicals owed a debt to the *Ladder*, the only lesbian journal before the 1970s. The *Ladder* was published by the Daughters of Bilitus (DOB) in San Francisco between 1956 and 1972 as a way for closeted lesbians to connect; it was considered so radical that newsstands sold it in a plain brown wrapper. In 1970 the *Ladder* declared itself a feminist periodical and became an important influence on the lesbian feminist publishing movement. Lesbian feminists played a pivotal role in starting bookstores and in writing and producing women's literature. According to the sociologist Junko Onosaka, "Without lesbian feminists, disseminating women's words might have been extremely difficult, if not impossible."[15]

Women visited feminist bookstores to see themselves in the books, and the way books were displayed simplified their search. It was important to stock books by and about African American and Latina women, and equally important to make those collections visible. Bruckman recalled that "how we featured books had a big effect on who came. Pretty early on, we moved the African American section front and center, created a Latina section, and created an Asian American section." They always had sections devoted to gay and lesbian issues, violence and sexual abuse, and women's health—whatever topics addressed the needs of the community.[16]

Feminist bookstores did more than assemble books about women in one place; they convinced readers, publishers, and literary critics that women's literature, and the demand for it, existed. In the process they taught women to expect books that would meet their needs for new identities.[17] Carol Seajay reported that one of things they did best was to "create a kind of literacy." By that she meant that women found something they needed from the books in her San Francisco store, Old Wives' Tales, and used them as tools in their own lives. The store carried a wide enough range of books that every woman who came in could find something that spoke to her. Seajay herself had found images of strong, independent women in novels by Toni Morrison, Alice Walker, and Zora Neale Hurston. By providing such role models, feminist bookstores created activists for the larger feminist movement.[18] In Seajay's opinion, one of the major successes of the women's movement was that it "created a literacy revolution among women."[19]

In their 1973 *New Woman's Survival Catalog*, Kristen Grimstad and Susan Rennie celebrated feminist bookstores for spreading the gospel of the women's movement. Unlike mainstream bookstores that might have only one shelf of "women's lib" books in their entire collection—or none at all—feminist bookstores were filled with hundreds of books, magazines, pamphlets, political tracts, and nonsexist children's literature from feminist and counterculture presses. Some also carried a collection of overtly antifeminist publications by Phyllis Schlafly and Maribel Morgan to illustrate the conservative attitudes they had to fight.[20] More than just the holdings separated traditional from feminist bookstores, though. In their travels around the country, Grimstad and Rennie sensed a distinctive ambience that reflected the spirit of the women's movement. Browsers could stay all day and read without being pressured to buy, and staff members were knowledgeable about women's publications and eager to help. Best of all, they reported, "Not at these stores any of that put-down crap from would-be-Thomas-Wolfe clerks who can't even make it into the copy-editing department of a publishing house, or those equally chauvinistic hip Left males."[21]

A Feminist Revolution in Literacy

According to the British historian Belinda Jack, women who read have been a source of anxiety for men since the Roman poet Juvenal confessed "I loathe the woman . . . who quotes lines I've never heard."[22] But more than male vanity was at stake when it came to women's literacy. A woman who could read might threaten the social order, especially if it was one that denied women access to books. Major world religions from ancient Christianity to contemporary Islam have challenged women's rights to literacy. During the Reformation the Catholic Church resisted translating the Bible from Latin into the vernacular, which would have made it more accessible to large numbers of women. Before the US Civil War, slaves were forbidden to read, and their owners could be punished for teaching them. Those in power have always known that subversive reading material can fuel a revolution, whether in private homes or in national politics. In the 1970s in the United States, feminist bookstores were repositories of revolutionary writings.[23]

These bookstores introduced a generation of women to women's writing, voices, and visions, creating what Onosaka, echoing Seajay, calls a "feminist revolution in literacy." Women already knew how to read and write, of course, but publishing and distributing their own work was a radical act. Feminist bookstores sustained and enriched the women's movement when they disseminated literature by women of differing cultures, ethnicities, races, and sexual preferences. They contained knowledge women could translate into action in their personal lives. By reading, customers learned how to recognize sexual harassment, fight against job discrimination, and take care of their own health. If the purpose of the Second Wave was to empower women through knowledge, feminist bookstores were key sites in that process.[24]

Except for classics like Simone de Beauvoir's *The Second Sex* or Virginia Woolf's *A Room of One's Own*, feminist bookstores initially had trouble finding enough publications by and about women. Most mainstream publishers avoided women's work for fear it would be too controversial or unprofitable. It was up to women, then, to publish, advertise, and distribute their own work. *Our Bodies, Ourselves* paved the way. The Boston Women's Health Book Collective chose the name for their educational booklet based on the abortion rights slogan, "Our bodies, ourselves, our right to decide." The New England Free Press published the bound newsprint pages in 1970 and sold two hundred fifty thousand copies in the first year. By 1980 it had sold two million copies in fourteen languages.[25] At its fortieth anniversary in 2011, when the total number of copies sold was four million, *Time* magazine listed

Our Bodies, Ourselves as one of the most influential nonfiction books of our day.[26]

All-woman publishing houses, many of them lesbian, began appearing in the 1970s: the Women's Press Collective and Feminist Press in 1970; Daughters, Inc., and Diana Press in 1972; and Persephone Press in 1976. By the middle of the decade, these presses together had sold one hundred fifty thousand copies of their titles.[27] Rita Mae Brown published two of her earliest works, *The Hand That Cradles the Rock* (1971) and *A Plain Brown Rapper* (1976), with Diana Press in Oakland. Brown's most famous novel, the autobiographical *Rubyfruit Jungle*, was published by Daughters, Inc., in 1973. *Rubyfruit Jungle* gained notoriety outside feminist circles for its candid portrayal of a lesbian's coming of age and coming out. Word of mouth resulted in sixty thousand sales by 1975 and the sale of paperback rights to Bantam for $250,000, making Daughters, Inc., highly visible. Brown's book symbolized the important role lesbians would play in feminist publishing.[28]

June Arnold and Carol Seajay were the most significant actors in developing the network that produced women's literature. Arnold organized the first Women in Print Conference, and Seajay, who attended that 1976 conference as owner of Old Wives' Tales, founded the *Feminist Bookstores Newsletter* (later called the *Feminist Bookstore News* [*FBN*]). In 1974 Helaine Harris and Cynthia Gair established the Women in Distribution (WIND) company as a clearinghouse for lesbian feminist publications; thanks to Arnold and Seajay, WIND soon had more titles to distribute to more bookstores.[29]

In the early 1970s Arnold and Parke Bowman established Daughters, Inc., in Vermont.[30] In January 1976, while Arnold was attending a meeting of feminist publishers in San Francisco, several of the attendees gathered at the Bacchanal, a lesbian feminist bar. There they came up with the idea to contact all the women involved with feminist magazines and newspapers, bookstores, publishing houses, distribution, and printing, and get them together in the same place. By that summer Arnold had organized the first Women in Print Conference with the help of Charlotte Bunch, founder of *Quest: A Feminist Quarterly*, Coletta Reid of Diana Press, and Nancy Stockwell of the journal *Plexus*.[31] They chose Omaha, Nebraska, as the site of the conference so that women from all over the country could drive to a central location; no one had the money to fly. From August 29 to September 5, 1976, 132 women from eighty organizations attended workshops and traded information day and night.[32]

Janis Kelly wrote an article in the November 1976 issue of *off our backs* that gave the conference a positive, if not glowing, review. Kelly recounted arriving at the Camp Harriet Harding campground and meeting Jean

Mountaingrove (of *WomanSpirit*, a magazine of feminist spirituality) at the pool. Here, said Mountaingrove, "are the women you always wanted to meet, all standing around nude."[33] Two types of workshops were offered: one type for learning skills like bookkeeping, setting up a shipping room, layout and design, and investigative reporting; and the other type for discussing political issues such as deciding what to publish, printing for underground groups, separatism, and the politics of organizational structure. Kelly attended the newspaper skills workshops and learned that there were as many approaches to designing layout as there were feminist newspapers. *Off our backs*, *Big Mama Rag*, *Feminary*, and *Sister Courage* each used a different system.[34] At the conference activists made connections that fueled the women's movement and the bookstore network, accelerating the growth of both.[35]

The conference experienced numerous mundane problems associated with housing and feeding more than one hundred women. Kelly vowed to bring her own toilet paper to the next conference and declared, "If I never see another lentil, I'll die happy." But there were also vexing instances of "dyke chauvinism" in which some attendees felt that lesbian separatists paraded their moral superiority over straight and bisexual women. And then there was the issue of power. Kelly acknowledged that women's publishing was gaining influence but warned readers about its potential to corrupt. The alliances formed at the conference did enhance activists' capacity to share information and do their jobs more effectively. The abuse of power would occur if anyone, or any group, tried to monopolize it for authoritarian purposes. Danger lurked in the tendency to establish institutions, which could become conservative and concerned only with their own survival.[36]

The conference was a success in Kelly's opinion. In the end, she said, "I got a tremendous amount of energy out of this conference. . . . I learned a lot of things, both practical and theoretical. I was put on the spot and forced to think about what I'm really doing. And I was reminded again of the power that exists in an all-woman environment, when energy is not wasted on dealing with men."[37]

Carol Seajay was equally invigorated by the Women in Print Conference. She had arrived from San Francisco asking whether it would be possible to open a bookstore with only $6,000. Seajay had worked at the nation's first feminist bookstore in Oakland. Called ICI: A Woman's Place, it opened in 1970 at 5251 Broadway. The Information Center Incorporated (ICI) collective sought to claim public space for the feminist movement by gathering under one roof everything they could find devoted to women's writing. In addition to literary publications, ICI carried the first issue of *Female Studies*, a collection of women's studies syllabi and resources.[38] Seajay thought

San Francisco needed a similar place. At the conference, Seajay heard from Bruckman and from Karyn London of New York's Womanbooks that it was, indeed, possible to open a bookstore with $6,000. Seajay and her partner Paula Wallace, who had already applied for a loan from the San Francisco Feminist Federal Credit Union, learned that it had been approved. With an additional $2,000 loan from Wallace's parents, they opened Old Wives' Tales at 532 Valencia Street at 16th Street on Halloween 1976, less than two months after the Women in Print Conference.[39]

In addition to serving the San Francisco feminist community, Seajay would make a major contribution to the national revolution in women's literacy. Those attending the conference, especially those running bookstores, wanted to find a way to stay in touch. Seajay volunteered for the job and started *FBN* in October, before she and Wallace opened their bookstore. On a borrowed typewriter, Seajay typed the copy for the twelve-to-twenty-page newsletters on stencils, designed the layout, borrowed a car to drive to a collective in Santa Rosa to use their Gestetner stencil-method printers, then addressed and mailed the newsletter to about two dozen bookstores.[40] *FBN* quickly became a way for all the small presses to notify bookstore owners about their publications. *FBN* also printed lists of new books by and for women from mainstream and feminist presses, and encouraged store owners to lobby major publishing houses to keep issuing important books about to go out of print. Seajay injected a strong editorial voice with suggestions that owners pay the feminist publishers first and let the mainstream companies wait if money was tight at the end of the month—as it always was.[41]

Every issue of *FBN* included letters in which bookstore owners shared information or sought advice. The second issue, which appeared in November 1976, devoted the first four pages to letters. Some thanked Seajay for her efforts; one requested a complete list of all feminist bookstores. In parentheses Seajay replied, "Yep, give us a couple issues for our address list to stabilize, and we'll do it." Another asked about the value of paid newspaper advertising, lamenting that people were still surprised to find their store nearly two years after it opened. "(That happens at A Woman's Place in Oakland after 5 years, too. C.)" was Seajay's response. Lyndall, a member of the Full Moon collective, had the nerve to criticize Seajay's spelling and punctuation in the first issue, because, she noted, she had been "a editor" [sic]. Lyndall also found fault with the way it had been distributed: "Gauuugh! You're using first class postage!?" "(Checking out the bulk permit idea—C)." In the fourth paragraph of her letter, Lyndall conceded that she was impressed that Seajay had produced the newsletter so quickly. She even volunteered to "do the shitwork on the next issue" if she were needed. The rest of that issue provided new titles and book lists especially for Native American, black, and young women.[42]

One of the letter writers asked whether there were any other distributors of women's books besides Women in Distribution (WIND). She complained that they did not properly write invoices or pack books and even made mistakes in calculating percentages. Seajay acknowledged her own problems with WIND (books had arrived damaged) but defended the company on the grounds that it was improving.[43] But WIND was trying to accomplish the impossible; it declared bankruptcy in 1979. At the time it was the distributor for nearly two hundred small presses, for which it stocked every title. WIND was an especially crucial link in the network of feminist lesbian publishing, and its closure threatened the entire industry. When it ceased distribution, Seajay worked nonstop with Helaine Harris and Cynthia Gair to put out an emergency issue of *FBN* listing the addresses and discount terms for every lesbian and feminist publisher WIND had done business with and explaining how to conduct transactions when ordering from dozens of publishers instead of from a single source.[44]

During the 1970s interdisciplinary women's studies programs grew more quickly than university bookstores and libraries could stock their book requests. By 1971, 127 institutions were offering a total of more than six hundred women's studies courses, many of which depended on feminist bookstores for their materials. The historian Kristen Hogan identified feminist bookstores as spaces that significantly contributed to the development of women's studies.[45] Seajay saw women's studies and feminist bookstores as inseparable: "How could you be a feminist in San Francisco and take a women's studies class and not go to the women's bookstore? It's like you had to. It was like breathing, you had to; it [the bookstore] was as important as anything you would read."[46]

By organizing texts related to women's studies scholarship, bookstores fueled the development of women's studies. Rita Arditti, the cofounder of New Words in Cambridge and a biologist by training, acquired an appreciation of interdisciplinarity by reading women's contributions to literature, history, science, and philosophy and by ordering for the bookstore. She understood how women's studies encompassed all these fields. Arditti's contributions to the growth of women's studies was acknowledged in 2004 when she gave the keynote address at the annual conference of the National Women's Studies Association (established in 1977).[47]

Gilda Bruckman, another cofounder of New Words, perceived a natural alliance between the scholars teaching women's studies courses and the bookstore. Sometimes faculty members visited the store looking for course ideas, and New Words provided books for the students in those courses. The founders also sent letters offering their services to local women's studies departments. Sales of women's studies materials became a reliable source of revenue for New Words. Other feminist bookstores reported less successful ventures. At New York's Womanbooks and Austin's BookWoman, the logistics of stocking textbooks that might be returned created financial burdens. But most stores persevered in maintaining a connection to academia. Staff members at BookWoman carried books to classrooms to sell so that students could save time, and the owner of Portland, Oregon's, In Other Words had a personal relationship with the chair of the Women's Studies Department at Portland State University.[48]

Feminist bookstores transformed women's lives. And like women's centers, they created oases for women in vast urban landscapes. Sisterhood in Los Angeles and New Words in Boston were two of those places.

Sisterhood Bookstore in Los Angeles

UCLA graduates Simone Gold, Gahan Kelley, and Adele Wallace each had a slightly different explanation for the motivation behind the decision to start a bookstore. For Adele, it was the closing of the Crenshaw Women's Center: "After it closed it left a void because women didn't know where to get hold of feminist books and information." According to Simone, "We envisioned it to be a movement place, multi-faceted, with everything in the way of books and materials related to women, the women's movement, and community. And we wanted it to be a place where people could sit down and have coffee, rap, or read." For Gahan, "We also imagined it to be an information center."[49] They named their store for Robin Morgan's anthology *Sisterhood Is Powerful*, and word spread quickly; within a few weeks, according to Simone, "it seemed like everyone in the women's movement" had stopped in.[50]

The partners never thought of Sisterhood as a business, but as activism. They invested $2,000 each in the store, money they raised within their families.[51] Gahan drew blueprints for bookshelves and selected pine at the lumber store, and the partners and their husbands stained the wood. Gahan built the shelves to slant just enough to make the titles easy to read and the books easy to reach. The seventy-two paperback books and some magazines they had in stock generated $3,000 gross in the first month.[52] Less than six months after Sisterhood opened at 1915 Westwood Boulevard in 1972, it had outgrown its cramped space and moved a mile north to 1351 Westwood. The new location on the corner of Rochester Avenue had a display window facing the intersection, with "Sisterhood Bookstore" written in large script across the

Figure 8. Sisterhood bookstore, 1351 Westwood Boulevard, Los Angeles, ca. 1975. Drawing by Reed Gyovai Muehlman based on photograph by Marsha Spain Fuller and details from Sisterhood website photos, http://www.inkwellweb.com/Sisterhood/Sisterhood%20story.htm. URL no longer active.

top of a big bay window (see figure 8). An Indonesian restaurant occupied the upstairs and a copy shop was next door. Since the area was zoned for retail, the owners never experienced problems with the city government.[53]

The partners chose the Westwood neighborhood, near UCLA, because it was "the place where everything was happening" in the early 1970s. Westwood Boulevard was home to a row of independent booksellers specializing in antiquarian, French, art, and fiction collections. Sisterhood became "*the* center of women's culture and women's empowerment in Los Angeles."[54] It quickly gained a reputation as the only place in the city to buy women's and lesbian books. It sold only books written by women, played only women's music, invited only women to speak, and sold feminist posters, including the one with an avenging angel holding a banner proclaiming "Fuck Housework."[55] Many of the political posters they carried, like "Women are not chicks," were produced by the Chicago Women's Graphics Collective.[56]

Each of the founders was married when they opened the store. A January 1973 article in the *Los Angeles Herald Examiner* thought it worth mentioning that they were "all Mrs.'s as well as Ms.'s."[57] And they were mothers. Adele's daughter, Amanda, spent a lot of time in a baby seat on the counter during her infancy, and Simone's daughter Emily virtually grew up at Sisterhood.[58] Everyone's personal lives changed over the next few years, however. Gahan left in 1978 to start a new venture with her then life partner (now spouse). Simone got divorced and returned to her birth name, Wallace. Adele had been briefly married to Simone's brother; thus her married name was Wallace, the one she kept after her divorce so that she and her daughter would have the same last name.[59] For all of its existence, Sisterhood was run by former sisters-in-law.

In preparation for moving to the larger place, the trio tried to borrow money at a bank, but they were turned down. Male loan officers at one bank denied them qualification for Visa and Master Charge because they had no credit references. They finally found a female manager in another bank who helped them open accounts.[60] Once in their new location, they continued to expand over the years by renovating the space. The three women rotated their working hours and stayed open six days a week and some evenings for special events. The store was financially successful its first year, but the partners deferred their salaries until the second year.[61]

Sisterhood Bookstore was to be more than just a place to buy books. The store carried crafts, music, art, posters, and jewelry made by and for feminists. The owners imagined their place to be a community information center, which it quickly became. In addition to maintaining a bulletin board, they made phone referrals for women seeking help with rape, emergency housing, and domestic violence problems. Perhaps most important, since the 1970s marked the coming out of an open lesbian culture in Los Angeles, Sisterhood carried books and music by and about lesbians.[62]

Lesbians felt comfortable in the store, which sponsored readings by the well-known lesbian authors Adrienne Rich and Rita Mae Brown. The section on lesbian titles grew with the bookstore.[63] The author Terri de la Peña discovered Sisterhood in 1983, when she went to listen to local Latina writers reading from their work. It was the first time she had met another Latina writer, and she had never met another lesbian Latina writer. De la Peña was drawn into the Sisterhood circle. One of her novels identified Sisterhood by name as a special place for lesbian feminists. De la Peña's protagonist reveled in books by notable lesbians like Jane Rule, Audre Lorde, and Adrienne Rich. "Whenever I feel discouraged, alienated," she said, "I stand here and look at all these books, remember these writers, and my spirits rise."[64]

In a small room at the back called the "flyer room," women could find notices for roommates, housing, doctors, psychotherapists, and C-R groups. Customers were encouraged to post announcements about political, community, and cultural events and to pick up free newsletters. According to Simone, the flyer room was at the heart of the store's political agenda.[65] Sisterhood sold tickets to women's events, especially women's music festivals featuring performers like Sweet Honey in the Rock and Holly Near. Simone remembers that one of their biggest events was a book signing with Lily

Tomlin and her life partner, writer-producer Jane Wagner. They talked about *The Search for Signs of Intelligent Life in the Universe*, based on the one-woman show Wagner had written for Tomlin. They sold hundreds of copies of the book. Regular customer Angela Brinskele, who waited in the rain for hours to see the event, remembers that the store ran out of copies; Adele and Simone rushed out to other bookstores to buy books for those in line.[66]

Another book signing was less successful. Early in Barbara Kingsolver's career, her publisher called to ask if Kingsolver could do a reading three days later, a weekday, at 4:00 p.m. The owners scrambled to pull together the event, but they could muster only four attendees, one of whom was Adele. Nearly a decade later, when Adele met (the now famous) Kingsolver at an American Booksellers Association convention, Kingsolver remembered Sisterhood as the place where only four people had shown up for her reading. This was a minor crisis, however, compared with the major one that was narrowly averted. When Adele was on her way to open the store one night for an appearance by Gloria Steinem, she realized she had advertised the wrong date; Steinem was due the *following* night. Women were lined up around the block by the time Adele reached the store. She went inside and closed the door. Just at the moment when she could no longer delay admitting her mistake, the electricity in the entire building went off. Adele stepped outside and announced that the event would have to be rescheduled for the following night due to the power outage. People went home, Steinem arrived the next night, and all went smoothly.[67]

Sisterhood catered primarily to women, but occasionally men would wander in. Adele divided them into two categories. There were the "funky younger guys who are into men's C-R," including students conducting research on feminist topics. They were welcome. It was the other category that the owners despised: "men over 40—more often than not bastards—who usually . . . just come in to hassle . . . their first line is always the same, 'Are men allowed in here?' Then they giggle because they think they're so witty." This scenario happened often enough that Adele considered printing a sign saying, "Yes, men are allowed in here" to ward off the nerve-grating snicker.[68]

In 1973, the same year Sisterhood moved to the larger location on Westwood, they opened a branch in the original Woman's Building. It was the former Chouinard Art Institute building at 743 South Grandview Avenue that housed the Feminist Studio Workshop created by Judy Chicago, Sheila de Bretteville, and Arlene Raven. The trio advertised the workshop as open for classes, but when students showed up, they were asked to put on overalls and completely rebuild the interior of the entire building. The "nasty little room" that had been promised to Sisterhood was "transformed into a glorious, heavenly space" that dazzled Simone.[69] The eighteen-thousand-square-foot building, a "feminist acropolis," also housed Womanspace's art galleries, the publications *Lesbian Tide* and *Sister*, the Associated Women's Press, the Los Angeles Women's Switchboard (a referral service), Los Angeles NOW, and a feminist restaurant.[70]

Adele described the clientele at the Woman's Building as a cross section of "committed feminists, women artists, curious vagrants wandering in from [MacArthur] park, and local women office workers experiencing their first tremors of feminist consciousness during their lunch hour."[71] When the Building's lease ran out after a year, Simone lamented all the work that had been wasted, remarking that it was a "great disappointment and huge loss, especially after the amount of energy that went into the creation of the space."[72] After a fund-raising campaign, the Woman's Building found a new location on North Spring Street in the warehouse district north of China-town, and Sisterhood moved with them. The bookstore sponsored readings by Angela Davis, Alice Walker, and Anaïs Nin, among other famous writers, but such special events could not offset the lack of foot traffic in the more isolated location. Sisterhood closed its Woman's Building branch in 1979.[73]

In contrast, business at the Westwood store was strong. Feminist titles were proliferating, and when UCLA launched its Women's Studies Department in the late 1970s, Sisterhood carried textbooks for its classes.[74] A former UCLA student, Carla C., remembered her first encounter: "The best thing my professor ever did . . . was send me here to buy my books. I was nervous when I first stepped in because I had never been somewhere that has so many proud, strong, female, and lesbian women's voices. It took only a few minutes to get over my fear and feel at home."[75]

In 1981, when a room adjacent to the bookstore became available, Adele and Simone removed a wall at the west end and doubled its space. They had no plans or professional drawings; they just "dreamed it up as they went along."[76] The resulting long and narrow space had several advantages. There were now more windows along the Rochester Avenue side, so people waiting in line for an event could see into the store. For especially popular programs, movable bookshelves were pushed aside and the windows were left open so people on the sidewalk could hear. The expansion allowed the partners to enlarge several sections, including children's books and guides to nonsexist child rearing. The renovation raised the back of the store two feet higher than the rest of the store. The result was a stagelike setting for readings and book signings. Its elevation made speakers visible from the front of the store, as well as to those outside.[77] Sabina Tubal, the author of *Sarah the Priestess*, thought it made the back "look like a shrine" to women (see figure 9).[78]

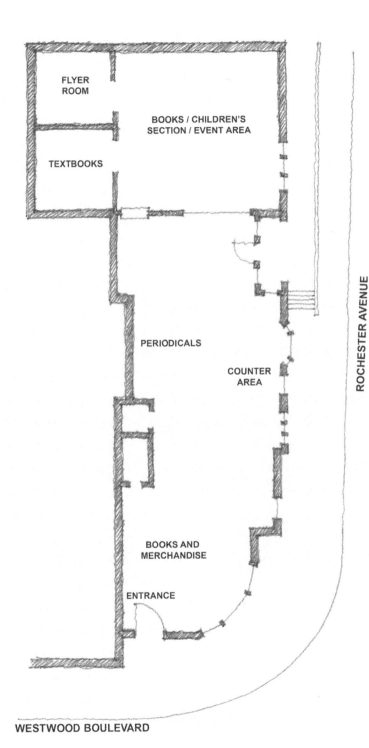

FLYER
ROOM

BOOKS / CHILDREN'S
SECTION / EVENT AREA

TEXTBOOKS

PERIODICALS

COUNTER
AREA

ROCHESTER AVENUE

BOOKS AND
MERCHANDISE

ENTRANCE

WESTWOOD BOULEVARD

FIGURE 9. Sisterhood Bookstore floor plan, ca. 1981. Drawing by Reed Gyovai Muehlman based on image in Wes Joe's unpublished submission to the Los Angeles Cultural Heritage Commission for historic designation for Sisterhood Bookstore.

Making any changes to the store was a financial risk because the founders had only a month-to-month lease with landlords who refused to invest
in the property. The brother and sister who inherited the store from their
mother seemed to know little about management. Broken windows stayed
broken, carpets became dirtier and dirtier and lighting fixtures more and
more outdated. Adele and Simone were hesitant to make expensive changes
in such a precarious situation. As a result, the place was comfortably shabby
through most of its existence.[79]

Simone and Adele conducted all their business at the counter on the
Rochester Avenue side of the building. They made a conscious decision to
avoid operating in back offices, believing it to be "too corporate." Since they
were fully visible to customers, though, they were constantly interrupted
by women who needed reading advice or just wanted to talk. Simone was
frequently hindered during phone conversations with a publisher's representative or while filling out orders for new books. In retrospect she regretted
their decision to adhere to feminist principles of transparency since they
accomplished so little work and also wished they had devoted the counter
space to stocking books.[80]

In 1997 Sisterhood held a celebration of its twenty-fifth anniversary.
Adele and Simone were surprised they had stayed in business so long. Simone
assumed that "the women's movement would take off and that after a short
time there wouldn't be a need for a women's bookstore because 51% of the
inventory of every bookstore would consist of books by and about women;
51% of the art sections would reflect books by women artists; and 51% of the
literature would be women's literature. It seemed so obvious."[81]

In honor of the anniversary, Adele and Simone solicited reminiscences
from current and former customers. Simone remembered Sisterhood as a
place where conversations got started, where women met their life partners, and where they came to understand parts of their lives through books
about sexual abuse, domestic violence, or incest. Women realized their common experiences with other women; for many, the bookstore changed their
lives. The first time women walked in, they stood in the front room, looked
around, saw images of women on books, posters, and bumper stickers, and
heard feminist music. The deeper women went into the store, the more
intense the experience became. Simone saw this experience play out "day
after day, year after year."[82] Testimonials that poured into their website confirmed her assessment:

> Sisterhood has been an anchor for me. . . . The sweet scent of incense
> and ink; the sight of all those books celebrating women, even the creak

of the wood floor under the carpet signal safety and nurturing of my lesbian soul. —Leslie R.[83]

Sisterhood Bookstore means a tremendous amount to me. Many times, it has kept me going!! Seemingly an oasis; a sanctuary in a typical patriarchal U.S. city. —Lisa K.[84]

You anchored our exciting new movement—to a reader like me, the existence of a bookstore for and about us made our revolution real, visible, permanent. —Harriet P.[85]

Sisterhood bookstore has meant that if I needed a source to open my mind, I could find it at your bookstore; if I needed a place to open my eyes, I could come to you. If I wanted to empower myself, I only needed to look to you for guidance, support, and understanding. It is because of you that I came to call myself, proudly, feminist and womyn. —Suzan N-K.[86]

Sisterhood closed a few years later for economic reasons. Competition from bookstore chains was one factor. A forty-three-thousand-square-foot Borders Bookstore opened directly across the street from Sisterhood in 1994; its underground parking garage was an appealing amenity in crowded Westwood. The other competitor for their business was Amazon.com. Sales at Sisterhood dropped by almost half soon after the company was founded in 1995.[87]

On June 15, 1999, the *Los Angeles Times* ran an article headlined "Beaten by the Big Guys: Sisterhood Bookstore in Westwood Gets Ready to Close Its Doors on a 27-Year Commitment to the Diversity as well as the Commonality of Women's Experience." Journalist Lynell George reminded sympathetic readers that Sisterhood was probably the first place they had heard—not just read—Gloria Steinem, Rita Mae Brown, Barbara Kingsolver, and Alice Walker. Discovering these writers did more than awaken a feminist perspective; it politicized the women who shopped there. According to George, "Sisterhood Bookstore opened its doors with shelves and spinner-racks full of border-shattering titles to edify and enlighten women who were attempting to define themselves outside of the predesigned boundaries of daughter, homemaker."[88] Soon after the article appeared, Sisterhood closed. It was not forgotten, however. In 2009 friends of the store launched a campaign directed at the Los Angeles Cultural Heritage Commission to have it designated one of the city's Historic-Cultural Monuments. The application argued that

"Sisterhood offered resources that sustained feminist identity and activism and that legitimized women's voices. This encouraged individual women to express their own voices, to educate themselves, and to explore their own potential."[89] As of July 2015, the designation had not been granted.[90]

Boston's New Words

In April 1974 Rita Arditti, Gilda Bruckman, Mary Lowry, and Jean MacRae opened New Words Bookstore at 419 Washington Street in Somerville. The four women came from different backgrounds. Arditti was working at Union Theological Graduate School as a faculty resource administrator; Bruckman's field was English literature; and Lowry was a licensed optician with retail experience. MacRae was attending Harvard Divinity School, one of the few women in the classroom there.[91] Like the founders of Sisterhood, the women who founded New Words had to use their own money. Collectively Arditti and her colleagues raised $7,000 for legal fees, necessary repairs, furnishings, and initial book stock. Over the next two years they borrowed $15,000 to finance a move and the expansion of their stock. A small loan, $700, came from the Massachusetts Feminist Federal Credit Union.[92]

The first location was in a rented back room of a restaurant, Peasant Stock, which specialized in French cooking; Julia Child lived around the corner. Doors connecting the restaurant and the bookstore were typically closed, but New Words staff wandered in and out of the kitchen, helping themselves to coffee and lunch. One stipulation of the rental agreement was that the bookstore would remain open on Saturday nights to give restaurant customers a place to gather while waiting for a table.[93]

By 1976 the store needed larger quarters and moved to a triple-decker house at 186 Hampshire Street in Inman Square. The building was owned by Melvin Chalfen, who liked to rent to progressive organizations. The building was also home to the Goddard Cambridge Graduate Program in Women's Studies, the Massachusetts Feminist Federal Credit Union, and Focus Counseling for women. The Women's Community Health Center was down the block, and across the street from the health center was the women's restaurant Bread and Roses. A women's craft store called Gypsy Wagon was one block in the other direction. Bruckman remembers that the critical mass of feminist places empowered women. They created for themselves a "feminist heaven" and joked about taking over Inman Square.[94]

New Words occupied a former apartment on the first floor and had use of the basement; the space included a bathroom that was available to anyone, not just customers. An enlarged bay window displaying books, huge yellow wooden numbers at the third-floor level, and a sign made the place easy to find. The building and its sign, in fact, appeared as the store's logo on flyers and tote bags.[95]

The space had been renovated to remove some walls and doors, so the store had three rooms of nooks and crannies that made it feel cozy. The owners brought in director's chairs to encourage people to sit and read for as long as they liked. The office was the only section with a closed door; otherwise customers could see from one space to another. Women painted the walls, built bookshelves, and fixed the plumbing. Bruckman remembers that the store had decent lighting, but that the inefficient heating system made it cold in the winter, and that incoming book orders were unpacked at the front desk because there was no storage room; keeping the sales desk neat for customers was a constant challenge. The founders eventually acquired a fourth room in the back for readings and social events. They also installed a wheelchair ramp and widened aisles between bookshelves to allow access to wheelchair users.[96]

When the store submitted its first book order to Paperback Booksmith, most of the requests were for two or three copies of titles like Jane

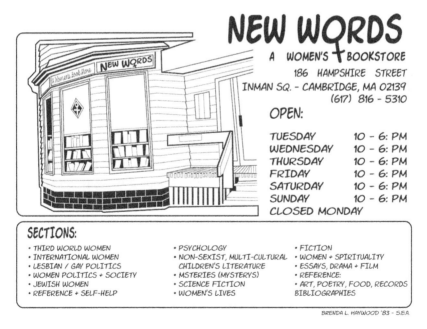

FIGURE 10. New Words poster, 1983. Drawing by Reed Gyovai Muehlman based on a flyer designed by Brenda L. Haywood, 1983. Records of New Words, Schlesinger Library, Radcliffe Institute, Harvard University, collection MC 619, carton 23, folder 7.

Austen's *Emma* or Kate Chopin's *The Awakening*. Some titles were so popular they rated five copies, such as African American Congresswoman Shirley Chisholm's *The Good Fight*, Doris Lessing's *The Four-Gated City*, and Sylvia Plath's *Ariel*. There was a big demand for *Free to Be You and Me*, published in 1972 by the actress Marlo Thomas. The book contained stories by celebrities encouraging boys and girls to achieve whatever they wanted regardless of gender stereotypes. Released with an accompanying record, the project was funded by the Ms. Foundation for Women. But the ten copies of the nonsexist children's book were a far second to Virginia Woolf's *A Room of One's Own*, which warranted twenty copies. Novels, poetry, autobiographies, and essays filled out the cross-disciplinary collection.[97]

The clientele was mostly women, some of whom brought their mothers. Therapists—male and female—came in occasionally looking for books about childhood sexual abuse for their patients. Faculty from local universities created entire courses in women's studies based on what they found at New Words, giving the store significant influence over the earliest women's studies curricula. And Bruckman remembers a nice guy who came in repeatedly to buy books by and about lesbians for his sister, who lived in the Midwest and could find nothing in her local bookstores.[98]

The alternative newspaper the *Boston Phoenix* featured a story about feminist businesses, including New Words, in December 1974. In a letter to the editors, Bruckman and her colleagues complimented journalist Karen Lindsay for portraying women's "evolving consciousness of work and self-support" fairly, but they objected to the headline, "Cashing In on Capitalism." Instead, they argued, if the editors were seeking alliterative appeal, they should have used "Coping with Capitalism." New Words was part of the women's community committed to eliminating exploitation; it was not out to profit from the movement but to support it. Although operating within a capitalist economy, the founders attempted to overcome its most dehumanizing effects: "In so doing we are able to withdraw our support (i.e. labor) from patriarchal businesses and invest our energy in work which benefits ourselves and other women."[99]

Aside from contributing to the women's community, the founders concentrated on changing the processes by which people were accustomed to working. Instead of a strict division of labor, for example, everyone staffing the store shared responsibilities and gained the experience necessary to operate a successful business. Decisions were never final as they were thought to be in the "men's world" of rules and regulations; they could be revisited at any time. According to an early account of the venture, this process resulted in an "absence of pressure, tension, everyday aggravation at New Words, a lovely sense of calm."[100]

News of the bookstore spread rapidly through the national feminist network. Within a year of its opening, letters were coming in from women in Salt Lake City, Cincinnati, and North Bay (New York) seeking advice about starting or expanding a store. The women in Cincinnati had once lived in Boston and had visited New Words; they asked for a booklist and pointers on contacting publishers.[101] The woman from North Bay learned of New Words through Kristen Grimstad and Susan Rennie's *The New Woman's Survival Sourcebook* and needed information about start-up costs and book wholesalers.[102] The woman in Salt Lake City ran a new feminist bookstore called The Open Book located in the basement of an old home. Feeling isolated in Salt Lake, she wanted recommendations for titles and contact with other feminist booksellers around the country.[103] The bookstore once received an inquiry from a member of a Latin American Feminist Women's Group in Paris, wanting to know if the store would like to carry its publication *Nosotras*. The French group had learned of New Words from Mary Daly, then visiting Paris.[104]

Women also wrote suggesting books to carry. Suzy McKee Charnas, a feminist science-fiction writer living in New Mexico, lamented the lack of science fiction that appealed to women, noting that most of the genre consisted of "shallow, sexist, pre-adolescent books." But, she argued, science fiction was a vehicle for imagining the world differently and could be used to raise women's consciousness of inequalities and their solutions. Charnas included a copy of her *Walk to the End of the World* and a list of other science-fiction titles by and about women. She ended the letter by noting that "women writers need women readers," especially in traditionally male fields that were undergoing a transformation.[105]

On the store's second birthday, the founders issued a statement to the feminist community reiterating their primary goal of meeting local women's need for access to the writings of the feminist movement and to the art, music, and literature created by women. They also reminded readers of their commitment to work cooperatively and share equally in the decision-making and daily operations of the store. The Women's Law Commune helped with incorporation documents, and women volunteered to design, paint, and do minor carpentry before they opened. Women's groups used the store for meetings and special events. Because of ongoing contacts with these groups, New Words became a clearinghouse for all kinds of information.[106]

Almost from the beginning the cofounders received salaries: four dollars per hour in 1974 and five dollars per hour four years later. Everyone worked a different number of hours depending on how much income they needed and how much time they could commit to the store. It was an important tenet of the movement that women be paid for their work, and New Words complied. They avoided accepting volunteers except in special circumstances, as they did in January 1977 when a crew of about twenty women moved the contents of the Washington Street store to its new location on Hampshire Street. Starting in 1977 employees received health insurance and three weeks of vacation annually. Although the store had registered as a for-profit organization, it was that in name only. As the founders admitted in their fourth birthday statement, "In reality profit is not an immediate issue."[107]

Despite precarious financial standing, New Words always paid its bills to women's presses and suppliers first, often immediately on receipt, to maximize the cash available to women's businesses. The store also made small grants to women's organizations, like the Women's Community Health Center and the domestic violence shelters Transition House and RESPOND. The founders vowed to increase that financial help when the store became profitable.[108] But their first priority, following Carol Seajay's advice, was to support small alternative presses, and feminist, gay, and Third World publishers. Self-published books and books published by community groups could also find a place on the shelves, as could nonsexist and nonracist children's books. Almost anything written by or about women was acceptable as long as it did not degrade or devalue them.[109]

In 1981 New Words held readings and performances in the basement of their building; the space was also used by a regular Women's Craft Market and various women's organizations.[110] By the mid-1980s the store had significantly increased its offerings (see figure 11). Books on Third World and Native American women, gay and lesbian politics, Jewish women, and women and alcohol had joined the original categories of fiction, biography, and poetry. The music section expanded, along with the selection of feminist journals and periodicals, from a few shelves to an entire wall. The most popular authors were May Sarton, Alice Walker, Audre Lorde, Adrienne Rich, and Rita Mae Brown; staff members had their own favorite discoveries of off-print or overlooked titles, one of which was Zora Neale Hurston's *Their Eyes Were Watching God*.[111]

Bruckman described New Words as a politicized gathering space for the feminist community. It was an important social nexus for the exchange of information about significant events, such as an abortion clinic shooting. Many relationships began and ended at the store, and there were often spontaneous reunions of old friends (some of them ex-partners). Like Sisterhood, New Words had dozens of bulletin boards with information about services

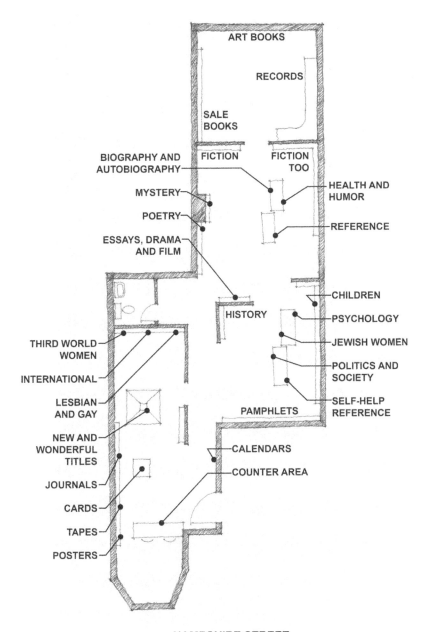

ART BOOKS

RECORDS

SALE BOOKS

BIOGRAPHY AND AUTOBIOGRAPHY

FICTION

FICTION TOO

MYSTERY

HEALTH AND HUMOR

POETRY

REFERENCE

ESSAYS, DRAMA AND FILM

CHILDREN

HISTORY

PSYCHOLOGY

THIRD WORLD WOMEN

JEWISH WOMEN

INTERNATIONAL

POLITICS AND SOCIETY

LESBIAN AND GAY

SELF-HELP REFERENCE

NEW AND WONDERFUL TITLES

PAMPHLETS

CALENDARS

JOURNALS

COUNTER AREA

CARDS

TAPES

POSTERS

HAMPSHIRE STREET

FIGURE 11. New Words Bookstore floor plan. Drawing by Reed Gyovai Muehlman based on undated diagram. Records of New Words, Schlesinger Library, Radcliffe Institute, Harvard University, collection MC 619, carton 23, folder 7.

and events. The store's main feature, though—its overwhelming display of works by and about women—reminded customers just how much they were a part of a larger women's world.[112]

In 1999 the women operating the store created New Words Live, a non-profit that sponsored weekly readings. In 2000 the Ford Foundation granted them $75,000 to examine the "cultural and community role of a feminist bookstore and multiple scenarios for the future of New Words and New Words Live." After conducting interviews and focus groups under the grant, New Words closed as a bookstore in October 2002 and reopened as the Center for New Words, which was expected to become a "premier regional center for the cultivation of women's and girls' writing." A new bookstore was to anchor the center, and the possibility of a women's café was discussed.[113] The Center for New Words closed at the end of 2009, spinning off one of its main projects, Women, Action, and the Media (WAM!), into a separate nonprofit organization.[114]

In November 2002 the *Boston Phoenix* ran an article more laudatory of the bookstore than its 1974 article had been. Citing the bookstore's nearly three decades as the hub of the city's and the region's feminist resource network, it recalled New Words in its early days as "an oasis where no one snickered when a customer asked for a book about breast cancer, or inquired where one might find shelter for battered women or a support group for lesbians with kids." Further, New Words was the only place in the 1970s seeking links between women's literature, political activism, and the emerging women's movement.[115]

"Trying to Find a Language for Myself"

A young feminist struggling to understand her own sexuality during the early 1970s recalled her first visit to a feminist bookstore: "I didn't know what to call myself, and I didn't know what name worked for me. . . . I'd look through all the books, and then I'd go to the lesbian section. . . . I didn't go in looking to buy something, but maybe to find something that sounded familiar . . . that resonated with my experience . . . trying to find a language for myself."[116] This woman's experience echoed those of others seeking out feminist bookstores during the height of the women's movement. The books, and the people in the store, helped women understand who they were and what they wanted to become. Visiting a feminist bookstore was a significant event in the coming-out process for lesbians: it was a safe place to connect with other lesbians in addition to the "paper lesbians" they read about in books.[117] As Carol Seajay observed, "With the lesbian books it was most easy to see: you can watch somebody come out, cut off her hair, become a dyke!"[118]

Lesbians found the courage to come out by reading the novels of Rita Mae Brown. Novice poets discovered Sylvia Plath, hopeful musicians could buy albums by Meg Christian, Holly Near, and Cris Williamson, and aspiring artists could admire posters created by the Chicago Women's Graphics Collective. Movement publications like *off our backs* and *Big Mama Rag* carried national and international news on women's issues. Students from local colleges bought books for women's studies courses, and victims of incest recognized themselves, and found strength in, books written by other survivors. A curious woman might walk in the door unsure of her attitude toward feminism, but she typically walked out as a convert.

New Words and Sisterhood were only two, but two of the longest-lived, of the feminist bookstores that have vanished. The mid-1990s marked the high point, when there were more than 140; by 2002 approximately three-quarters of them had gone out of business.[119] They all fell prey to chain store and Internet competition. But in their heyday, feminist bookstores were not just a retail experience, they were, in the words of Seajay, "a manifestation of a MOVEMENT."[120]

Individual bookstores could never have flourished without the support of numerous people and institutions. First, lesbians played a significant role in the early days. Some opened bookstores and others wrote poetry, music, and novels for an audience emerging from the closet. Many of these same lesbian feminists organized the first Women in Print Conference, which gave birth to the *FBN*, which in turn connected book women during the crucial early days. WIND helped by streamlining the ordering process for publications from hundreds of feminist sources. Finally, women's studies programs (with or without lesbian content) contributed to the growth of feminist bookstores by ordering publications for their students.

A continent apart from each other, Sisterhood and New Words catered to different local communities but to the same national and international audiences. They shared a similar trajectory from beginning to end, starting with the personal savings of dedicated co-owners and prospering (or at least prevailing) over time due to the decades-long commitments of their founders. They carried much more than books by and about women. Hundreds of well-known and lesser-known authors presented their work within their walls. Women could find resources, unavailable elsewhere, in a safe environment. Themes of safety and the bookstore as an oasis from a hostile world pervade the recollections of founders and customers.

Most important was the sense of community they cultivated. Women who visited feminist bookstores knew they were with others like themselves, even if they were not yet clear about who they were or who they were becoming. Some apolitical women might be discovering that they were feminists and some straight women that they were lesbians; when the two occurred simultaneously it was a dramatic experience. Despite the schisms that plagued (or energized, depending on one's perspective) the movement, feminist bookstores welcomed women of all persuasions under one roof. These were the glory days of feminist community-building, and it happened in bookstores. Simone Wallace laments the loss of a women's community today. How, she asks, do we make places like that again? And how do the pioneering founders find anything equally as fulfilling as operating a feminist bookstore? The bookstores did more than transform the lives of readers; they also gave enormous meaning to their founders' lives.[121]

CHAPTER 4

Feminist Health Clinics
Promoting Reproductive Rights

The cornerstones of reproductive rights are access to safe abortions and birth control methods and the ability to reject forced sterilization. According to the philosopher David Held, reproductive rights signify "the very basis of the possibility of effective participation of women in both civil society and the polity."[1] Women's opportunities in the public realm are directly correlated with their ability to control their own fertility. The activists who opened the first feminist health clinics understood that vital connection.

In 1971 Carol Downer and Lorraine Rothman founded a self-help clinic in Los Angeles. It was the first in the nation, earning the title Self-Help Clinic One. Downer explained its philosophy for the July 1973 special health-care issue of the Women's Center publication *Sister:* "The goal of the Self-Help Clinic is to take women's medicine back into our own hands. The strategy is to take back the power over our own bodies, both everyday types of control which information and self-knowledge gives [*sic*] us, and we also want to acquire special skills and knowledge which will allow us collectively to independently provide our own health care."[2]

The magazine's cover featured a speculum-wielding Wonder Woman vanquishing male figures representing the American Medical Association, Sigmund Freud, and the Catholic Church. Self-Help Clinic One grew from a single back room in the Women's Center at 1027 South Crenshaw

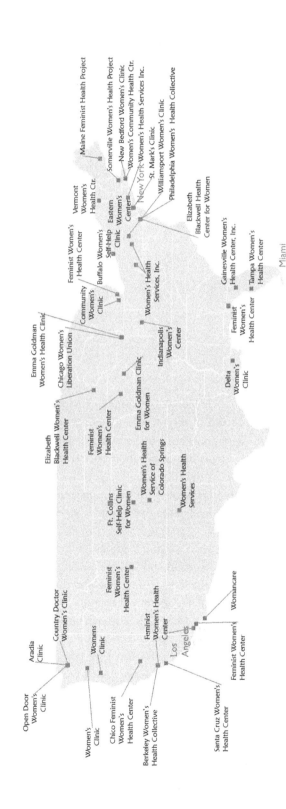

FIGURE 12. Map of feminist health clinics, ca. 1975. Map by Lucas Lyons. Source: Appendix D.

Boulevard to the entire side of the duplex. When the Women's Center closed in 1972, the clinic was renamed the Feminist Women's Health Center (FWHC) and took over both sides of the building. Soon the FWHC expanded into a two-story house at 746 South Crenshaw, where staff installed state-of-the-art communications equipment: five push-button lines on a rotary telephone.[3] When the lease at 746 South Crenshaw expired in July 1974, the FWHC moved to the second floor of an office building at 1112 South Crenshaw Boulevard.[4] Throughout its history, it stayed near its initial location and avoided any disruption in access for women who needed its services.

In 1975 the women's health movement in the United States included more than twelve hundred groups.[5] Warnings about dangerous obstetrical practices and the side effects of certain drugs spread quickly via C-R groups and mimeographed sheets distributed in women's centers. Grassroots activities that began locally in the United States soon had a national and global reach, with women's health organizations in Australia, Canada, Europe, Great Britain, and Mexico. In the United States, 110 clinics and centers delivered women's health services by 1978 (see figure 12 and appendix D for a partial list).[6]

The Road to Reproductive Rights

In *Woman's Body, Woman's Right* (1990), the historian Linda Gordon places the contemporary struggle for reproductive rights in the context of the longer US social movement for birth control, which began in the late nineteenth century with feminists' demands for "voluntary motherhood."[7] Women can avoid having children by using contraception, by having an abortion, or by sterilization, but legal access to all three methods has not always been available. The government, influenced by cultural assumptions about proper sexual activity for women, has regulated all three at some point in US history. Men's reproductive functions, in contrast, have been exempt from legal control.[8]

Women, most of them white, led the mid-twentieth-century battle for reproductive rights. African American women were hesitant to join the fight because of its all-consuming focus on legalizing abortion; they were more concerned about forced sterilization. Middle-class white women, for their part, were slow to recognize sterilization abuse as a feminist concern. Since whites typically encountered resistance from private doctors if they sought the operation, they failed to understand that doctors often sterilized women of color without their consent.

Sheryl Burt Ruzek's *The Women's Health Movement: Feminist Alternatives to Medical Control* (1978), written as the movement was unfolding, is the starting point for statistics and stories about the early days. Two subsequent books testify to the movement's longevity: Sandra Morgen's *Into Our Own Hands: The Women's Health Movement in the United States, 1969–1990* (2002) and Jennifer Nelson's *Women of Color and the Reproductive Rights Movement* (2003). I have drawn from these histories for the following sections on contraception, abortion, and sterilization.

Contraception

Question: What do you call couples who use the rhythm method? Answer: Parents. This joke circulated in the 1970s among feminists frustrated with the Catholic Church's stance on birth control.[9] Scheduling intercourse to coincide with "safe" days of her menstrual period is risky even if a woman could time her cycle perfectly, which few can do with certainty over the entire span of their reproductive years. Yet that is what the church demanded of Catholic couples. In 1965 one-third of Catholic women who used contraception relied on the rhythm method compared with 5 percent of Protestant women.[10] Since the rhythm method has a high failure rate, devout Catholics found it more difficult to control their fertility than women of other religions. Non-Catholic women could practice the rhythm method, of course, but they could also in good conscience use diaphragms, spermicidal gels, or condoms, all of which were somewhat more reliable than the rhythm method.[11] But these were difficult to find. Until 1965 laws in thirty states prevented married couples from obtaining birth control products or information through the mail. Before the Supreme Court declared those laws in violation of couples' rights to privacy in its 1965 decision *Griswold v. Connecticut*, thousands of women seeking contraception were acting illegally.[12]

When oral contraceptives came on the market in 1960, the event was due to the efforts of the birth control pioneer Margaret Sanger. In the 1950s she and the wealthy heiress Katherine McCormick recruited the physicians Gregory Pincus and John Rock to develop the technology.[13] The Pill was heralded as the first technique that could be used separately from the act of sexual intercourse, unlike a diaphragm or condom, and be completely under a woman's control. If used properly, it also had a lower failure rate than other contraceptives. This was the solution Sanger had been searching for since 1912.[14] As a visiting nurse in New York City's tenements, she was constantly tending to women seeking relief from unwanted pregnancies. Sanger's own mother had eighteen pregnancies, bore eleven children, and died at the age of forty.[15] Like her radical mentor, the socialist Emma Goldman, Sanger saw compulsory motherhood as a threat to women's freedom. She and Goldman coined the phrase "birth control" to signal the value of individual autonomy and to mimic the language of the Industrial Workers of the World (IWW), "workers' control."[16]

Within a few years of its release, the Pill became highly controversial. Journalist Barbara Seaman published a book in 1969 that challenged the Pill's safety and condemned the medical-pharmaceutical industry for developing it. In *The Doctor's Case against the Pill*, Seaman accused physicians of patronizing women patients and blamed the pharmaceutical industry for making exorbitant profits. She demanded that they share information about the side effects of oral contraceptives. In 1970 Congressional hearings into the safety of the Pill were followed one year later by Food and Drug Administration requirements that manufacturers provide full disclosure about its hazards. Product inserts with information about side effects became standard practice largely as a result of Seaman's work.[17] The hearings were also responsible for bringing together the women who created the National Women's Health Network (NWHN) in 1975. Located in Washington, DC, the NWHN served as an information clearinghouse for feminist clinics, provided testimony to Congress, and published a newsletter on health policy and legislation.[18]

Before she began sponsoring development of the Pill, Sanger founded Planned Parenthood Federation of America in 1942 when her American Birth Control League (established in 1921) merged with its successor, the Birth Control Federation of America.[19] Planned Parenthood established the first clinics in the country to dispense birth control and offer abortion services. The Griswold in *Griswold v. Connecticut* was Estelle Griswold, the president of the Planned Parenthood League of Connecticut, who opened a clinic to dispense contraceptives specifically to test Connecticut's law.[20]

Although it was successful in reducing unwanted pregnancies for thousands of women, Planned Parenthood saw its reputation among feminists suffer when it became associated with population control. The phrase *population control* evoked images of forced sterilization characteristic of earlier eugenics movements, especially among African Americans.[21] Other women of color had similar concerns. In 1937, fearing that overpopulation in the US territory of Puerto Rico would lead to the island's economic decline, the US Eugenics Board designed a government-funded program for population control. By 1968 more than one-third of Puerto Rican women of childbearing age had been sterilized—ten times the continental US rate.[22]

The relationship between African Americans and the birth control movement, including Planned Parenthood, waxed and waned over the twentieth
century. In 1925 the National Urban League asked the Birth Control Federation of America to open a clinic in the Columbus Hill district of the
Bronx, and black women's clubs supported family-planning clinics in black
neighborhoods. The black press promoted family planning as an avenue
to racial uplift. By the 1930s, however, birth control had become associated with eugenics and the Ku Klux Klan. African Americans perceived it
as another tool—like lynching—that whites could use to control them.[23]
Perhaps in an effort to improve its reputation in the African American community, in 1966 Planned Parenthood gave one of its first Margaret Sanger
Awards to the Rev. Martin Luther King Jr. for his dedication to social justice
and human dignity.[24] In his acceptance speech, King likened Sanger's nonviolent campaign for birth control to the civil rights movement and urged
the Negro to embrace family planning as a "profoundly important ingredient
in his [sic] quest for security and a decent life."[25]

By the time he accepted the award, King was no longer the only voice of
authority speaking for African Americans. Stokely Carmichael was advo-
cating Black Power and drawing younger disciples. An anti–birth-control
resolution passed at the 1967 Black Power conference, and two years later
the editors of a black radical newsletter claimed, "For us to speak in favor
of birth control for Afro-Americans would be comparable to speaking in
favor of genocide." The Urban League reversed its earlier support for family
planning, and the head of the Florida NAACP stated publicly that black
women needed to produce more babies. Until African Americans com-
prised one-third of the US population, he argued, they would be unable to
challenge the white power structure. The head of the Pittsburgh NAACP
declared that the local family-planning clinic was an instrument of genocide.[26] Surveys from the early 1970s found that more than half of all black
women believed that the survival of the race depended on higher birth rates,
and one-third believed birth control was a form of genocide.[27]

Like white feminists who rejected male leadership in the New Left, many
African American women asserted their independence from black male radicals on the issue of reproductive rights. When black men shut down family
planning clinics in Cleveland and Pittsburgh, black feminists reopened them.
Frances Beal, head of the Black Women's Liberation Committee of the Student Nonviolent Coordinating Committee (SNCC), declared in 1969 that
"Black women have the right and responsibility to determine when it is in
the interest of the struggle to have children or not to have them and this
right must not be relinquished." Shirley Chisholm, the first black woman

in Congress, made her position equally clear: "To label family planning and legal abortion programs 'genocide' is male rhetoric, for male ears."[28] African American women faced a dilemma similar to that experienced by Catholic women contemplating the Pill: a culture from which they drew strength was adamantly opposed to reproductive rights.

Byllye Avery, an African American activist in Gainesville, Florida, was known as someone who could provide women with the telephone number of a New York City doctor who performed abortions. In 1970 the only grounds for a legal abortion in Florida was to preserve the life of the pregnant woman.[29] After the *Roe v. Wade* decision in 1973, Avery and her friends "used to all gather . . . around a kitchen table and dream about having a women's health center." In 1974 they opened the Gainesville Women's Health Clinic. Because the Gainesville Medical Society had denied Planned Parenthood's request to open a clinic providing abortions, Avery's group did not ask permission; they just opened the clinic. Its doctors performed abortions in an environment deliberately designed to be "pleasing, beautiful, more homey and friendly" than sterile medical complexes. Like other feminist clinics, the Gainesville clinic rejected the power hierarchy that kept women from understanding the procedure they would undergo. Staff members fully informed the patients and spent as much time with them as necessary.[30]

In 1983 Avery, by then a board member of the NWHN, organized the First National Conference on Black Women's Health Issues at Spelman College in Atlanta. The conference drew two thousand participants and marked the official birth of the Black Women's Health Project (BWHP) and its newsletter, *Vital Signs*. The Project adopted a slogan made famous by militant activist Fannie Lou Hamer: "We are sick and tired of being sick and tired." The organization applied self-help strategies through "sister circle" groups promoting mental, physical, and spiritual awareness. In 1984 the group incorporated and changed its name to the National Black Women's Health Project (NBWHP), purchasing a national headquarters in Atlanta.[31]

Abortion

Feminist health clinics emerged after the Pill had improved contraceptive effectiveness, but before abortion was available without a doctor's recommendation. Part of their mission, therefore, was to help women sidestep the law. Women whose periods were slightly late could request "menstrual extraction" at the L.A. clinic. Menstrual extraction (ME) was effectively an early abortion performed within a few days of a missed period. Rothman developed a kit of tubes and a vacuum bottle she called the "Del-Em"

method to perform the procedure.[32] According to Rothman, ME was significantly different from early abortion because the woman using it "is participating in a home health care method and is not being subjected to medical
treatment. The woman controls all aspects of her menstrual extraction."[33]
ME was also much less expensive than a hospital abortion, which could cost
several hundred dollars. The price for ME was fifty dollars.[34]

Abortion was legal in several states before *Roe v. Wade*, but access was
restricted. When the US Centers for Disease Control started collecting
statistics in 1969, all but one (Mississippi) of the eleven states it surveyed
required a physician's approval. Forcible rape was grounds for approval in
all eleven states, but statutory rape was not. Neither Georgia nor Mississippi
considered incest appropriate justification. Most states prohibited abortion
after a certain number of weeks of pregnancy, and several had residency
requirements to prevent women from crossing state lines for abortions.[35] In
New York State, although abortion laws were more liberal than elsewhere, a
woman was required to have letters from two psychiatrists attesting that her
life would be at risk if the pregnancy were carried to term. Those letters
then went to the Committee on Therapeutic Abortions at her gynecologist's
hospital. Most hospitals had a quota, since none wanted to become known as
abortion mills, and appeals were often denied.[36]

Given the difficulty of obtaining legal abortions, women seeking to ter-
minate pregnancies turned to other options. For many in Illinois, it was
Chicago's Jane network. In Illinois, as in Florida, legal abortion was allowed
only when a physician determined it was necessary to save the woman's
life.[37] Jane was the code name for a group of feminists operating as The
Abortion Counseling Service of Women's Liberation. Organized in 1969,
Jane operated by word of mouth. Women called 643–3844 and were told a
time and location (the Front) to meet a contact. They would then be taken
to an apartment (the Place) for the abortion, after which they were returned
to the Front. The two functions were separated, and few records were kept, to
protect patients' confidentiality in case of a raid.[38]

Those precautions failed when seven members of Jane were arrested in
1972. Acting on a tip from an informant, police staked out the building at
5532 South Everett Street in Hyde Park. When a group of women left, they
were followed to apartment 11F at 7251 South Shore Drive. There the police
found three bedrooms set up as operating rooms, with abortions in progress.
Officers noted that patients were charged about $100 for an abortion, about
fifteen procedures per day were performed, and the defendants "had apparently been trained by a physician." The last assumption was wrong. Initially
the abortions had been performed by Nick, a man presenting himself as a

doctor. But when Jane's members discovered he lacked medical credentials, they decided they could do the abortions themselves. Several women trained with Nick before dismissing him completely. When Jane ceased operations in 1973, the group had performed more than eleven thousand illegal—but safe—abortions.[39] By the time the "Jane Seven" came to trial, *Roe v. Wade* was law and the charges against them were dropped.[40]

Women without access to Jane or a service like it were subject to dangerous procedures that could result in serious complications or death.[41] Recognition of the risks associated with "back alley" abortions drove feminists to launch numerous nonprofits to challenge abortion laws. One of the first was the Association to Repeal Abortion Laws (ARAL) founded by Patricia Maginnis, author with Lana Clark Phelan of *The Abortion Handbook* (1969). In 1966 Maginnis, Phelan, and Rowena Gurner—the Army of Three—handed out leaflets on San Francisco street corners with names of abortion doctors in Mexico and Japan. This was the beginning of the first open, and illegal, abortion referral service in the nation. Like-minded activists adopted the name and political stance of ARAL when they formed the National Association for Repeal of Abortion Laws (NARAL) in 1969. After *Roe v. Wade*, the acronym stood for National Abortion Rights Action League.[42]

Carol Downer, who considers Maginnis and Phelan her earliest mentors, points out that many other organizations were actively fighting for abortion reform in the late 1960s. The YWCA, the California Committee on Therapeutic Abortions, and the American College of Obstetricians and Gynecologists were among them. The American Law Institute also published a model abortion law in 1971 followed by California and nine other states.[43] Downer reminds us that the women's movement did not single-handedly transform abortion laws, although it "provided muscle in the fight."[44]

Protestant religious organizations joined the crusade. Howard Moody, minister at Judson Memorial (Baptist) Church in New York City, formed the Clergy Consultation Service on Abortion (CCS) in 1967 to help women obtain safe abortions. When Moody and his colleagues discovered that the vast majority of abortion deaths in New York City occurred among blacks and Puerto Ricans, they invoked "higher laws and moral obligations transcending legal codes," declaring it their "pastoral responsibility and religious duty to give aid and assistance to all women with problem pregnancies."[45] Ministers at other churches adopted the same policies, and by July 1970 the CCS was operating in twenty states.[46]

These organizations celebrated the *Roe v. Wade* decision in January 1973. They understood, though, that it was merely the beginning of another struggle. The bureaucratic medical delivery system would take longer to change.

Members of the CCS predicted that the victory would require vigilance.[47] They were correct. Before a year had passed, Senators Jesse Helms, Henry Hyde, and Robert Dornan proposed a "human life amendment" (HLA) to the Constitution that would give the unborn fetus greater rights than the woman carrying it. The Catholic archbishop of Boston agreed with the sponsors that no circumstance, not even to save the mother's life, would qualify as grounds for abortion. Passage of the HLA became the top priority for the National Right to Life Committee (the largest anti-abortion organization in the US). NOW mounted a major campaign to defeat it, using Jesse Helms's own words to warn that even birth control would be criminalized under the HLA. Helms stipulated that "any constitutional amendment that allows *abortions previous to implantation* will fail to protect the whole biological lifespan of human beings" (emphasis added). Under this definition, contraception would qualify as an abortion because its purpose was to prevent implantation. The HLA never passed, but Hyde soon succeeded in strictly limiting federal funding for poor women seeking abortions.[48]

In 1976 Congress passed the Hyde Amendment banning the use of Medicaid and other federal funds to pay for abortions. Unless she could prove her life was in danger, a poor woman covered by Medicaid no longer had access to an abortion. Medicaid, however, would pay 90 percent of the cost of sterilization.[49] The law penalized black women, whose poverty rates were much higher than white women's. African American feminists interpreted passage of the Hyde Amendment as a failure of white feminists to mobilize on behalf of poor black women, which created a wedge between white and black feminists.[50]

African American women responded by joining reproductive rights organizations like the Committee for Abortion Rights and Against Sterilization Abuse (CARASA). Brenda Joyner of the Tallahassee FWHC understood the racist undertones, and duplicity, of the Hyde Amendment: "The government will not pay for a $200 or $300 abortion procedure for a poor woman on Medicaid. But it will pay for a $2,000 to $3,000 sterilization procedure for that same poor woman."[51] Joyner had identified a flash point among African American women: forced sterilization.

Sterilization

Black women had reason to be angry about sterilization abuse. US Senate testimony in 1973 revealed that federal funds had been used to perform two thousand involuntary sterilizations in the previous year, many of them on African American women.[52] The Relf sisters put faces to those numbers.

In 1973 two black sisters, ages twelve and fourteen and deemed mentally incompetent, were sterilized without consent in Montgomery, Alabama. Their mother, who could neither read nor write, had mistakenly signed an X on the sterilization release form, believing she was granting permission for contraceptive injections of Depo-Provera. The operations were paid for by federal funds administered by the Montgomery Community Action Committee. The Southern Poverty Law Center sued on the Relfs' behalf. The judge in the case concluded that untold numbers of poor women had been coerced into sterilization under the mistaken belief that welfare benefits would be withdrawn if they refused.[53]

At least one poor woman was proved correct in that belief. Nial Ruth Cox sued the state of North Carolina because she assented to sterilization (which she had been told was temporary) after authorities threatened to cut off her family's welfare payments if she refused the operation. In neighboring South Carolina Dr. Clovis Pierce insisted that pregnant patients on welfare who had two or more children submit to "voluntary" sterilization before he would deliver their babies. Pierce was quoted as saying he was "tired of people running around and having babies and paying for them with my taxes." At the time he made that statement, Dr. Pierce had received approximately $60,000 of taxpayer's money for performing sterilizations.[54]

Cox's lawsuit prompted African American, Native American, and Puerto Rican women to come forward with more complaints about forced sterilization. Dr. Helen Rodriguez-Trias, of Puerto Rican heritage, was familiar with the extensive sterilization program the government had conducted in Puerto Rico decades earlier. She became a strong advocate for abolishing forced sterilization and was a founding member of CARASA and New York's Committee to End Sterilization Abuse (CESA).[55] The West Coast Committee Against Forced Sterilization and Chicago's CESA joined them to take on multiple cases. Planned Parenthood, the American Civil Liberties Union (ACLU), NOW, and the National Black Feminist Organization (NBFO) also entered the fight. In 1974 the Department of Health, Education and Welfare (later Health and Human Services) responded by drawing up guidelines to ensure informed consent, a 72-hour waiting period, and prohibition of sterilizations on women under twenty-one. Yet one year later few hospitals were in compliance with government regulations and some were completely ignorant of them.[56]

Sterilization abuse took several forms. It could be trickery like that which resulted in sterilization of the Relf girls. It could occur when a doctor insisted on a tubal ligation or hysterectomy as a condition for delivering a baby. Or it could happen without the woman's consent. The voting rights activist and founder of the Mississippi Freedom Democratic Party Fannie Lou Hamer experienced the latter. When Hamer checked into the hospital in Sunflower County, Mississippi, to have a small uterine tumor removed, the doctor performed a complete hysterectomy without medical justification and without her knowledge. She later discovered that 60 percent of black women in the county had been victims, as she had, of a "Mississippi appendectomy."[57]

Just as the Relf case mobilized African Americans, *Madrigal v. Quilligan* energized Mexican Americans. In 1973 Dr. Bernard Rosenfield, a resident at County General Hospital in Los Angeles, discovered an explosion in the number of sterilizations performed between 1968 and 1970. Dr. Rosenfield found little evidence of informed consent. Instead, he observed obstetricians urging uneducated patients to have tubal ligations, often so that doctors could gain surgical experience. Mexican American feminists learned of the practice and recruited more than one hundred women who had been forcibly sterilized. In 1978 ten of these women, all low-income Spanish-speaking immigrants, brought suit against the hospital. One of the plaintiffs, Dolores Madrigal, had signed a consent form to be sterilized after a medical assistant informed her, falsely, that her husband had already signed it. Other plaintiffs testified that they had been approached while in the last hours of a difficult labor when they were under stress, had been told they already had too many children, or had been denied a hernia repair unless they signed. In three cases, no consent was obtained. But the judge decided in favor of Dr. Quilligan, head of obstetrics and gynecology at County General, declaring that the defendants had acted in good faith and intended no harm.[58]

Activists saw feminist health clinics as women's only hope to combat the medical profession's abuse of their reproductive rights. None were more adamant about the power of self-help than Carol Downer and Lorraine Rothman.

Los Angeles Self-Help Clinic One

The idea for the clinic took shape on April 7, 1971, at Everywoman's Bookstore in Los Angeles, where women dedicated to medical self-help regularly met.[59] Downer, a mother of six, believed that if mothers could care for their children with basic first aid knowledge, they could also take care of themselves with the proper training. Women with inflammation of the cervix (cervicitis), for example, were typically treated by cauterization. Yet the condition usually resolved itself over time. A woman could prevent costly visits to the doctor's office, and possibly unnecessary procedures, if she checked her cervix regularly. To demonstrate the technique that night, Downer lifted her skirt, inserted a speculum into her vagina, and revealed her cervix for all the women to see.[60]

Later that year Downer and Rothman opened a clinic in the back bedroom of the Los Angeles Women's Center on South Crenshaw Boulevard.[61] The front room on the south side of the building was used on Tuesdays for the Women's Abortion Referral Service (WARS). Staff members performed uterine checks and counseled women about the upcoming procedure, then accompanied them to San Vicente Hospital where doctors would perform the abortions.[62] Some feminists were critical of abortion referral services because they received fees from hospitals. But defenders of the practice pointed out their advantages. Abortions were so lucrative that hospitals agreed to pay fees to referral services. If it was a feminist service, the fees paid rent and telephone expenses, financed abortions for indigent women, and compensated staff for time spent counseling women. Nonfeminist services, on the other hand, made profits that went into "some man's pocket."[63]

Downer and Rothman toured abortion clinics in New York City to collect ideas for their own facility. They found that each client would come through the front door into the waiting area. She would then progress through a series of stations, staffed by medical specialists, to have her blood drawn, change into a hospital gown, and have a pelvic exam, followed by anesthesia and the abortion. After recovery, she would leave by the back door. Downer and Rothman were determined to avoid that layout in the self-help clinic, later renamed the Feminist Women's Health Center (FWHC). They arranged for patients to sit around the stations and talk with each other, providing cheese and crackers if the wait was long. After her abortion, a woman would come back out into the waiting room where others could see that she was fine. This created a loop of peer counseling among patients that began when they walked in the door. The clinic layout empowered women to ask questions, observe how other women were doing, and support each other.[64]

The staff tried to ensure a comfortable and supportive environment that was as different as possible from a typical medical facility. They wanted to distinguish their place from the free clinics, run mainly by men, which were grimy, bare, and furnished with "ten-minute chairs" in which no one could sit for long. The FWHC was decorated with pictures on the walls and—a woman's touch—on the ceiling over the examination table so patients could focus on a calming landscape scene when their feet were in the stirrups. Rugs covered the floor of the living/waiting room, plants were scattered about, and comfortable chairs were arranged in a circle to facilitate conversations.[65]

Within two months of the 1973 *Roe v. Wade* decision, the FWHC opened Women's Choice Clinic at its two Crenshaw Boulevard locations and began offering abortions. Physicians performed therapeutic abortions up to ten weeks after conception using vacuum aspiration and a local anesthetic. Women were counseled by staff both before and after the abortion, and staff accompanied them into the procedure room for emotional support and to explain each step of the process. Free pregnancy screenings and birth control information were available five days a week. Patients had two choices when they came to the clinic. They could make an appointment to be examined by a woman gynecologist and female lay workers who demonstrated self-examination techniques. Or they could choose the less conventional option of scheduling an appointment with several other women at the same time and, in addition to being treated by the doctor, observe the treatment of other women. Fees for services were on a sliding scale.[66]

Like other self-help pioneers, Downer and Rothman had a revolutionary agenda: women educated about their bodies should seize control of their health care from doctors and place it in their own hands, where it belonged. The first step was to alert women to their rights as consumers of existing health services. As a visitor from the Milwaukee Women's Health Collective discovered, the FWHC was more than a clinic. "It's a political organization that, as part of its politics and as a way to sustain itself, does provide abortion services and well-woman participatory gynecological services and pregnancy counseling."[67] Indeed, staff discussed politics daily, sometimes in meetings that lasted for hours. They all sat in a circle, on couches or on the floor, figuring out as they went how to run the clinic democratically.[68]

Political discussions were about more than the internal functioning of the FWHC. The clinic was also an operating base for political activity and engagement with the neighborhood. Refusing to just "sit inside the four walls" waiting for patients, staff members attended every community meeting—about police brutality, for example. They advocated for reproductive rights and gave interviews to the media when abortion was in the news. With its "Women's Choice Clinic" sign clearly visible from the street, the center became the symbol of legalized abortion. These were the ways in which the FWHC became influential in the public dialogue about abortion rights.[69]

Downer believed in a concept that was controversial among feminists: organizational structure. Running an effective clinic, Downer insisted, required such bureaucratic concessions as sign-in sheets, in- and out-baskets, trainings sessions, and personnel files. But she was quick to point out that it was an open structure inviting maximum participation in making clinic policy. Downer was committed to the ideals of egalitarianism, and to making the structure work for staff and patients, rather than having them fit the structure. One of the guiding tenets of the clinic was collective control over the workplace by full-time staff members, with no outside board of directors or separate management structure.[70]

The founders took a collective approach to family life as well. One of the advantages of working at the Los Angeles FWHC, compared with any other type of clinic, was free on-site child care.[71] Children were loosely supervised by everyone, until one day they set a sofa on fire. Downer and Rothman decided it was time to hire someone to watch the kids. They let the children interview the candidates; the kids asked applicants if they would be allowed to curse and where they would take them on field trips.[72] Staff furnished the room with toys, a TV, and equipment older children could use when they came to the FWHC after school. Some of the women also shared housing. Living communally stretched their small wages, as did the food provided at the center. Staff members could have breakfast there, and snacks were available all day. One of the best benefits, though, was free membership in a gym two blocks away. Staff members took their own health seriously; gym time counted as work time.[73]

Francie Hornstein, who worked with Downer and Rothman, published a column for feminist newsletters titled "Assertiveness in the Doctor's Office." The list of thirteen suggestions started with "All people have a legal right to read their own medical charts and records" and "You have the right to full and complete explanations of all examinations, treatments, and medications." It included reminders that married women have rights to medical treatment without the consent of their spouses, and that it is the patient's right to read literature accompanying medications. Hornstein recommended a firm stand on the politics of language. "If you are addressed by your first name by office personnel (including the doctor) you should feel free to relate to them on a first name basis also."[74] Physicians assumed then—and some still do—that a female patient would use his title, while he was free to patronize her by using her first name regardless of her age. This practice tapped into feminists' anger at being called "girls" or "chicks" instead of women. For feminists, rejecting the familiarity implied by first names was crucial to leveling the balance of power. Hornstein was committed to revolution. In 1974 she told an interviewer that "Unlike most Free Clinics, our goal is *not* to provide an alternative health delivery system. . . . We do not want to coexist with the medical establishment, we want to take it over."[75]

The same year the clinic opened, Downer and Rothman embarked on a twenty-six-city tour to spread the gospel of self-help. They took with them a slide show illustrating cervical self-examination, childbirth, abortion, birth control, menopause, and other subjects related to women's health.[76] The trip was prompted by their experience at a NOW conference at the Marina Hotel in Los Angeles where they had been prevented from demonstrating the ME technique. Although Downer and Rothman had been invited, conference organizers decided that the spectacle was too radical; the event took place in a hotel room instead of in a conference venue. (Downer would eventually give the demonstration at the 1973 NOW convention in Washington, DC). Madeline Schwenk of Chicago's Jane underground abortion referral network was at the 1971 conference and asked Downer and Rothman to teach self-examination techniques to Jane's members.[77] These experiences convinced Downer and Rothman that they had to reach a larger audience. At the invitation of NOW members across the country, they traveled by bus from Los Angeles to Wichita, Kansas City, Iowa City, Detroit, and Chicago, then to New Jersey, Brooklyn, and Providence, Rhode Island.[78]

It turned out to be a busy year. Carol Downer and staff member Colleen Wilson were arrested in September for practicing medicine without a license. The grounds? Downer had helped activist Z. Budapest insert yogurt into her vagina, a common home remedy for a yeast infection. Wilson had fit a woman with a diaphragm. Downer and Wilson spent several hours in jail before being released on $500 bond each.[79] Wilson pleaded guilty; she was fined $250, given 25 days' suspended sentence, and put on two years of probation. Downer pleaded not guilty and went to trial.[80] *Time* magazine predicted the case would become a "feminist cause célèbre."[81]

To arrest the two women the Los Angeles Police Department had raided the FWHC based on information from undercover witnesses. Two uniformed policemen and eight plainclothesmen conducted a "gynecological treasure hunt." They confiscated a fifty-foot extension cord, plastic specula, syringes and tubes, birth control pills, diaphragms, a pie tin, and a measuring cup. One of the informants was an ex-nun who had attended the session at which the yogurt incident took place. The other, the policewoman Sharon Dalton, reported that on April 28 Downer had offered to perform an abortion for her. In fact, Downer had flown to Portland, Oregon, that day to conduct a workshop at the American Psychological Association conference. At the time Downer was employed full time by the California Department of Corrections, Parole, and Community Services Unit. Things looked grim until the unit's secretary brought the plane tickets to court. Downer remembers that up to that moment, "the trial had not been going well, especially after Sharon Dalton's testimony. After Jenny [the secretary] testified, the entire atmosphere of the courtroom changed."[82]

The FWHC issued a press release expressing its outrage at the arrests, but it also conveyed the sense of absurdity surrounding "the great yogurt conspiracy." Reporting that the premises had been searched and files and equipment seized, the statement noted that "police also attempted to confiscate a carton of strawberry yogurt, but were deterred by the strenuous objection of one of the center staff members, who stated, 'You can't have that; it's my breakfast.'" Los Angeles Deputy City Attorney David M. Schacter was indignant that women at the clinic had been practicing medicine. He insisted that all the procedures should have been performed by a physician, demanding, "Who are they to diagnose a yeast infection and prescribe yogurt for it?" To the clinic staff, Schacter's attitude was characteristic of men's monopolistic control of women's bodies. "The male-dominated medical profession would make Tampax a prescription item, if they thought they could get away with it" was one of Downer's more caustic remarks.[83]

News of the raid spread immediately through the feminist media. *The Monthly Extract: An Irregular Periodical*, published by the Feminist Gynecological Self-Help Clinics of America, issued an appeal for legal defense funds in its September 1972 newsletter.[84] The newsletter urged women to publicize the self-help clinic concept and the arrest through multiple efforts. They were to copy a sample press release, pass the word to feminist groups, and discuss the issue in C-R groups and meetings. The emergency appeal was also sent to presidents of all chapters of NOW. The newsletter emphasized that the charges concerned "every woman with a body that she wants to own and control." After all, the editors pointed out, "Much as a man has immediate access to his own penis, a woman can now have immediate access to her own cervix. IS THAT ILLEGAL?"[85] The fund-raising appeal garnered $1,200 within a few months. Robin Morgan, the poet and editor of *Sisterhood Is Powerful*, contributed $1,000 of that amount.[86]

Downer relished the trial. It was an opportunity to publicize the FWHC's efforts and focus public attention on women's health needs. Downer sent a "Dear Sister" letter to all feminist groups urging them to join her at the Los Angeles County Courthouse on November 27, 1972, at 9:00 a.m. Mindful of the costs their attendance might incur, the letter noted that women who needed child care or had parking problems should contact the FWHC for help. Downer anticipated a *"resounding victory for Sisterhood!"* Her feminist attorneys Diane Wayne and Jeannette Christy requested, and got, a woman judge. This was a major accomplishment given the scarcity of women judges at the time. Downer closed her appeal with the language of rights: "This trial is a direct threat to our rights to know our own bodies. We not only expect to win, but we also want to give emphatic notice to all who would deny us this right that *we will control our own bodies!"*[87]

Downer's prediction of a successful outcome was correct. After nine hours of deliberation, a jury of three black women, one white woman, and eight white men acquitted Downer of practicing medicine, which in California was defined as "diagnosing and treating a disease."[88] Attorney Wayne had argued that the statute was so vague that she wouldn't be able to discuss a cold with a friend or offer her a tissue. Wayne further pointed out that "half the mothers in the county could be charged with diagnosing that their children had the measles." This test case set a precedent for other self-help clinics to operate legally. The infamous "yogurt bust" reveals just how far authorities would go to eliminate the threat of clinics that gave women control of their health. Had Downer been unable to prove that she was out of town that day and been convicted, it would have been a serious setback to the women's health movement.[89]

Authorities would continue to harass the clinic. In October 1975 a representative of the state Health Department made an unannounced visit to investigate a complaint that nonphysicians were performing abortions. The representative found no evidence that unlicensed personnel were performing abortions but did report that staff members were performing pelvic exams, which she considered to be practicing medicine without a license. The clinic, however, was in full compliance with state regulations.[90]

In 1976 the California Board of Medical Quality Assurance recommended that the District Attorney file criminal charges against the clinic for practicing medicine without a license.[91] The news quickly reached the East Coast. The second annual report of the Boston Women's Community Health Center carried an appeal for letters of support, reminding readers that women must stand together to gain control over their bodies: "We must fight when our rights are violated."[92] The California Department of Consumer Affairs, at the behest of the Board of Medical Quality Assurance, also conducted an investigation in 1976, prompting the resignation of three physicians and loss of access to the hospital where second-trimester abortions were performed.[93]

In 1979 a news crew from the Los Angeles CBS affiliate KNX-TV arrived unannounced at the FWHC to film an anti-abortion program. In addition to filming women entering and leaving the clinic, the team sent in a reporter claiming to be pregnant to demand an abortion, disrupting a clinic session in the process.[94] Staff members were furious. They wrote directly to CBS President William Paley to demand the program not be shown. The feminist abortion-rights network flew into action, writing Paley and KNX-TV General Manager Van Gordon Sauter to express their objections to the harassment.[95] The May 5–11 issue of *TV Guide* ran a sensational headline advertising the upcoming show "Abortion without Pregnancy," hosted by KNX-TV News coanchor Connie Chung.[96] Ultimately three shows were aired, each five minutes long. The first addressed the supposed inaccuracies of the two-minute urine test that led to unnecessary abortions. The second and third shows were less critical and more informational, talking about the FWHC and what women should know about obtaining a clinic abortion. Feminists considered the calmer tone and educational content of the second part of the series evidence of their successful letter-writing campaign.[97]

In 1982 an employee of the California Department of Health Services took a secretarial job at the Women's Choice Clinic under false pretenses. The information she reported back to her bosses reached Kathy MacManus of *New West* magazine, who wrote an article condemning the clinic. State investigators tried to shut it down based on alleged violations of professional practice, political indoctrination of staff members, and unlawful billing practices. The FWHC sued the magazine for libel and won. Jack Shoemaker, the lead investigator in the Department of Health Services' investigation of MacManus's charges, was so livid over the FWHC victory that he had a nervous breakdown. He later claimed his emotional distress as a work disability.[98]

The Los Angeles FWHC promoted feminist goals by treating every woman with respect for her opinions and needs. Instead of using the painful dilation and curettage (D&C) to perform an abortion, FWHC staff relied on the gentler vacuum aspiration method. They accepted fees for services, gave speeches, and engaged in fund-raising to achieve financial independence from government sources. The FWHC was a place established by, serving, and run by women.[99] The Los Angeles FWHC became the model for dozens of "Self-Help Clinics-in-a-suitcase," as Downer called them.[100]

Other Feminist Women's Health Centers in California

Feminist health clinics around the country used the Los Angeles "famous Self-Help Clinic # 1" as their model.[101] Two clinics, one in Oakland and the other in Orange County, were originally part of the Los Angeles FWHC.[102] Chico, Sacramento, and San Diego also opened FWHCs. By 1974 the FWHC network of Feminist Women's Health Centers had expanded beyond California to include Boston, Detroit, and Tallahassee (Florida).[103] Boston's Women's Community Health Center became a member in 1974.[104] They were all connected through National Women's Health Network (NWHN) newsletters, conferences, and visits between facilities. Nonprofit FWHCs operated under three priorities that distinguished them from commercial clinics: sharing knowledge, taking control of one's body, and breaking down the boundaries between practitioners and patients.[105]

Each FWHC offered free courses in cervical self-examination, pregnancy screening, and counseling. FWHCs also maintained twenty-four-hour emergency hotlines. Under the guidance of medical directors, centers ran seven-week sessions to train lay health practitioners. Sessions cost $150 and were limited to six women who learned telephone counseling, how to conduct workshops on health care and self-help, and general business skills. All the clinics were decorated with an eye toward making women feel comfortable. In the Sacramento clinic, the walls were lined with black and white photographs of smiling women who had had abortions.[106]

In the early years the California FWHCs pooled their resources to rent an apartment in Sacramento to lobby legislators. They had to educate lawmakers about everything concerning abortion clinics, from billing procedures to the effect of building codes. A proposed law requiring clinics to have eight-foot-wide hallways, for example, would have restricted abortions only to hospitals, since many FWHCs were in former homes or buildings with narrow hallways.[107] The FWHC campaign was effective in blocking the legislation and in winning allies for future battles.[108] But in 1974 internal political differences split the centers into three separate groups that seldom worked together.[109]

In 1973 a threat to the self-help movement caused alarm among members of the Oakland FWHC. In a letter that began "The medical establishment is rapidly stealing Menstrual Extraction from us," center codirector Laura Brown warned that national and international population control organizations were studying ME as a form of birth control for women in developing countries. This was a direct assault on feminist values because doctors would control the method. Members of the Oakland FWHC reaffirmed their commitment to women's control of ME at the November conference of the American Public Health Association in San Francisco.[110]

Brown made a formal statement at the conference that expressed how seriously the threat was perceived: "Menstrual Extraction is the next logical step after self-examination in the move for us to control our own lives. The male medical establishment is attempting to coopt menstrual extraction to control women. The purpose of the Menstrual Extraction Review [journal] is to publicly proclaim that Menstrual Extraction is every Woman's right."[111]

By 1976, however, instead of expressing the sentiments of all FWHCs, the Oakland clinic was seriously out of step with its sister organizations. Directors of the Oakland FWHC had sold the center's assets to the profit-making California Feminist Corporation (Cal-Fem Corp). Staff at other FWHCs

were enraged. A jointly signed letter from the Los Angeles, Chico, Tallahassee, Detroit, and Orange County FWHCs denounced Oakland for
robbing the feminist community of money, time, and energy in order to
make a profit. The Oakland "sell-out" resulted in layoffs of full-time staff
(previously the decision-makers) and the hiring of less expensive part-time
workers. The letter accused Oakland directors of a power grab from the
top, violating every principle of grassroots organization. The worst insult
was that their move mimicked the male power structure. The letter ended
by announcing that the other FWHCs were no longer associating with the
Oakland Cal-Fem Corp. The letter declared that the Oakland FWHC was
not, in fact, a feminist center.[112]

This would be only one of the rifts that befell California FWHCs.
A crisis erupted when Downer and Rothman returned from their 1971
cross-country proselytizing trip. According to Z. Budapest, "whose vagina
was exhibit A" at Downer's trial for practicing medicine without a license,
Downer and Rothman demanded that staff members devote *all* their time,
including weekends if asked, to the clinic. Most of the women involved
in the self-help movement volunteered their time or received meager salaries through the federal Comprehensive Employment and Training Act
(CETA) that paid for employees of nonprofit organizations.[113] They all
worked hard for very little money. When asked about work weeks of
fifty-five hours or more, Downer responded that most staff "feel privileged to do our political work fulltime and get paid for it."[114] Although
some feminists believed all services should be free, thereby requiring volunteer labor, the FWHC believed women should be paid a living wage
for "devoting their energies to the movement."[115] In 1972 participants in
the first conference of feminist self-help clinics agreed that they must pay
themselves, even if only to reimburse personal expenses. Echoing Virginia
Woolf's lament from an earlier era, one attendee conceded that the "subject of funding never fails to impress on my consciousness the total abject
poverty of all women."[116]

Downer's ultimatum caught the staff by surprise. Five women who could
not or would not make that sacrifice left the group after an emotional
late-night meeting. They decided to open their own FWHC in Redondo
Beach and rented space from a woman with a licensed laboratory who needed
help paying rent on the building. But Budapest complained: "FWHC lowered the knife on our necks. Carol [Downer] forbade the Lab Technician
sister to rent to us, or she will lose her accounts with the FWHC and Orange
County. This, the Lab sister could not afford and pulled out. Unbelieving
this counterrevolutionary blackmailing and power manipulating, I called up

FWHC and talked to Francie [Hornstein]. It was true, they didn't want us to open a clinic within L.A. County no less."[117]

Budapest was livid. In an open letter to the feminist community in *Sister*, she accused Downer and Rothman of monopolizing the feminist clinic concept. Budapest fumed that "revolutionaries get turned into ingrown groups or clichés and perverters of democratic procedures when they allow themselves territorialism." She acknowledged that she had admired the FWHC as the first woman-controlled clinic but never would have believed they expected to remain the only one in Los Angeles County. "Others will follow," Budapest warned, "as Herstory cannot be stopped—not even by those who started it."[118]

Budapest was right. In 1974 a group of feminists opened the Westside Women's Health Center at 1711 Ocean Park Boulevard in Santa Monica. It still exists today, at the same location, under the name Westside Family Health Center.[119] The Los Angeles FWHC closed in 1984.

The Women's Community Health Center in Boston

The Women's Community Health Center (WCHC) opened in Cambridge in 1974 as a joint effort between the Boston Women's Health Book Collective, the Los Angeles FWHC, and several activists with an interest in women's health. The Health Book Collective, formed by members of Bread and Roses, is particularly significant. It published *Women and Their Bodies* in 1970, which was renamed *Our Bodies, Ourselves* in 1971. This classic manual, and the group, were the East Coast pioneers in the women's health movement. Subtitled *A Course by and for Women*, the 136-page stapled newsprint booklet was written by members of the Collective "to be used by our sisters to increase consciousness about ourselves as women, to build our movement, to begin to struggle collectively for adequate health care."[120] The chapter on abortion in the 1971 edition began with the declaration "Abortion is our right—our right as women to control our own bodies."[121]

Before women could mobilize to demand their rights, they needed to understand their own reproductive systems. *Our Bodies, Ourselves* included information on anatomy, venereal disease, sexuality, pregnancy, birth control, and abortion. Moreover, it was a scathing attack on the entire capitalist male medical establishment. According to its authors, doctors treated women as if they were "stupid, mindless creatures, unable to follow instructions." Women needed to take responsibility for their own health care so doctors could no longer "control the knowledge and thereby control the patient."[122]

Activists in Los Angeles and Boston were in frequent contact. Jennifer Burgess, a "self-helper at large" involved with the original Los Angeles clinic and those in Oakland and Orange County, attended a women's health meeting in Worcester, Massachusetts, in August 1973. There she met Cookie Avrin, a member of a Boston feminist group who wanted to start a health center. After Burgess moved to Boston, she, Avrin, and Terry Plumb organized the First Annual Women's Health Conference at the Boston YWCA. Burgess, Avrin, Plumb, and four other conference attendees established the Women's Community Health Center.[123]

The group initially met once a week, then twice a week, trying to figure out how a health center owned and controlled by women would operate. Members were united by their belief that good medical care was a human right that should be free. Rejecting the hierarchy of existing medical clinics, they also agreed to follow democratic procedures of decision-making. An early meeting was run collectively because no one wanted to chair it.[124] In deciding how the center would function financially, members agreed on nonprofit status to allow tax-deductible donations.[125] They also grappled with the fee schedule. Rigid fees would conflict with the goal of making the center available to all women, while a sliding scale would require them to make value judgments about other women's ability to pay. Both the rigid and sliding scales were incompatible with the organizers' political ideal of equality. In the end, they assumed that women who could pay more than the suggested fee would do so in order to finance the center for those who could not afford the fee. That assumption proved to be overly optimistic, but the clinic operated on this philosophy despite the financial hardship it imposed.[126]

In January 1974 the Los Angeles FWHC began to contribute fifty dollars a week toward the WCHC's start-up costs. In February the WCHC filed for incorporation as a nonprofit woman-owned and -controlled self-help clinic. In March Robin Morgan read her poetry at a benefit that raised $700.[127] By April 1974 the clinic had opened in rented quarters at 137 Hampshire Street in Cambridge, thanks in part to a $5,000 grant from the Women's Health Book Collective (see figure 13).[128]

That summer the center hired a female doctor and began offering gynecological services, including first-trimester abortions. Reflecting a less violent time in the history of abortion services, the WCHC held open houses for friends and community members to acquaint them with its facilities and mission. The speed with which the Cambridge clinic moved from concept to reality—nine months, appropriately enough—was a testament to the energy and commitment of its founders.[129]

women's community health

center inc.
137 hampshire st.
cambridge, ma. 02139
617.547.2302

WOMENS
COMMUNITY
HEALTH

FIGURE 13. Women's Community Health Center, 137 Hampshire Street, Cambridge, MA, ca. 1980. Drawing by Reed Gyovai Muehlman based on newsletter image. Women's Community Health Center, Third Annual Report, Women's Community Health Center Records, Schlesinger Library, Radcliffe Institute, Harvard University, collection MC 512, carton 1, folder 13.

The WCHC's first annual report included a "herstory" of the clinic's origins. De- (or re-) gendering traditional language signaled the group's feminist roots. Lest there be any doubt about the center's radical politics, the report included its mission statement:

> The Women's Community Health Center is a woman-owned and controlled nonprofit health center operated by a collective of women. We are working toward the time when all women will control our bodies and our lives. Since knowledge is the key to control, we must educate ourselves in new ways and take hold of formerly forbidden medical knowledge. For us, as women, control over what is done to our bodies is a major issue; this means creating new models of health care which nurture, rather than destroy, our growing strength.[130]

The "formerly forbidden medical knowledge" was a reference to doctors' failure to take women patients seriously. The Center was especially concerned about doctors' refusal to inform patients about the side effects and long-term consequences of taking the Pill, using intrauterine devices (IUDs), or taking diethylstilbestrol (DES), a synthetic estrogen prescribed to prevent miscarriages. Part of the problem was that doctors themselves lacked knowledge about the Pill's long-term effects; another was that "informed consent" was a novel concept in medicine at the time.[131]

In 1975 the WCHC began the application process for a license to operate as a clinic independently of the licensing of its physicians. Clinic licensing required, first, obtaining a Certificate of Need from the state Department of Public Health demonstrating demand for their services in the surrounding community. Proof of proper zoning and an affiliation with a back-up hospital were also required. After the Certificate of Need was granted, city and state building inspections had to grant a Certificate of Occupancy, followed by a Department of Public Health inspection. A clinic license could be obtained only after all six conditions were met. On May 1 the WCHC submitted its application for a Certificate of Need with a seventy-page document that included thirty letters of support from local agencies and residents; Mount Auburn Hospital would be its affiliate. This was the beginning of a licensure effort that would take countless letters, phone calls, and visits to local and state agencies over the next three years.[132]

In June 1975 the WCHC received a Certificate of Need. In November the Department of Public Health sent an inspector to the WCHC. The inspector listed several areas in which the center needed to comply with state regulations, one of which was that it could not call itself a "health center" or advertise medical services until licensed. In January 1976 they opened under the name Women's Community Health. A second public health inspection occurred in March 1976, at which additional demands were made. Then a new inspector visited in April 1977, making new demands that contradicted the earlier reports and threatening to close down the WCHC. As with the Building Department, Public Health claimed to have lost documents relevant to the application. WCHC staff members had copies of all transactions and mailing receipts to suggest otherwise.[133]

The Cambridge Building Department was especially intransigent. It was responsible for approving the Certificate of Occupancy, the second step in opening the clinic. One Department member assured WCHC that the clinic was properly zoned, one told them it was not, and a third said he was unsure. The department repeatedly lost WCHC's application, eventually demanding a total of five applications between May 1975 and January 1976. It also sent out inspectors on four different visits, each time saying they had lost the earlier inspection report. The department finally granted the Certificate of Occupancy in May 1976. Within two months, however, the Massachusetts Department of Public Safety informed WCHC of new building regulations that were in conflict with those required by the City of Cambridge. WCHC was told to hire an architect to design the necessary changes. When they presented the architectural plans, they were told nothing could happen until their zoning status was clarified.[134]

Zoning was a problem because the word *clinic* was missing from the Cambridge zoning regulations. The WCHC was located in a residential area, which earlier had been zoned as a business district. A different clinic that operated in the same neighborhood had experienced no difficulty in obtaining a license. Yet in January 1976 the Cambridge Legal Department declared the WCHC to be improperly zoned. In order to move forward with the licensing process, the WCHC agreed to be classified as a "community center" that offered some medical services. The compromise was possible because the WCHC was a nonprofit, tax-exempt organization that included the words "community" and "center" in its name.[135]

After presenting its case to the Board of Zoning Appeals in May 1977, the WCHC was declared appropriately zoned. The victory went beyond the single case of the WCHC. Based on their arguments, the city included the definition of *clinic* and *community center* in its new zoning regulations. Clinics connected with a community center, such as WCHC, had the fewest land use restrictions and could exist even in residential neighborhoods. The zoning battle had taken two years.[136]

The WCHC was, finally, fully licensed in April 1978. Licensure had come at an enormous cost of time and money. Along the way, the center was threatened with closure by "compulsory pregnancy" advocates (anti-abortionists) who charged that the WCHC was an "unlicensed illegal abortion clinic." One of the strongest opponents of the clinic was State Representative Raymond Flynn (later mayor of Boston), a member of the House Post Audit Committee, which pressured the Department of Public Health to reverse its policy of allowing clinics to operate while applying for licensure.[137]

In 1978 the WCHC moved to 639 Massachusetts Avenue in Cambridge to avoid the prohibitive costs of bringing the Hampshire Street facility up to code. Organizers had to raise $30,000 to renovate the new space properly. But it was worth it. According to staff members, "The new offices are a concrete and daily reminder that the work done by Women's Community Health Center is recognized as an essential part of women's struggle to control our lives."[138] Members, though, were angry over all the obstacles placed in their way. The 1978 *Annual Report* noted that "the difficulties encountered [during the licensing process] reflect ways that bureaucratic red tape can be used for conscious harassment. [The clinic] was subjected to this harassment because as an anti-capitalist, feminist self-help center it threatens the medical establishment and ultimately our political and economic system."[139]

The system eventually won, however. Constantly underfunded, the WCHC was unable to pay its bills. It closed and filed for bankruptcy in 1981. The organizers did not go quietly. In a last-ditch fund-raising letter announcing their imminent closing, they claimed that the center was "a victim of the New Right and depression economics" and declared that they were "enraged that so many years of good, hard, productive work" still left them with no other option.[140]

Women's Health in Women's Hands

The Los Angeles and Boston feminist clinics were not alone in facing external threats. By 1976 conflicts had become so common that Downer, Hornstein, and Rothman created Women Acting Together to Combat Harassment (WATCH), an umbrella organization to document attacks and mobilize resources for clinics across the country involved in lawsuits.[141] In a study of fifty feminist health clinics, the sociologist Sandra Morgen found crises to be the norm. She estimated that one clinic spent almost half of its organizational life in battles with local and state officials. Building inspections, zoning ordinances, and public health reviews all determined whether a clinic could secure a health department license. The process was long and costly; it also exposed clinics to intense scrutiny. Feminist clinics were subject to the same government budget cutbacks as other grassroots organizations during the 1980s, but few others were targets of extreme violence. Abortion clinics were bombed, set on fire, and vandalized. Staff members and doctors were threatened. All this took a toll on clinics' ability to deliver medical care.[142]

Internal conflicts also disrupted the unity of the women's health movement and individual clinics. Bureaucracy and hierarchy were anathema to feminists, but collective group decision-making could be tedious, and sometimes disastrous, for an organization. Emphasis on democratic processes often worked better in theory than in practice. An emotionally charged workplace was inevitable given the number of clients with emergencies, and the periodic sieges from outside forces were stressful. Tensions erupted when white middle-class founders were accused of racism, class bias, and homophobia by black, working-class, or lesbian staff members.[143] In fact, founders of the self-help movement prided themselves on their working-class origins. Their lack of academic or professional credentials gave them the freedom to speak out without fear of reprisal from professional organizations.[144] According to Carol Downer, "Self-Help comes out of a lower-class consciousness, an everyday common-sense understanding that social change is not going to be welcomed by the status-quo."[145]

Clinic manifestos were filled with the language of rights: from the Oakland FWHC, "Menstrual Extraction is every Woman's right"; from the *Monthly Extract*, "We must fight when our rights are violated" (referring to official harassment of clinics); from *Our Bodies, Ourselves*, "Abortion is our right—our right as women to control our own bodies." The two Supreme Court cases that granted women reproductive rights, *Griswold v. Connecticut* and *Roe v. Wade*, were both based on rights to privacy rather than rights to autonomy. Ironically, rights couched in the language of privacy have done much to give women more potential for public lives. Above all, reproductive rights granted women bodily integrity, a basic criterion for full citizenship. Carol Downer thinks *Roe v. Wade* was a mistake. Not because it legalized abortion, for which she had campaigned relentlessly, but because the Supreme Court decision of 1973 was cast in the language of a constitutional right to privacy rather than a woman's right to control her body.[146] Other feminists have also found fault with *Roe v. Wade*, pointing out that it established a woman's "negative right" to freedom from government constraint, rather than a "positive right" recognizing a woman's prerogative to choose.[147]

Women needed medical knowledge about their own bodies before they could defy doctors who patronized them, or, at worst, sterilized them without their consent. Feminist self-help clinics taught women how to take charge of their health. In the clinics, "women's knowledge" challenged men's control. Clinics also lobbied vigorously to legalize abortion and prevent forced sterilization. By 1974 feminist health clinics had inscribed these rights on the urban landscape in more than two hundred cities around the world. Their campaigns came at a cost. Clinic staff suffered police raids, arrests, and harassment.[148]

The Los Angeles FWHC closed in 1984. Like other feminist health centers, many of its functions were absorbed by hospitals and health maintenance organizations (HMOs).[149] Operating constantly on the brink of financial crisis, many clinics might have closed sooner had it not been for Robin Morgan's deep pockets at various fundraisers, and salaries subsidized by federal programs like CETA. In 1975 there were at least forty-two clinics in nineteen states. In 2010 only fifteen feminist health clinics were still operating.[150]

Individual clinics closed, but the women's health movement prospered. Advocacy organizations created in the early days still exist, and others are emerging. The mission of the NWHN continues to be to "improve the health of all women by developing and promoting a critical analysis of health issues in order to affect policy and support consumer decision-making."[151] The National Black Women's Health Project, later called the Black Women's Health Imperative, has become increasingly active internationally.[152] Our

Bodies Ourselves (formerly the Boston Women's Health Book Collective) identifies itself as a "non-profit, public interest women's health education, advocacy, and consulting organization."[153] An evolving website named after Fannie Lou Hamer's "Mississippi appendectomy" is devoted to disseminating information about women of color and forced sterilizations. The collective longevity of these pioneering groups is a testament to the impact they made on health care for women.[154]

The spaces the feminist clinics occupied may have been small, but their symbolic value was much larger: they enhanced women's capacity to engage in public life by giving women the ability to control whether or when to become pregnant. The road to reproductive rights was paved by feminists like Carol Downer who insisted on women's rights to control knowledge about their own bodies as the first step toward changing women's rights in other realms. Downer is still preaching the gospel of self-help on her website Women's Health in Women's Hands.[155]

CHAPTER 5

Domestic Violence Shelters

Protecting Bodily Integrity

Battered women who stay in violent relationships are denied bodily integrity, a "free citizen's first and greatest right."[1] They also lack freedom of movement. If women cannot move and act freely in the public sphere, of if they are intimidated in the privacy of their homes, their ability to act as citizens is limited.[2] The feminist philosopher Sandra Bartky points out that citizens give up their prerogative to use violence; they expect the government to protect them from unwarranted physical injury at the hands of others. Yet for most of history the law has failed to protect women attacked by intimate partners, leading Bartky to question whether women who are repeatedly beaten are *bona fide* citizens of the state at all.[3]

In the early 1970s activists who were angered by this assault on women's basic rights—and by public silence on the issue—established the first domestic violence shelters. Shelters were places of refuge; they provided physical locations from which to organize and served as bases for political thought and action.[4]

Mary Marecek, program director of the RESPOND shelter in Somerville, Massachusetts, saw similarities between shelters and stations on the Underground Railroad:

> The shelter movement is not unlike the underground railroads of Harriet Tubman. The houses provide the route of escape for thousands

of women who have lived with violence and have no other route of escape. Just as oppressed people followed the north star to freedom from enslavement, victims of domestic violence seek safe passage from the bondage of fear and abuse. The shelter movement is a moment in herstory—one in which women who have been liberated from this oppression help those who are not.[5]

Domestic violence shelters shared another similarity with Underground Railroad stops: the secrecy of their locations. Just as slaves had to be hidden from bounty hunters or owners who came looking for their property, abused women needed to hide from their assailants. Only a small network of trusted allies could direct the way to a safe haven for people who feared for their lives. Confidentiality was paramount; once it was violated a location had to be abandoned. Thus this chapter includes only one image: the first RESPOND shelter at 24 Walnut Street in a residential neighborhood off Union Square in Somerville, Massachusetts (see figure 14). The building is no longer used as a shelter.

FIGURE 14. Original RESPOND domestic violence shelter, 24 Walnut Street, Somerville, MA. Drawing by Reed Gyovai Muehlman based on photograph by the author. No longer in use.

The Political and Social Construction of Domestic Violence

Shelters were new in the 1970s, but wife abuse is at least as old as the country itself. The family was so vital to the success of the Puritans' mission that domestic violence was considered "wicked carriage"—sinful behavior subject to punishment. Believing that disruptive family life threatened social order, the Puritans kept watch on one another for violations of proper conduct. They also relied on the moral influence of the pulpit. Religious leader Cotton Mather preached that for "a man to beat his wife was as bad as any Sacriledge. Any such a Rascal were better buried alive, than show his Head among his Neighbours anymore."[6] Domestic violence was thus very much a public concern in colonial North America. Then the topic faded from public view for nearly two centuries.

A formal movement against domestic violence in the United States emerged again in the late nineteenth century, when "child saving" charities acknowledged that fathers who beat their children often beat their wives as well. Whether wife battering is considered a public issue warranting intervention or a personal problem to be resolved within the family has fluctuated over time. According to the historian Linda Gordon, for more than one hundred years public concern with domestic violence grew when feminism was strongest and ebbed when it was weakest. Between 1875 and 1910, when suffragists were campaigning for the vote, and again during the Progressive Era (1910–30), reformers seized on wife beating as a deplorable practice. During the Great Depression, when economic hardship took priority, and during the 1940s and 1950s when family values were paramount, attention to domestic violence waned. The rebirth of feminism in the 1960s and 1970s "forced open the doors of closets that hid family problems."[7]

Those problems needed to be named in order to become the objects of public policy and legal interventions. Dispelling public perceptions that wife abuse was the woman's fault, and a problem only among the poor and minorities, was the first step. Second Wave feminists began to publicize their three basic assumptions about domestic violence. First, women of any race, ethnicity, class, or age are equally subject to assault. Second, women are innocent victims of their partners' rage; and third, the men are deliberate offenders who repeatedly inflict serious physical harm on their partners. "Wife abuse," then, was a label for "severe, frequent, and continuing violence [by men toward women] that escalates over time and is unstoppable."[8] Initially wife abuse meant physical assault; feminists would later include psychological aggression as well.

Husbands of all races and classes strike their wives. In her memoir, Betty Friedan revealed that she had been a battered wife. Her husband Carl began beating her soon after *The Feminine Mystique* was published. The more famous she became, the more frequently he hit her, until she finally divorced him in 1969.[9] Husbands who feel threatened by the increasing independence of their wives may strike them to remind both partners who has the greater power. Or husbands may attack their wives to make them afraid to leave, thus ensuring the continuation of domestic and sexual services. Attitudes differ about whether alcohol is responsible for domestic violence. Some see it as the primary cause. Others argue that drinking merely gives men license to be aggressive without taking responsibility for their actions. Above all, men use physical violence, both inside and outside of marriage, to maintain control over women.[10]

The earliest definitions of domestic violence assumed heterosexual couples as the norm. Del Martin, the author of *Battered Wives* (1976), defined battered wives as "any woman who is beaten by her mate, whether legally married or not, and the word 'husband' applies to the man in the couple."[11] Feminist psychologist Lenore Walker added a caveat about patterns of abuse in *The Battered Woman* (1979): "Any woman may find herself in an abusive relationship with a man once. If it occurs a second time and she remains in the situation, she is defined as a battered woman."[12] For Mildred Pagelow, the author of *Woman-Battering: Victims and Their Experiences* (1981), battered women were adults who were physically abused to the point of pain or injury or "were forced into involuntary action or restrained by force from voluntary action by adult men with whom they have or had established relationships, usually involving sexual intimacy, whether or not within a married state."[13]

These definitions underscore the low profile of same-sex intimate violence when the battered women's movement began; the original shelters seldom dealt with lesbian relationships, even as increasing numbers of gays and lesbians were coming out.[14] Lesbians may have been less likely to seek shelters, or staff may have been less likely to admit them based on lesbians' failure to fit the model of a "real" battered woman.[15] Acknowledging that women abused other women would also have challenged the feminist theory that domestic violence was the product of male domination in a patriarchal society. As the movement matured, however, understanding grew that power and control were as central to abuse as gender.[16]

During the 1970s it was difficult to estimate the national incidence of wife battering. "Wife abuse" was not an official category on police reports, court rosters, or emergency hospital admission files; police recorded calls for help as "domestic disputes." Statistics from police departments in Boston,

Chicago, Detroit, and New York indicated, however, that domestic disturbances outranked any other type of call to the police. A 1972 study of Family Court records in New York State, extrapolated to the nation, estimated that more than one million cases of domestic violence occurred each year.[17]

Feminists initially paid more attention to rape than to domestic violence. The first rape crisis hotlines were formed before the first battered women's shelters, for example, although both projects drew from the same principles and gathered power in C–R groups.[18] In 1971 the New York Radical Feminists held a public rally called a "speak-out" against rape that energized local feminist collectives to organize anti-rape actions.[19] Demonstrators at that event declared that violence was a form of domination between people of unequal power, and that rape was an act of violence, not passion. Susan Brownmiller's *Against Our Will: Men, Women, and Rape* (1975) shattered other myths about rape: that women invited rape by dressing provocatively, actually liked to be raped, and meant yes when they said no. Brownmiller and other feminists declared that socializing women to be passive and men to be dominant fed into a legal system that blamed the victim and allowed rapists to go free. Much of the same ideology applied to battered women.[20]

An example of the early invisibility, even to feminists, of domestic violence is Kirsten Grimstad and Susan Rennie's 1973 edition of *The New Woman's Survival Catalog*. No mention was made of domestic violence, although the book included fifteen pages on issues of rape. In their updated 1975 *New Woman's Survival Sourcebook*, however, they introduced two pages on wife battering in addition to the section on rape and its prevention.[21] NOW declared marital violence a major issue in 1975 and initiated its Women against Violence against Women campaign. Within the year local chapters of NOW were publishing materials on wife beating. The Ann Arbor, Michigan, chapter developed instructions for a "wife assault task force" and distributed counselor training manuals.[22] The Delaware Council for Women produced a *Resource Booklet for Battered Spouses* after a statewide NOW conference.[23]

By the end of the 1970s domestic violence had become a major feminist issue. Betsy Warrior was at its center as one of the founders of the shelter Transition House in Cambridge. Warrior became an activist in 1968 when, as Betsy Mahoney, she joined Roxanne Dunbar and Dana Densmore in Boston's Female Liberation Front (later known as Cell 16). When members of the group began to write down their thoughts, Mahoney chose the pen name Betsy Luthuli in honor of the Zulu chief Albert John Luthuli but soon changed it to Betsy Warrior.[24] Influenced by living for seven years with a husband who beat her, Warrior believed marriage enslaved women. Working without wages and living in "perpetual economic bondage to males as a class," she noted, was obscured by sentimental myths of the sacredness of the family and contented wives. According to Warrior, society "determinedly ignored . . . the pervasive occupational hazard houseworkers are frequently victims of, resulting in emotional and physical injury and too often death. The beating of houseworkers by husbands and 'lovers' is a world wide phenomenon that occurs in no other occupation with such high frequency and degree. . . . At Transition House . . . we constantly see the physical scars that the stamp of slavery has left on women. . . . Wherever housewives are found, battered women are found."[25]

Wife battering was also making its way into mainstream US media, legislation, and government policy. The *New York Times* began to cover domestic violence with some regularity in 1976, and by 1978 articles on the subject appeared in major news magazines. Battering was a prominent topic at the 1976 International Tribunal on Crimes against Women held in Brussels.[26] In 1979 *U.S. News & World Report* identified more than 170 emergency shelters that had been opened nationally between 1975 and 1978. By 1980 laws in forty-five states and the District of Columbia addressed the legal rights of domestic violence victims and increased penalties for their assailants. Federal agencies granted millions of dollars to combat family violence; funding flowed through Community Development Block Grants (CDBG), the Comprehensive Employment and Training Act (CETA), Law Enforcement Assistance Administration (LEAA), and Volunteers in Service to America (VISTA).[27] Research on the causes of wife beating also began to appear in the 1970s. Much of it was conducted by sociologists at the University of New Hampshire's Family Violence Research Program with funding from the National Institutes of Mental Health.[28]

Domestic Violence and Women of Color

Women of color were virtually absent from the earliest discussions of domestic violence.[29] But Alice Walker's Pulitzer Prize–winning novel, *The Color Purple*, brought them to public attention. The book ignited a controversy in the black community when it was published in 1982. Reviewers criticized Walker for portraying the character Celie's emotional and psychological abuse at the hands of her husband, arguing that it was a false image of African American culture. But many black women recognized themselves in Celie.[30] Walker's book also addressed, with the nurturing relationship between Celie and Shug, the black lesbian experience.[31]

African American, Latina, and Asian women experience battering differently from white women. The intersection of race and/or ethnicity and gender exposes women of color to multiple forms of domination, only one of which is domestic violence. Racism and sexism interact to produce high rates of poverty and unemployment for women of color. Poor women in abusive relationships have few alternatives if they lack job skills or have no friends or family who can afford to shelter them, even temporarily. For these women, leaving an abusive relationship may be as much about economics as about overcoming psychological obstacles.[32]

Stereotypes about pathological violence in nonwhite communities also play a role in whether wives report battering. Why expose domestic abuse, this argument goes, when it only reinforces public perceptions that people of color engage in more violent behavior than whites? Critics of this perspective point out that the African American political community routinely discusses black-on-black crimes of homicide and gang violence but avoids placing wife beating in the same criminal category. Women of color may also be averse to exposing their private lives to the scrutiny of police they perceive as hostile. Finally, in an attempt to protect their kids from beatings, African American women, like other women, may sacrifice their own safety.[33]

Of all women of color, immigrants are least likely to seek help. Cultural practices, like protecting the family honor, may discourage them from taking action against abusive partners. Language barriers can prevent them from obtaining and acting on information about their rights, and they may depend on their husbands for information regarding their legal status. Intervention from the police could jeopardize the well-being of the entire family in the case of undocumented workers. Add to that a general distrust of the police among immigrants fearful of deportation, and it may be a rational choice when an immigrant woman stays with an abusive husband.[34]

The black lesbian activist and author Barbara Smith thinks that the campaign against domestic violence was a path by which African American women joined the predominantly white feminist movement. Volunteering in a shelter was often the first step an African-American woman would take in identifying common concerns. Boston's Combahee River Collective, of which Smith was a founding member, wanted to open a shelter for black women soon after the group formed in 1974.[35]

To achieve their goal, members of the collective formed a coalition with women and men that became Inquilinos Boricuas en Acción (Tenants in Action, IBA), a radical group working on affordable housing in Boston's South End. The area, plagued by inner city problems, was demographically and economically diverse. It was home to African Americans, Jews, and a large Latino population from Puerto Rico, Cuba, and the Dominican Republic. The IBA member Myrna Vazquez, a well-known actress in Puerto

Rico, promoted arts and culture to combat the violence associated with crime and drug abuse.

In the early1970s the collective and IBA found a four-story, eight-bedroom brownstone they could purchase cheaply from the city. To convert it to a women's shelter, contractors added another kitchen and bathroom. Offices were located on the first floor, and women seeking shelter stayed on the upper floors. While in residence, women had to sign a confidentiality agreement about the shelter's location, but they had keys to the door and could come and go as they liked. Volunteers staffed the house and offered services needed by women with physical, mental, and addiction problems. When Vazquez died suddenly in 1976, the shelter was named for her, and Casa Myrna Vazquez has been in continuous operation since.[36]

Battered Women and the Law

Mary Marecek, the author of *Say "NO!" to Violence*, warned that "Until women are in positions to write the laws, pass the laws and enforce the laws we will continue to live with violence."[37] The legal precedents that protected men from prosecution for wife abuse in the 1960s originated in eighteenth-century English laws, long before women had any influence on the legal system. Under the doctrine formulated by British Chief Justice Lord Hale, it was impossible to accuse a husband of raping his wife because she had given up the right to refuse his sexual demands by agreeing to the marriage contract. In a similar vein, William Blackstone's "unities" theory declared that husband and wife were one person, the legal existence of the wife being "suspended during marriage, incorporated into that of the husband," so that an injured wife could not take action without her husband's permission. Rape in general was considered a crime against another man's (father's or husband's) property rather than a violation of a woman's bodily integrity. Since a husband could not steal (i.e., rape) his own property (i.e., wife), marital rape became a legal impossibility. The United States formally recognized the right of a man to rape his wife (the "Hale doctrine") in the 1857 *Commonwealth v. Fogarty* decision. These same laws prevented victims of domestic violence from filing civil suits against their husbands for physical or psychological damages, which often included rape.[38]

Domestic violence was exempt from legal oversight for so long because, until the end of the nineteenth century, behavior within the family was considered private. Criminal law did not apply to family members, and a husband was ensured the right to chastise his wife with a stick "no thicker than his thumb." In 1864 a North Carolina court decided that the state should not interfere with domestic chastisement unless it resulted in permanent injury. Otherwise, the law would not "invade the domestic forum or go behind the curtain," leaving the couple to make up and "live together as man and wife should."[39]

The notion of privacy employed in the legal system reinforces the idea that personal experiences are unrelated to social and political structures. This interpretation of privacy also means that something should be kept secret. Most important, it means that laws and policies apply only to the public sphere, leaving private matters unregulated. According to the feminist lawyer Elizabeth Schneider, the concept of privacy reinforces violence against women, making it immune from sanction and part of the basic fabric of US family life. "Privacy says that what goes on in the violent relationship should not be the subject of state or community intervention. Privacy says that it is an individual and not a systemic problem. Privacy operates as a mask for inequality, protecting male violence against women."[40]

The logistics of obtaining protection have been historically difficult for women. Before the 1970s, tort law concerned with injury inflicted by individuals did not apply to family members.[41] Women could take out restraining orders against their abusers, but it was a lengthy, expensive process, and the orders were difficult to enforce. A woman could obtain a restraining order only after hiring an attorney and paying filing costs. Unless she was eligible for legal aid, she had to pay to have the order served on her husband at least ten days before the hearing, and she had to appear in court to testify against him. Husbands who violated a restraining order were subject to only a misdemeanor or contempt of court charge, and police seldom monitored compliance. Another barrier to appropriate punishment for the batterer was the practice of transferring domestic violence cases from criminal courts to family courts, where only civil procedures apply. Other avenues an abused wife might pursue, through the district attorney or a judge, were sufficiently intimidating that few women would even try.[42]

In 1974 activist Laura X began a campaign to criminalize marital rape. She assisted in the 1978 trial against John Rideout, the first husband to be criminally prosecuted for rape while still living with his wife. Although Rideout was acquitted, the case concentrated public attention on the issue. Starting with California in 1979, Laura X led the successful fight to repeal the marital rape exemption nationwide. It took more than a decade, but by 1993 marital rape had become a crime in all fifty states. Declaring that rape within marriage was as much a crime as rape outside marriage paved the way for treating assault and battery between intimates in the same way as that between strangers.[43]

Repeal of the marital rape exemption was one of several legal victories for battered women; tort law was also reformed to cover domestic abuse.[44] In 1976 four women filed a class action suit (*Scott v. Hart*) against the Oakland, California, police department for failing to respond to calls for help from physically abused women. The three years of litigation it took to win the case were followed by three years of monitoring and six months of police training. Other results were city funding for three local women's shelters, a Battered Women's Resource Card that police gave to victims of abuse to explain their rights, policy changes in the district attorney's office, and similar lawsuits in other states.[45]

Transforming the private troubles of domestic violence into a public issue demanding legal intervention was one of the greatest accomplishments of the Second Wave. It was the quintessential example of turning the personal into the political. In one decade, wife beating was brought out of the family closet and exposed to public scrutiny. Pressure from feminist groups, media coverage, and federal subsidies for research reached a critical mass that created a social movement against domestic violence. Unlike the societal response to other social movements, though, the public at large never identified wife abuse as a problem that demanded a solution. Rather, domestic violence was tolerated at numerous institutional levels, especially by law enforcement officials. The police considered domestic disputes a private matter and were reluctant to intervene until the 1970s. As long as women endured assaults and had nowhere else to go, the public knew little about domestic violence. It took feminists to construct it as a social problem and to propose solutions.

The Emergence of Shelters in the 1970s

The shelter movement started in London, England, in 1971 as a byproduct of community activism unrelated to domestic violence. The feminist Erin Pizzey and a group of friends were protesting rising food prices in their neighborhood. As they stood on street corners brandishing placards that listed food prices at different stores, they met numerous young mothers who said they felt isolated in their homes. Pizzey thought a community center would provide a place to temporarily escape their loneliness and identify common problems they could solve collectively. She pressured the local housing council into giving her and other activists an abandoned house at 2 Belmont Terrace. Volunteers transformed it into a comfortable place with a children's play area, a stove and sink in the kitchen, and a washing machine. Upstairs were a room for an office and a room with a bed. Chiswick Women's Aid had come to life. In addition to fulfilling its initial intent as an all-purpose gathering area, it increasingly became the destination for battered women and their families. A year after opening, the center was housing thirty-four women and children, who slept on mattresses laid in the hall and shared one toilet.[46]

There were few house rules, but one was that men were allowed in by invitation only. Another was that any woman who wanted a key could have one. All the women and children took responsibility for running the operation, avoiding the labels of "supervisor" and "client." Residents shared the tasks of keeping coal fires burning and cooking massive quantities of stews and soups. The washing machine was in constant use because laundromats were too expensive for women on relief. To raise enough money to keep the center open, residents held jumble sales of old clothes; the first one netted 70 pounds.[47]

By May 1973 the center was taking nearly one hundred calls a day from women seeking to escape violence at home. At any given time thirty women and children would be living there. When sympathetic executives at the Bovis Company agreed to fund the facility, the center was able to move to a larger house at 369 Chiswick High Road. Its new quarters had large rooms, a garden, and a finished basement converted to playrooms. Most important, it had three toilets. The center was licensed to hold thirty-six residents, but there were often one hundred women and children living in the house. Chiswick Women's Aid quickly added four more centers in London.[48]

All of the houses were crowded, but they shared a positive atmosphere. They were effective, according to Pizzey, because women and children living with violence are shut off from other people, whereas "Women's Aid forces them out of their isolation. When they come into the house they are crowded together with many others who've been through the same kind of suffering. They have to communicate. Often for the first time since they married they are talking to someone who understands what it's like, because she's been through the same herself. They can also listen and recognize what others have been through. They can see they're not alone."[49]

Pizzey railed against public silence and government indifference to family violence. She received publicity partly because her husband was an anchorman for the BBC. A television program about Chiswick Women's Aid titled *Scream Quietly or the Neighbors Will Hear* became the basis for Pizzey's book by that name.[50] When it was published in 1974, Women's Aid had five large houses that served 250 women and children. Pizzey thought the centers had grown so fast because they were run *by* battered women *for* battered women.[51] In her 1977 introduction to the US edition of the book, Pizzey noted that Women's Aid was the only place in England, and possibly the world, that would take in any woman escaping a violent relationship. By 1978 the National Women's Aid Federation, supported by local and national government funds, operated more than 150 refuges in the United Kingdom.[52]

In the US edition of *Scream Quietly*, Pizzey recounted how women visiting the shelter had spread the word about its work. Two women from Amsterdam, for example, lived in the refuge for a week soon after it opened. When they returned home, they sought help from the Dutch government to establish a similar center. They were told, though, that domestic violence was only an English problem. Outraged, the two women squatted in a derelict house; within a week fourteen mothers and their children were on the doorstep. The government relented and funded the refuge. Pizzey and her colleagues also traveled, giving lectures in France, Germany, Switzerland, and the United States; the shelter movement was soon an international phenomenon. By the time Pizzey reached the United States in 1977, she found refuges everywhere.[53]

Women's House in St. Paul, Minnesota, was among the first shelters in the US created by feminists, members of the Women's Advocates collective who had been in the antiwar movement together since the 1960s. In 1972 they started a telephone service giving legal advice to women, staffed by volunteers and two VISTA workers assigned through a legal aid office. The majority of calls came from women who had been assaulted by their husbands. Because local welfare and social service networks provided no emergency shelter for battered women, members of Women's Advocates opened their homes to let women and their children sleep on their living room floors.[54]

After two years of fund-raising, in 1974 the collective moved into a large Victorian house on Grand Avenue. The founders wanted to create a "politicizing" domestic space that was free of violence and demanded that law enforcement institutions support that goal. By the end of its first month of operation, "Women's House" had accommodated twenty-two women and fifteen children. Residents shared their experiences and made decisions about how to run the shelter. The only standing rule was that women could not reveal the location.[55] The shelter was always filled to capacity. By 1976 Women's Advocates planned to use CDBG funds to buy the house next door; within a decade they owned three adjacent houses.[56] One of the founders remembered that they discovered their politics in the process of discovering themselves. When they realized that the system failed to meet the needs of battered women, they "rushed in to save them," learning from the women they served, and from each other, how to become survivors: "The personal was political. Personally, I didn't call myself a feminist when we started. It sort of snuck up and embraced me as I lived it."[57]

The existence of local feminist groups like Women's Advocates was a significant predictor of programs for battered women. Grassroots groups were important in providing services, documenting needs, and pressuring policy makers to address the problem.[58] In 1977 the US Department of Health, Education, and Welfare (HEW),[59] in coordination with the activists who had demanded research on the issue, conducted a national survey of facilities for battered women. The resulting monograph was based on 163 groups that responded to a questionnaire about the number of women they served, funding, staffing and services, and organizational structure. The programs were sponsored by local chapters of NOW, church groups, and YWCAs; about 15 percent emerged out of C-R groups, rape crisis groups, or the National Coalition against Domestic Violence. The majority were organized along traditional lines of authority, with boards of directors and paid program directors. The programs begun by feminist groups, however, were nonhierarchical, democratic, and included battered women on the staff. In 1977 forty-seven thousand women and fourteen thousand children received shelter or other assistance from these groups. The average stay was two weeks. Funding came from donations and federal CETA funds that paid staff. Services included counseling, referral to social service agencies, transportation, and child care.[60]

By the early 1980s, due partly to the problems associated with a loose management style, fewer than half of the existing US domestic violence shelters had been founded by, or were related to, feminist groups. About one-quarter were started by church groups and another one-quarter to one-third by YWCA, Al-Anon, and other local civic organizations.[61]

Erin Pizzey mentioned a refuge in Boston during her 1977 visit to the United States, although her lecture tour did not take her to the city.[62] She may have heard of Casa Myrna established in the South End in the early 1970s, RESPOND, which began operations in 1975 in working-class Somerville, or Transition House, which opened in middle-class Cambridge in 1976. The latter two cities were just outside Boston's city limits.

Somerville's RESPOND

In 1974 four community activists publicly announced the idea for RESPOND, Responsible Escape for Somerville People through Options and New Developments. Anne Broussard, Pauline Dwyer, Jean Luce, and Maureen Varney, all single mothers, had been discussing the idea for several years.[63] According to Dwyer, they "met in barrooms and talked forever."[64] There was a lot to escape in Somerville in the early 1970s. Varney described the city as a densely populated blue-collar urban area with one of the highest rates of alcoholism in the country; overall, not a very pretty place. She and the others saw a need to give young women hope for a better life.[65] They envisioned an organization that could respond to four problems women faced: youth in crisis (teen runaways), young women in transition (single women seeking independence from their families), women in crisis (victims of wife battering), and housing for welfare recipients.[66]

Few of RESPOND's founders were members of NOW, which they considered anti-male. Instead, they were "flaming feminists who liked men."[67] Cofounder Maureen Varney noted that it was difficult to involve working-class women in the women's movement because "feminists do not always take into account the needs and problems that affect working-class women's daily lives. It is impossible for a woman to begin to recognize her own strengths and take more control over her life when she is constantly terrorized by her husband."[68]

Broussard and Dwyer asked Somerville Mayor Lester Ralph for a CETA worker who could coordinate a program to provide for the "shelter, health, education, and wellbeing of the women and children of Somerville."[69] The mayor granted their request and selected Jean Luce as planning coordinator for the nascent program. Before joining RESPOND, Luce had been a member of the Somerville Youth Coalition and the Neighborhood Youth Corps. Her full-time job with RESPOND included negotiating with funding agencies, working with the board of directors to set up job descriptions, and locating a permanent building for the organization.[70]

The founders added men to the board of directors to add legitimacy to the organization.[71] The Reverend DeForest Brown, Father William Leonard, and the attorney William Jerome joined their Monday evening meetings.[72] In 1974, with the help of Bill Jerome, the board filed for incorporation as a nonprofit, tax-exempt 501(c)3 organization. When that status was granted in 1975, the "S" in RESPOND was changed to stand for "Special" in recognition that its mission had expanded beyond Somerville.[73] Anne Broussard, then president of the board, started looking for office space. She found it at the Somerville Multi-Service Center at 1 Summer Street. The Reverend Paul Duhamel of the First Methodist Church, who operated the center in the church building, agreed to let the group use a desk and telephone.[74]

In January 1975 the *Somerville Journal* featured an article about RESPOND's multiple missions under the headline "New Program RESPONDs to Women's Crisis Needs." The Youth in Crisis would provide a facility, open twenty-four hours a day, where runaway teens could live temporarily and receive counseling. The Young Women in Transition component was an effort to give women an alternative to early marriage. Small groups of young women would live cooperatively in apartments paid for by their own earnings; they would work part time while continuing an education or vocational training. The program would provide a semi-sheltered environment for young women who lacked the resources to attend college or leave home. The Women in Crisis program was described as an emergency shelter where a woman and her children could go during a family crisis to talk with other women. Housing for Welfare Recipients would provide apartments where mothers receiving welfare could live with their children while establishing financial independence.[75] Housing, or at least temporary shelter, was the theme uniting all of these efforts.

The article encapsulated Somerville women's needs to escape from the streets, early marriage, domestic violence, and poverty. Whether one organization could address all these issues simultaneously was doubtful. As the board began to realize that its initial plans were too ambitious, Varney and Broussard were asked by members of NOW to join a panel on domestic violence. Varney had been thinking about the issue and reading about shelters in other countries. A year earlier she and Judy Sutfren had written a proposal for a women's crisis center in Somerville in which they mentioned shelters in England, Ireland, and Toronto.[76]

As word got out about the Women in Crisis program, RESPOND was overwhelmed by calls from battered women. Over the course of the year, board meeting minutes show an increasing attention to domestic violence; they also reflect the realization that the organization was being stretched thin. By the end of 1975 RESPOND's sole mission was supporting battered women and their children.[77]

Maureen Varney was the leading advocate for a shelter.[78] At the time she became involved with RESPOND, she was a counselor at the Somerville Women's Health Project and attending classes at the University of Massachusetts Boston.[79] A childhood memory influenced her commitment to providing refuge from domestic abuse. She recounted the incident in the proposal:

One of my most vivid memories is that of a fire in a block near my home. I rushed out to see if my home was in danger. To my horror, there were three children screaming from the third-floor windows, smoke billowing around their heads. Their mother, whose husband was drinking, left the children to seek help from the police. She had no phone and so it was necessary for her to travel through the snow to get police assistance. It isn't clear how the fire started, but I am sure that if the woman had a place to go at that time of night, she would not have left the children unattended.[80]

While others might have blamed the mother for leaving her children, Varney blamed a society that offered no options for women in crisis. She recognized that family violence was a difficult cycle to break. Battering one night could lead to repentance and new resolutions the next morning. Domestic abuse was especially difficult for working-class women who, for financial or psychological reasons, could not escape their husbands or community. A battered wife might feel too ashamed or guilty to approach friends and neighbors who knew her family. Someone who resorted to emergency rooms was treated as if *she* were the problem. And a wife might be reluctant to press charges against her husband because she knew he would be "sober and sorry" in the morning; she would also have to live with the consequences of having filed a complaint. Varney understood all these complicating factors. She wanted to create a place where "a woman can seek temporary refuge from the storms of her life."[81]

The women's crisis center Varney described would provide a "neutral shelter with a warm, supportive atmosphere within the Somerville community," a safe place where women subject to domestic violence could bring their children. The center would be staffed by volunteers, who were also available to offer counseling. Staff would direct a resident to agencies and resources that could help her assess her situation and consider her options. She would be referred to the Somerville Women's Health Project for medical care, for example, or Cambridge and Somerville Legal Services for legal advice. The crisis center would have two goals: to provide women with the mechanisms to take more control over their immediate situation and to teach other residents how to do the same.[82]

The proposal included an appendix with twenty-four questions about shelter start-up operations. They ranged from "How should a crisis center be run?" to "How do we get kids to and from school safely for long-term clients?" Practical logistics were important, but so was a more philosophical question: "Who is responsible for battered families: religious organizations, community people, private citizens, nonprofit groups such as RESPOND, public social service agencies?"[83] The founders did not wait for an answer. They moved forward with their plans.

At the time Varney and Sutfren wrote the proposal, the board was considering three or four buildings near Union Square for housing the crisis center. Until adequate funding was available, the center would be open only on weekends, when drinking was heaviest and the police department received the greatest number of domestic dispute calls. The limited weekend plan would allow the center to begin operating quickly.[84] Varney pushed the board for a May 1, 1975, opening.[85] They missed that deadline but started offering shelter in a four-room apartment at the Mystic River public housing project. Mayor Ralph, a progressive politician, gave them the apartment rent free.[86]

Once fully funded, the center would be open twenty-four hours a day, seven days a week, with a paid and volunteer staff. The plan was to establish contracts with the Department of Public Welfare so that its employees could come to the center to explain available services to residents. Staff encouraged residents to form support networks to help each other solve similar problems. A resident would stay, it was thought, from one day to three or four weeks, depending on her needs.[87]

Local media began to recognize Varney for her work with domestic abuse victims. In March 1975 Boston's television Channel 5 ran a special show, *Battered Women*, in which Varney served as a panel member and interviewer.[88] Eunice West of Channel 5 sent Varney a tape of the show, which RESPOND used to educate community groups about domestic violence.[89]

Varney and Sutfren presented the draft proposal for the crisis center to the board at the April 1975 meeting. The proposal was directed to smaller foundations interested in innovative or radical programs.[90] In early May, Jean Luce wrote to Lisa Leghorn and Betsy Warrior at the Cambridge Women's Center asking for advice about funding sources. Luce reported that RESPOND had formed a task force to start the center, and that several members of Al-Anon (a support group for families of alcoholics) were eager to volunteer. In that letter, Luce also thanked Leghorn and Warrior for writing an article on wife beating that had appeared in the *Boston Phoenix*.[91]

While they were seeking funding for the center, the founders met Marie Siraco. Siraco was assigned to RESPOND as a VISTA volunteer, becoming one of the pioneering members of the staff and continuing to work there while raising eight children. Siraco's knowledge of domestic abuse arose from her involvement with alcohol programs through the Catholic Church. Drinking and family violence were highly correlated, and women who attended Al-Anon meetings were often battered. Al-Anon and Alcoholics Anonymous were the only safe places to talk about the taboo subject of abuse. The first victims Siraco knew were sheltered at St. Catherine's Convent in Somerville through the auspices of Al-Anon.[92]

Siraco met with other women who were willing to speak about the violence they, or their friends, were trying to escape. They had all been in Al-Anon a few years and recognized that the support group was ill-equipped to solve the problem. "We knew that instant relief, while the battering was going on, was needed and [a] long term program was needed to keep the violence away." Siraco observed that battered women needed to make short-term decisions, like leaving an abusive husband, in order to eventually make long-term decisions.[93] Board members adopted Al-Anon's approach to the batterer; it supported women whether they chose to stay or leave.[94]

Alcohol played a significant role in sparking domestic violence, but Varney interpreted drinking as a symptom of larger social and economic problems. In her opinion,

> The working-class man receives little esteem from his job and compensates for this lack by drinking with his friends at the neighborhood bar. This same man is frequently laid off at work (particularly during the present economic period) which forces all family members into new roles as the wife takes over financial responsibility for the family. This increased stress leads to drunkenness and domestic violence. The man vents his frustration and anger at his position in society by abusing those who are even less powerful than he, his wife and children.[95]

Varney's class- and gender-based analysis is consistent with radical feminist interpretations of violence against women. Men use physical assault to assert their power over all women, married or otherwise. Like rape, domestic violence has structural roots in power relations between the sexes. As long as women possess fewer social, psychological, and economic resources than men, that power imbalance will persist. Varney formed her opinions, in part, by counseling battered women. Although she occasionally heard of women battering women, she was learning that violence was "mis-use of power and in our society unfortunately the power was predominantly on the side of the men."[96]

Varney and another volunteer, Martha Black, joined VISTA and became codirectors of RESPOND. Varney was the community educator, making presentations to doctors, nurses, and other professionals; Black worked directly with battered women. They took courses in co-counseling and started two groups to work with residents. Varney recalled that RESPOND was the "first and only group at that time dealing with the age old problem of battering. Domestic violence had not been addressed, recognized, or spoken about to any members of the professions or to police, family or even trusted friends."[97] The founders of RESPOND saw it as their responsibility to change public perceptions. They lobbied the legislature for domestic violence legislation, and one member convinced the local police department to add a domestic violence unit.[98]

In April 1975 the board member Frank Mazzola purchased a six-unit apartment building at 24 Walnut Street (see figure 14) with the understanding that RESPOND would buy it when members could afford to pay him.[99] Raising the money was arduous. It started in February with a performance of "Firesticks: A Journey into Self-Respect," a series of vignettes based on the personal experiences of seven women who, "with sensitivity, wit, and humor, share their lives and growing sense of respect for themselves as women."[100] The play was staged at the First Methodist Church Multi-Service Center, where RESPOND offices were located. The flyer advertising the event identified RESPOND as "a temporary live-in crisis center for women," avoiding the use of "domestic violence" or "abuse."[101]

Firesticks raised $266. The organizers did better with a rummage sale at the church in March, which netted $430. Bread and Roses Restaurant made RESPOND its "cause for the week" in March and generated $85. Combined with a bake sale, a small grant from Paperback Booksmith Community Action Fund, and several donations, RESPOND raised about $1,000 that year.[102] The most successful event of 1975 ($386) was an "Oldies but Goodies" dance where Harvard theologian Harvey Cox and his band entertained the crowd.[103] Substantial donations from unnamed sources generated $5,500 for a down payment on the building on Walnut Street; the Haymarket Foundation also awarded the organization $2,000.[104]

Maureen Varney and Jean Luce put up the rest of the money on behalf of RESPOND, and Frank Mazzola turned over the mortgage. Varney, a single mother of six children, used her house as collateral for the loan; Luce contributed her savings. Over the next few years Luce prepared numerous grant proposals asking for funding for the Refuge, as it was being called. She invoked the organization's good reputation within the community and explained the three components of their program. Weekly support groups served sixty women by encouraging them to build self-confidence and explore alternatives to living with violence. Emergency housing provided women with child care, someone to talk with, and information about medical, legal, and welfare resources. The Community Education component included newspaper, television, and radio coverage; in one year RESPOND offered dozens of workshops on domestic violence for hospital staff, community agencies, and women's groups.[105]

All those proposals paid off. The 1976–77 financial report had been brief, listing only three sources of income totaling $1,400.[106] In contrast, by 1977–78, RESPOND reported receiving $11,000 from CDBG funds and $2,000 from the Haymarket Foundation. CETA contributed $33,000 in the form of salaries for four staff members. CDBG money was used to hire a full-time program director.[107] In 1977 the Refuge sheltered twenty-five women and forty-six children; the average stay was about one month.[108]

But there was never enough money. A letter from Treasurer Janet McDonald to the board of directors, dated Christmas week 1979, reported that the financial position of the organization was "extremely grave." Payroll had been met more than once by individuals making personal loans to the organization. McDonald explained that they had been expecting $28,000 in CDBG funds from the city but had been informed in September that the grant had been denied. She reminded the board that "This is the same grant that over one year ago, as a result of women storming City Hall, exerting political pressure, getting TV coverage, was approved and the money was slated for Respond [sic]. We have not been able to bill against this money as yet and are now told the revised proposal is denied. In simple english [sic], WE ARE BEING SCREWED!! WHAT ARE WE GOING TO DO ABOUT IT?"[109]

An emergency board meeting was called for December 28. Women who had once depended on the shelter rallied to RESPOND's support. A January 3, 1980, letter to the editor of the *Somerville Journal* criticized the city for its failure to deliver the funds. A "former battered woman" wrote to express "outrage at the possibility of RESPOND having to close its doors because city bureaucracy is putting the agency's funding in jeopardy." She recounted how RESPOND had helped her and her children escape family violence and create a new life. She warned that "the City will commit an unforgivable crime if it lets RESPOND die."[110]

The money eventually came through. The Walnut Street house was quickly outgrown and the Refuge was moved to another residential neighborhood, where the mortgage was held by two other board members. The move generated opposition from the Somerville Board of Assessors, whose members objected to a nonprofit house in a residential neighborhood. Neighbors also complained, but the shelter remained.[111] Demand continued to grow, and there were typically more women and children than beds. Some staff members took families home with them if the shelter was full; others invited women over for the holidays. When recounting these days, founders of RESPOND acknowledged that the experience of starting a shelter had been of as much benefit to them as to the women they served; for the first time they realized their power to create a new institution. They all said they never anticipated that RESPOND would last so long, serve so many women, or become part of such a large social movement.[112]

Transition House in Cambridge

In January 1976 Chris Womendez and Cherie Jimenez, both mothers who had experienced domestic abuse, established a shelter for battered women in the small apartment they shared in Cambridge.[113] For the next six months Womendez and Jimenez fed and sheltered more than 150 women and children, sometimes as many as twenty-five at a time sleeping on mattresses on the living room and kitchen floors. The two women financed their Transition House (T House) with Aid to Families with Dependent Children (AFDC) checks, food stamps, and money from bake sales and private donations. Some victims of abuse were there only a few days before moving in with friends or relatives; others stayed a month or more until they could find permanent housing. There was no waiting list because women were never turned away. Women seeking shelter were of all races, nationalities, and social classes; about one-fourth were from the Cambridge area and the rest were referred from police or social service agencies throughout New England.[114]

Radical feminists Betsy Warrior and Lisa Leghorn were among the core group who joined Womendez and Jimenez in the early days of Transition House. Warrior and Leghorn were members of the Cambridge Women's Center, which initially sponsored the shelter. They coauthored two editions of the *Houseworker's Handbook* (1973–75), an analysis of women's economic status that linked wives' unpaid work in the home to domestic violence. Having divorced her husband for beating her, Warrior was motivated to form a support group for battered women; she also published nine editions of *The Battered Women's Directory* between 1975 and 1985.[115] Warrior was the coordinator of outreach and educational programs for Transition House, and Leghorn was its fund-raiser.[116]

The group closed the apartment in July 1976 to reorganize and find a larger facility. In September they reopened in a five-bedroom house that could accommodate twenty women and children at once. The vast majority of women who used the shelter were from lower middle-class, working-class, or poor families; about one-third were black, one-half were white, and about 10 percent were immigrants who spoke little English. Approximately one-half stayed for two to four weeks, until they could find jobs or welfare and private apartments or public housing. The others were there only a few days; very few women returned to the abusive situations. Women who stayed at T House typically left with the conviction that "no woman deserves to be beaten." Many dedicated themselves to helping others in the same situation, showing newcomers how to navigate legal aid and welfare offices or volunteering for training to work at the shelter.[117]

Transition House listed the Cambridge Women's Center as its formal address. The location of the shelter itself was, of course, confidential. The house provided up to six weeks of food and shelter for battered women; mothers with children were given priority. Residents were asked to pay a daily fee of $1.50 per family for rent and $1.25 per person per day for food to defray operating costs; women could obtain emergency food and rent vouchers from the Welfare Department if they had no other source of income. Staff at T House made referrals to legal, medical, and social services and provided information on housing and employment. The core group of twelve women supervised and coordinated activities; they and approximately forty volunteers staffed the house on a twenty-four-hour basis and provided child care. The crisis phone line was especially important. Women who called might need immediate help or information about legal options available to them.[118]

Everyone staffing the house took a training session in which they learned about welfare and legal advocacy, in addition to the history, philosophy, and operations of T House. Residents met nightly to discuss and coordinate the next day's activities. They also used this opportunity to address any problems between residents. Since women often arrived at the house traumatized, some with substance abuse problems, it was impossible to avoid interpersonal conflict. The volunteers met bimonthly to discuss problems and supervise committees dealing with volunteer training, fundraising, child care, house maintenance and repair, and community outreach. The enormous volume of the work required to keep Transition House open was accomplished predominantly by volunteers who donated hundreds of hours every year.[119]

Transition House gave a woman physical and emotional refuge, but it also taught her that "the craziness she's being forced to deal with isn't unique to her and her children, but that it's a political issue that touches all women directly and indirectly." Ideally, a woman would gain political awareness by viewing her own situation in a social and political framework. Staff members were recruited from among other battered women so that everyone's experience would be similar. Emphasis was on sharing stories as a way for women to gain strength and develop survival skills for life outside the violent relationship. Rules were made by residents and often changed with every turnover. The only unbreakable house rule was the one ensuring confidentiality of the location.[120]

The founders estimated that volunteers donated the equivalent of $99,000 worth of services per year. The volunteers most critical for daily operations were the women who staffed the house, in pairs, twenty-four hours a day, fifty-two weeks of the year. Bilingual volunteers were on call and produced foreign-language pamphlets and informational videos for non-English-speaking women. T House had reciprocal agreements with other women's institutions, sharing referrals and counseling with RESPOND, Casa Myrna Vazquez, and the Cambridge Women's Center. Local musicians raised money through benefit performances, and about twenty women with cars ran errands and picked up women in trouble, often in the middle of the night. A nurse practitioner was on twenty-four-hour call; child care workers, an accountant, and lawyers donated their services. People contributed furniture that women could take to their new homes, as well as appliances and radios. Local businesses donated sand, lumber, and wood chips to build a playground, and the Cambridge Food Co-op and Bread and Roses Women's Restaurant contributed food; the American Friends Service Committee sent clothing from its secondhand store. Clothing was especially important for women who had fled their homes with nothing but what they were wearing.[121]

Members of the core group engaged in constant community outreach. Over the course of one year, staff and residents of the house participated in nearly three hundred radio, television, and lecture events educating the public about domestic abuse. They spoke at churches, social service agencies, community associations, and college classes. Members gave keynote speeches at national conferences on wife abuse in Washington, DC, and Milwaukee. Like members of RESPOND, they prepared a card explaining women's rights for distribution by police officers responding to domestic incidents. At the time, Boston police reported receiving forty-five calls a day about domestic disputes. Transition House prepared videotapes and newsletters for national audiences. Their most effective video was *We Will Not Be Beaten*, shown at local women's centers and around the country. Staff also researched and drafted laws for the Massachusetts legislature mandating a state shelter for battered women, obligating the police to distribute the informational card, and giving battered women first priority in requests for emergency public housing.[122] Residents and staff members testified before the Massachusetts House of Representatives in support of these bills.[123]

By the spring of 1977 the demand for Transition House services had again outstripped its ability to provide them. Originally large enough for twenty, the house was accommodating closer to fifty women and children. For the first time, the founders were reluctant to publicize its telephone number for fear staff could not provide space for everyone in need. Staffers began to raise money for a larger house. Margaret Hunt requested $1,000 toward a down payment from the Boston/Cambridge Ministry in Higher Education. Hunt described their current house as always overcrowded and constantly in need of expensive repairs. She explained that they had $8,000 saved but would need $12,000 for the down payment. The 1976 financial statement included in the request revealed about $6,000 from small grants and $8,000—one half of all income that year—from private donations. Expenses totaled almost $9,000 for the year.[124]

The Ministry responded with a donation of $500. It was one of fifteen grants the house received between May 1976 and October 1977, out of seventy-five proposals submitted to organizations and individuals. The smallest was $100; the largest, $8,000, was from an anonymous donor. The Gardiner Howland Shaw Foundation contributed $7,000, and the Hyams Trust and the Charles Bacon Trust of the New England Merchants Bank contributed $5,000 each. Among those who rejected appeals were the Rockefeller Foundation, John Hancock Insurance, Arthur D. Little, the Junior League, and Catholic Charities. More surprising, perhaps, was a rejection from the Ms. Foundation for Women.[125] The Ms. Foundation did, however, grant money to print one thousand copies of the fourth edition of Betsy Warrior's pamphlet *Working on Wife Abuse.*[126]

The 1977 budget was supplemented with funding from CETA and the Massachusetts Department of Mental Health. Totaling approximately $16,000, these sources paid one full-time and two part-time salaries for women who were longtime volunteers at the house.[127] What they needed, though, was $51,000 to pay for a full-time house coordinator, a full-time fund raiser, two full-time staffers, and two full-time child care workers. The need for child care was acute. Children arriving at the shelter with their mothers were often traumatized, battered, and insecure. In an attempt to provide positive male role models, the shelter sought volunteers among men sensitive to the needs of children. Male and female child care workers played with the children and took them to parks, museums, and the zoo. The yard was small, so the staff renovated the basement for indoor day care. The most pressing need was for supervision from 9 a.m. to 5 p.m. on weekdays. Many of the children were out of school while their mothers relocated, and the mothers needed the freedom to visit agencies or get other help solving their immediate problems.[128]

In April 1977 Lisa Leghorn applied to the Cambridge Area 3 Planning Team for $300 to fund supervised summer trips for children staying at Transition House. During the winter children stayed inside in the basement play space; in the summer, however, they wanted to play outside. That was a problem. Many of the women staying at the shelter were from the Cambridge area. The location of the shelter was confidential, but violent husbands were known to hire private detectives to find their wives or offer a reward for their return. A woman walking to the store might be recognized by her husband or his friends, which was bad enough, but mothers were terrified that a father might see his children playing outside in the yard. Eight child care volunteers took children on short visits to the zoo or museums; Leghorn requested money for longer day trips to beaches and state parks.[129]

For all the sense of community they fostered, shelters had distinct disadvantages. The buildings were typically shabby and in disrepair. They were crowded, noisy, and hotbeds for contagious illnesses. Children often lacked adequate play spaces. Shelters were expensive, requiring constant fund-raising, and staff turnover was high due to the stress and heavy workload.[130]

Shelters as Redemptive Places

With the exception of their invisibility in the urban landscape, domestic violence shelters are similar to the redemptive places settlement house volunteers created in the nineteenth century. Both kinds of places combined aspects of private and public space, but shelters gave women a temporary respite from dangers *inside* the home rather than from external threats in the industrializing city. Second Wave activists established emergency shelters because municipalities failed to meet the need for them, much as settlement houses initially provided kindergartens, libraries, and public baths.

Were domestic violence shelters equivalent to stops on the Underground Railroad, as Mary Marecek claimed? Providers of both types of places took risks by offering aid to those on the run. Shelters gave victims of abuse a way out, but unlike escaping slaves, battered women often chose to return to their oppressors. And domestic violence still exists, whereas slavery in the United States was abolished long ago. Symbolically, however, domestic violence shelters were a statement that women would and could stand up for their rights to personal safety. For women seeking their help, shelters provided opportunities to change their lives. A physical space so thoroughly enmeshed in the problem itself, and in the lives of the victims and staff, was unique for most social movements. It is doubtful that a movement, rather than just a provision of a service, could have developed or been sustained without the actual shelter.[131]

RESPOND, Transition House, and Casa Myrna were still operating in 2015. They offer a twenty-four-hour crisis hotline, emergency housing, support services such as psychological and financial counseling, and educational programs in the community. Each of their websites has a safety exit for women who need to hide their activity if someone enters the room unexpectedly. Clicking the emergency exit takes the user immediately to the

Google home page, which contains no search history that would reveal the previous site.[132] Paradoxically, at the same time technology allows women to hide a virtual site, it has made it easier to find the physical shelter. Mobile phones and cars with Global Positioning System (GPS) capabilities can lead an abuser to the exact address. In response, some shelters have exchanged the pursuit of secrecy for that of security. Closed-circuit camera systems, key card entry, and perimeter fences make a shelter safer than in the past. Scattering shelter apartments through a large development is another approach: it gives the resident the option to admit or refuse entry to someone at the apartment door.[133]

RESPOND identifies 1974 as the year its "founding mothers" opened their homes to women escaping abuse; Transition House traces its origins to 1975, when "two survivors of intimate partner violence" opened their apartment to battered women. RESPOND's website reports that it is "New England's first domestic violence agency and the second oldest in the nation," while Transition House asserts that it was "New England's first (and the country's second) emergency shelter for battered women and their children."[134] It is unclear which shelter they considered the first in the nation; it was probably Women's House in St. Paul (1974) since that was the first shelter established by grassroots women activists.

Archival materials clearly identify 1974 as the year RESPOND was incorporated and January 1976 as the beginning of Transition House. But RESPOND did not open a shelter in the Mystic River public housing project until 1975, the same year Frank Mazzola bought the apartment building at 24 Walnut Street. Correspondence further deepens the confusion. In a letter dated May 7, 1976, Jean Luce, the planning coordinator of RESPOND, made a funding appeal to an unnamed donor on behalf of Transition House. Luce explained that RESPOND had been staffing a crisis line and offering support services to abused women but could not provide housing: "Emergency refuge, we are not able to provide and find that there are very few viable places for 'battered women' to go when danger is imminent. Thanks to the group of women in Cambridge who opened Transition House for this purpose, we now have a near-by place to send our women. Since it has opened in January 1976, Transition House has housed over one hundred women and children needing emergency housing; most of them escaping danger of physical abuse at home."[135]

The official website and archival materials claim 1974 as the year RESPOND was founded, and that it had opened a shelter in 1975, yet in 1976 Luce reported that only Transition House was providing shelter. Such confusion reflects the interwoven nature of the services feminists offered, the number of organizations that overlapped in membership, and the speed of institutional change.

The shelters' competing claims are reminiscent of a similar disagreement between two settlement house leaders more than one hundred years ago. Jane Addams and Ellen Gates Starr founded Hull-House Settlement in Chicago on September 18, 1889, while Vida Scudder of the College Settlements Association founded the College Settlement in New York City on September 1 of the same year.[136] Hull-House, of course, became internationally renowned due to Addams's high public profile. By comparison, College Settlement was relatively obscure. Scudder lacked Addams's reputation, but she could legitimately claim—as she did twice in her memoirs—that College Settlement had opened two weeks before Hull-House.[137]

Domestic violence shelters share other characteristics with redemptive places. Most important, they are refuges where women can feel safe in the supportive company of other women. Shelters encourage abused women to share their stories so they can understand the similarities that unite them. As soon as battered women walk through the door of a shelter, they are no longer helpless victims but members of a community of support.[138]

Like boardinghouses created by the YWCA and the National Association of Colored Women (NACW), domestic violence shelters were new spaces in the urban landscape. In the 1970s activists created shelters because welfare, social service, and medical agencies were blind to the existence of domestic violence, just as nineteenth-century municipalities were unresponsive to immigrants' needs for libraries and kindergartens before settlement house workers put them on the public agenda. Women in the late nineteenth century had to rely on men to purchase the properties they converted into vocational schools and settlement houses. Women at mid-twentieth century were still denied credit, making RESPOND's founders dependent on Frank Mazzola to buy the Walnut Street building for them. Adding men to their boards of directors enhanced the legitimacy of organizations in both eras.

The women who opened the first shelters in London and Boston were community activists with the ability to get things done. They had autonomy and they demonstrated agency. In contrast, the victims of spousal abuse possessed neither. They were economically or emotionally dependent on their abusers and lacked the resources to escape repeated bouts of violence. Most battered women need safety, support, and recognition that their problem is social and political, not individual.[139] By creating shelters, feminists offered victims an exit that could build their self-esteem and lead to greater autonomy. In doing so they challenged the very foundation on which gender inequality is based. Wife battering is the most extreme and brutal expression of the oppression of women in a patriarchal society, a type of violence that is an integral element in the structure of female subordination. Male violence creates fear that undermines women's ability to move and act freely in the public sphere. When feminists demanded that wives have a right to physical safety, they took a step toward affirming full citizenship for all women.

CHAPTER 6

After the Second Wave

Necessary Spaces

Second Wave feminists, intent on improving women's rights, expanded the range of spaces available to women beyond the home. Reformers accomplished this feat by desegregating formerly all-male spaces in their quest for equality, while radical activists created feminist places in which women could be independent of men. Both approaches were critical for improving women's status. The gains of the 1970s, though, require another kind of spatial institution if they are to be maintained: places that provide the services women performed before the majority entered the labor force. Spaces where women can receive intellectual and psychological support, health care tailored to their needs, and protection from male violence are necessary, but insufficient, for improving and maintaining women's rights. There must also be substitutes for domestic work.

In this final chapter, I propose that there is continuing value in women-only spaces, not just in the United States but throughout the world. In these spaces, women have a voice; their concerns are heard and their priorities come first. Second, I review the ways in which desegregated all-male spaces and feminist places built women's rights into the US city, and I explain why sites substituting for women's care work are central to women's ability to maintain those rights. Third, I review women's current status, lamenting the continued threats to reproductive rights but celebrating the possibilities inherent in Third Wave feminism.

The Value of Women-Only Spaces

Single-sex spaces are valuable for women only if they are voluntary. Mandatory segregation of the sexes limits women's opportunities, thus benefiting men, but segregation by choice can be liberating. Feminist places were empowering because there women proved that they could gain strength and take care of themselves apart from men. It was exhilarating to escape the enforced domesticity of the 1950s. Women took control of their bodies and responsibility for their own intellectual development. The look and feel of the places reflected women's efforts to create a sense of community as well as deliver services. Themes of comfort and safety appeared repeatedly; feminist places were "oases in a masculine city." These features are missing from mandatory gendered spaces that give men an advantage.[1]

Feminist places were predominantly for women only, but there were exceptions. Bookstores were open to men, and they carried nonsexist children's books to attract mothers and their kids. Domestic violence shelters were often filled with more children than mothers, since many residents had large families. What made a place feminist was that it catered primarily to women and their needs, promoted a feminist political agenda, and was controlled by women.

Complicating any discussion of "women-only" spaces is the ambiguous definition of "woman." Transgender individuals were fewer in number in the 1970s than in later years, but equally controversial. The 1973 West Coast Lesbian Conference in Los Angeles erupted into conflicting factions over whether a male-to-female transsexual folk singer should be allowed to perform. Although transgender women are more numerous in the early twenty-first century, and the public is generally more receptive to lesbian, gay, bisexual, and transgender (LGBT) rights, the status accorded to transgender women is still a matter of hot debate among radical feminists. Many trans women claim to be women because they have "women's brains in men's bodies" and have altered their physical appearance accordingly. Radical feminists reject the idea that anyone born male has experienced the same oppression as women. The groups Radfems Respond, Radfems Rise Up, and ecofeminists in the organization Deep Green Resistance exclude trans women from their events based on the belief that someone born with male privilege cannot lose it through surgery any more than a white person can know what it is like to be black by darkening her skin color.[2] Response from trans women has been fierce. They have posted violent messages on Twitter and Tumblr and have boycotted events held by trans-exclusionary radical feminists (TERFs). Both factions are small in number but have generated media attention because the fracas puts radical feminists "on the wrong side of a sexual-rights issue."[3]

Finally, the value of women-only spaces depends on their transitional nature. This applies to the places themselves and to the women who use them. Residents of a domestic violence shelter, for example, are there temporarily. With the exception of the Cambridge Women's Center, Casa Myrna, RESPOND, and Transition House, all the places described here have ceased to exist. Prolonged financial troubles and a shrinking volunteer base depleted the energy of even the most ardent feminists, and one place after another closed. The buildings they once occupied have been converted to other uses or demolished. In Los Angeles, Sisterhood Bookstore's building is a packing and mailing shop, and the first feminist health clinic has become a used car outlet. The triple-decker that housed New Words Bookstore in Boston is a yoga studio. The era of Second Wave feminist place-making is over.

A combination of factors accounts for the absence of such places in twenty-first-century cities. Sisterhood and New Words fell victim to big-box and online retailing competition, while many mainstream health-care facilities have added special programs for women. Another reason is rising real estate prices. City property was cheap in the 1970s compared to the exceedingly high rents it commands in the early twenty-first century. But an optimistic interpretation of the decline in feminist places would be that they accomplished what they set out to do. The medical profession has become more responsive to women's needs, through hospital birthing centers and midlife health services. Bookstores, whether physical or virtual, carry extensive collections of materials by and about women. Women's centers became less important as women entered the labor force and gained access to resources and networks through their jobs. Viewed from this perspective, feminist places that began as radical spaces for women only became obsolete as they fostered the integration of formerly male spaces. Liberation was the first step toward equality.

Two women-only spaces remain critical to women's rights, however. Until unwanted pregnancies and domestic abuse are eliminated, abortion clinics and domestic violence shelters will remain necessary women-only spaces. One cannot obtain an abortion or hide from an abuser online.

Women-only spaces in other countries have emerged as women have gained more political power. Two examples from the global North stand out. In the late 1970s German feminists believed that women became isolated when they lacked a workplace connection. In response, they created Mother Centers to reconcile the distinction between private and public spheres by giving at-home mothers a place to meet other mothers and their children. These centers support women's needs for social contact at the same time that they introduce children to life outside the home. The centers are often described as "public living rooms" that allow women and children to claim public space. Created from pilot programs in three cities, the grassroots movement has grown to include more than four hundred locally organized and publicly funded Mother Centers operating in German cities and rural areas.[4]

In addition to the social needs they fill, Mother Centers challenge the marginalization of women from public life due to their primary responsibility for care work. Most important, Mother Centers foster community cohesion and civic rebuilding in places destabilized by war, poverty, or political upheaval. The movement spread to Bosnia, the Czech Republic, Cameroon, and seventeen other countries. In the early twenty-first century, there are eight hundred fifty Mother Centers worldwide.[5]

The second example of a contemporary women-only space is cooperative housing in Canada. In 1979 a group of Toronto women formed a board to incorporate two housing cooperatives for low-income women. A thirty-unit concrete-block townhouse opened for occupancy in 1982 and was named the Constance Hamilton Co-op in honor of the first female city councilor in Toronto. Each unit is three stories high and varies in size from one to three bedrooms. A six-bedroom transitional house for homeless single women is attached. The second co-op, the Beguinage, opened in 1985. The name is taken from the medieval beguinage, a walled urban community of Beguines (secular nuns) who were economically independent and exempt from most rules of the Catholic Church.[6] Similar to the Constance Hamilton project, the Beguinage consists of twenty-eight stacked townhouses with a mix of one-, two-, and three-bedroom units. Residents take on property management themselves, acquiring administrative, financial, and maintenance skills.[7]

Both cooperatives are located in downtown Toronto. The Constance Hamilton project obtained a small amount of land on an industrial site redeveloped by the City of Toronto Housing Department to accommodate four nonprofit cooperatives. The Beguinage is situated on a site that had been cleared for urban renewal and was restricted to development for nonprofit housing. Thus the cooperatives occupy prime downtown real estate, with nearby public transit and a range of services. Their location maximizes opportunities for residents' employment, a social life with friends and family outside the co-ops, and access to medical facilities and cultural events. Constance Hamilton Co-op and the Beguinage offer more than safe and affordable shelter; they also give low-income women a foothold in the center of the city.[8]

The global South has success stories as well. The first All-Women Police Stations (AWPSs) were introduced in India's southern states of Kerala and Tamil Nadu in 1973. Women filing complaints about domestic violence or sexual harassment found little sympathy, and sometimes additional abuse, at the hands of male police officers. AWPSs are staffed by women who investigate crimes against women and deal with cases in which women are the accused. In 2011 the state cabinet of Patna authorized one AWPS for each of its thirty-eight revenue districts and two police districts. In 2012 the Thrissur district announced the opening of its first AWPS to "curtail violence against women and find quick solutions in cases involving them."[9] By 2015 India had 518 AWPSs; Tamil Nadu had 199, the highest number of any state in the country, and Maharashtra was the only state with none.[10]

India is also the site of women-only public transit. Ladies Specials trains were the idea of Mamata Banerjee, the minister of railways. She introduced them in selected cities in 2009 to protect women from "Eve-teasing," a form of sexual harassment that ranges from catcalls to groping.[11] For some young girls, such experiences are closer to sexual assault. They report that men have slapped them on the rear, touched their breasts, deliberately brushed against them, and followed them home while making lewd sexual remarks.[12] Women complained so loudly that the government introduced eight women-only commuter trains in Calcutta, Chennai, Mumbai, and New Delhi. These Ladies Specials reflect, according to a railway official, women's growing assertiveness.[13]

Women in Chennai and Mumbai who need safe transportation for trips not covered by the train may choose a women-only taxi service. In Chennai, Go For Pink Ladies Call Taxi Service employs five women drivers who cater only to women and children.[14] Two taxi services for women and their families in Mumbai started operating in 2007. Women drivers, most from lower middle-class backgrounds, earn good wages. Their ability to become earners for their families enhances their self-confidence, and taking their vehicle home increases their prestige.[15] The pink taxi has also become popular in Mexico, Russia, Lebanon, and other countries.[16] Beirut's Banet (Girl) Taxi fleet of fifteen pink late-model Peugeots offers twenty-four-hour service. Banet Taxis cater to conservative Muslim women seeking to avoid public transportation. Most of the customers live in Beirut, but Muslim women from the Persian Gulf States visiting during the peak summer tourist season also use the taxis.[17]

Women in African countries have created spaces of employment for women whose lives have been scarred by war and famine. The program Amani ya Juu (which means "peace from above" in Swahili) teaches displaced women to sew and sells their products internationally. Amani began in Nairobi, Kenya, in 1996 as a Christian ministry. Four women who were refugees from civil wars in surrounding countries came together to sew placemats for sale to hotels and shops. The women worked in one of their homes, becoming so successful that they expanded to a large production building which includes a shop to sell their wares and a garden café. The center offers a "sensory experience of peace . . . to hurting women looking for a place to heal."[18]

Visitors took the Amani model back home to Burundi, Kenya, Liberia, Rwanda, and Uganda. Amani Uganda initially occupied one room of a strip in the Cerelene district of Gulu; seven women sewed and four babies played in the twelve-by-twelve-foot space. All of the women were mothers who often kept their children with them during the day. The organization eventually found a spacious house in a quiet location in Pece; it has a kitchen and a bathroom, both of which were lacking in the original facility. Women describe it as a beautiful place where they feel free and where their children have a safe place to play.[19]

In contrast to these examples of single-sex places created and controlled by women are the mandatory spaces to which women are consigned by some Muslim cultures. After the 1979 Islamic Revolution, women in Iran were segregated from men in nearly all aspects of their lives. Former President Mahmud Ahmadinejad was a staunch proponent of segregating the sexes. When he was mayor of Tehran, Ahmadinejad introduced male- and female-only elevators in the city; soon there were female-only buses and taxis.[20]

In May 2008 Tehran Mayor Mohammad Baqir Ghalibaf declared the official opening of the women-only Mothers' Paradise. Located on fifty hilly acres in the northern district of the city, the park is hidden from male view by thirteen-foot high walls. Inside, women shed their obligatory headscarves and don jogging shorts and tank tops. They can take outdoor aerobics classes, ride bicycles, or learn archery. An all-female staff of janitors, gardeners, and security guards creates a sense of safety inside the walls; male guards patrol outside the gates. The park was instantly popular. So many women visited—an average of one thousand per day—that another park was opened in August, and the mayor's office announced plans for more. The mayor's adviser boasted that the park was not about segregation, but about providing women with equal opportunities in the city.[21]

Iranian feminists disagree. For the sociologist Nayereh Tavakoli, women-only parks give women opportunities, but not *equal* opportunities, since that would mean similar access to any park in the city.[22] The name of the park, Mothers' Paradise, implies that respectable women have no identity other than as mothers.[23] The lawyer and women's rights activist Nasrin Sotoudeh speculates whether "in the short-term future, we may see entire cities being divided into women's sections and men's sections. Or how about creating women-only and men-only cities? The [sex-segregated park] contradicts the international convention on human rights."[24]

Women-only cities as a feminist utopian vision date back at least to Charlotte Perkins Gilman's *Herland* (1915). The towns in futuristic Herland, free of dirt, smoke, and noise, "lay among the green groves and gardens like a broken rosary of pink coral." Large public buildings were interspersed among smaller dwellings scattered around parks and squares. Male time travelers from the early twentieth century were impressed. These towns were nothing like the ones at home, where men had made an "offensive mess in the face of nature."[25] In the 1970s, separatist lesbians established "womyn's lands" where they could live surrounded by other women. But because any city that excludes one-half of the population is unviable in the twenty-first century, women need to continually build on, and protect, their rights to the sexually integrated city.

At the same time, women need to defend single-sex places where their voices are heard. In the United States, abortion clinics and domestic violence shelters prioritize women's needs. Internationally, women (and their children) come first in Mother Centers, AWPSs, and Amani workshops. Women can go to these facilities when they need to be taken seriously and be taken care of. They may stay temporarily or long term depending on their situation. Places that rank women's rights as their most important goal are all too rare.

Building Women's Rights into the City

Second Wave feminists built women's rights into the city in two ways. Reformers successfully integrated a number of male spaces. Those that generated the most attention were bars, restaurants, and country clubs, perhaps because members of the media thought it was a silly goal. After all, women were welcome if accompanied by a man. Yet feminists recognized that their exclusion symbolized a woman's dependence on a man for a respectable identity, thereby writing "male supremacy and heteronormativity onto the social, physical, and economic landscape of US cities."[26] But more than symbolism was involved. Men conducted business in these places, striking deals and making connections that strengthened the "old boy network." During the 1970s, before many women held professional degrees, their networks were small to nonexistent. If middle-class women wanted to get ahead, it helped to talk to men in informal settings. White working-class women could find out about jobs if they were members of a union, but they had fewer places to network for economic gain than their husbands, who might belong to the Elks or the Masonic lodge. The church and the National Association of Colored Women's Clubs were the primary resources for African American women.

In addition to integrating bars and clubs, reform feminists used Title IX, a federal law passed in 1972, to gain access to high school and college sports. Title IX also required that women be given equal opportunities in all facets of public education. The number of women in college classrooms and professional schools increased dramatically as discriminatory practices were dismantled. Female faculty benefited as well; thousands received raises to compensate for salaries that were lower than those of their male colleagues. Given the number of veterans taking advantage of the GI Bill immediately after World War II, and how few women attended college before 1970, the transformation of colleges from predominantly male to predominantly female institutions was a significant accomplishment. Between 1970 and 2001, women increased their representation among undergraduates from 42 to 56 percent of the total.[27] Title IX is as close as the federal government has come to providing the same higher-educational benefits for women that it did for veterans.[28]

Professional schools have graduated so many (white middle-class) women that in the early twenty-first century female physicians and attorneys are practicing in numbers unimaginable to our grandmothers. Women are no longer only the nurse or a patient in a doctor's office, or only the stenographer in a courtroom. Less has changed for working-class women and women of color. They are still mostly relegated to sex-segregated occupations that pay less than men's, partly due to differences in unionization. If they are in the same jobs as men, though, they are legally guaranteed equal pay; whether they actually receive it depends on the ethics of the employer.

Radical activists recognized the importance of legal victories, but their energies went toward building newly won rights into the city. When *Roe v. Wade* granted women reproductive autonomy in 1973, thanks largely to the efforts of reform feminists, activists were ready to provide abortions in their own health clinics. Staff at the Los Angeles Feminist Women's Health Center switched quickly from counseling women about how to find an abortion to actually performing the procedure. The FWHC differed from hospitals in its appearance, feel, and insistence on educating women about the medical process they would undergo.

In at least one instance a feminist place preceded, and initiated, legislation of behalf of women. The Violence Against Women Act (VAWA) passed by Congress in 1994 established domestic violence and sexual assault as crimes like any other violent crime. The VAWA has funded educational programs, services for victims, and rape crisis centers. Its passage is attributed to 1970s grassroots organizations that lobbied for attitudinal changes toward domestic violence among the public and law enforcement agencies.[29] One of those grassroots organizations would have been RESPOND, whose members successfully petitioned for one of the first domestic violence police units in the country.

Anger over multiple injustices fueled feminists' determination to claim their rights, and activists modified existing urban spaces to do that. They converted houses and storefronts into places that served women's needs. Founders battled legal and financial obstacles to establish and operate feminist places in Boston, Los Angeles, and other cities. Finances proved to be especially difficult. Almost wholly dependent on volunteers, most feminist places experienced growth in demand for their services that outstripped their ability to deliver. Domestic violence shelters constantly needed more beds, clinics never had enough examination rooms and supplies, and bookstores lacked space for the explosion of women's writing.

Feminist places provided physical and emotional safety. Women in C-R groups were free to say what they wanted without fear of interruption or censure. Customers repeatedly described feeling safe in bookstores, likening them to an oasis in a hostile masculine city. Lesbians, especially, felt at home in bookstores run by other women, many of whom were also lesbians. Domestic violence shelters had the most overt safety agenda; they gave refuge to women who had nowhere else to turn. Feminist places were about control over one's own body, opinions, and space; and they built strong local women's communities. Women's centers, bookstores, clinics, and domestic violence shelters were places women could gather to be with other women who shared their views. The breadth of the network is revealed in the map in figure 15. Created from the addresses of women's centers, bookstores, and clinics listed in appendices B, C, and D, the map omits only domestic violence shelters. The places on this map did not exist before the 1970s. They all came to fruition because activists demanded their rights.

Despite differences between reformers and radicals, straight and lesbian women, those from the middle class and those from the working class, whites and women of color, mothers and those without kids, participants in the Second Wave accomplished a significant expansion of the places women could occupy. Reform feminists forced open the doors of colleges and workplaces

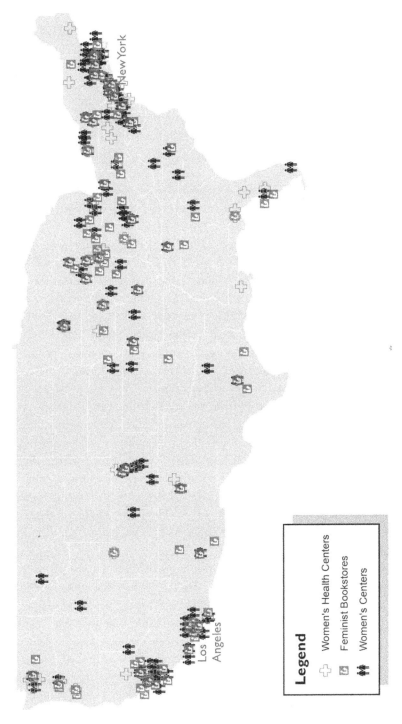

Figure 15. Feminist places in the continental United States, 1970s. Map by Lucas Lyons. Sources: Appendixes B, C, and D.

so that women could pursue formerly masculine education and occupations. Women in the 1970s took full advantage of new opportunities provided by federal legislation. But to do that, some needed the courage to challenge traditionally gendered expectations. And if they were to succeed in new roles, they had to have access to contraception and abortion. Radical activists created feminist places where women could acquire these and more: a liberation of mind, body, and spirit. Feminist spaces occasionally admitted men, but they were controlled by women who gave women's needs the highest priority. Controlling their own space, whether rented or owned, was of utmost importance.

The deliberate spatial changes initiated by Second Wave feminists have largely disappeared, but the unintended spatial consequences are all around us. We see them when we eat at a fast-food restaurant, drop off our kids or elderly parents at a day-care facility, or visit a family member in hospice. Employed women need these spaces if they are to maintain the rights earned during the 1970s. The conundrum, of course, is that more than three-quarters of employees in hospitals, health-related services, and social services are women.[30] Many of these jobs pay low wages, have few or no benefits, and lack opportunities for advancement. Household work that was undervalued when the majority of women performed it in private has become underpaid work performed by poor women in public.

The sites of care work are depressingly similar. Every fast-food restaurant chain has a logo recognizable from the street or interstate highway, as do KinderCare facilities. Buildings are "purpose built," as architects call them, designed to deliver specific services. Both the interiors and exteriors have been standardized to attract customers, feed or care for them efficiently, and speed them on their way; their sole mission is to maximize profits. Adult day service centers may be more personalized, but they still share similarities in layout dictated by licensing regulations. Buildings that house substitutes for care work have little meaning for either staff or the people who use them because the buildings all look alike.

Women need substitutes for their domestic labor if they are to be active in the public realm, but existing inequalities of gender, race, ethnicity, nationality, and social class are reinforced when caretaking is left to the private market. Middle-class employed women often hire women of color, many of whom are immigrants, as substitute caregivers. Immigrant women may be "transnational mothers" who have left their own families in their country of origin. Although nannies and maids work in the homes of the wealthy, many more care workers are employed in child care facilities, nursing homes, and adult day service centers. Thus we have created yet another era of gender inequality. Feminist theorists who argue for citizenship rights based on care work tackle this problem in the abstract, while "living wage" campaigns attempt to address its reality. The fate of care workers, the majority of whom are women, is a significant issue with global implications.[31]

A "care deficit" is growing due to increasing demand from aging baby boomers and the shrinking supply of caregivers resulting from smaller family size and women's employment.[32] But more than demographics drives the care crisis. The deficit has arisen due to the privatized and gendered nature of caretaking: Families, not the larger society, are responsible for caring, and women and other subordinate groups are assigned primary responsibility for caregiving.[33] For a brief period in history, the US government, in partnership with private industry, supplied extensive support for employed women. World War II made it acceptable, even patriotic, for Rosie the Riveter to take a job and leave her children with professional babysitters. In 1943 she was able to do that in Vanport City, Oregon ("Kaiserville"), built by the Kaiser Company for its shipyard employees. The new town, completed in ten months, housed forty thousand people. It included two child care centers open twenty-four hours a day, seven days a week—just like the shipyard. Between 1943 and 1945 the Swan Island and Oregonship centers served more than four thousand children; average daily attendance was close to three hundred children. The centers provided infirmaries, child-sized bathtubs, and prepared food to take home—all services that made mothers' jobs easier. They were located between neighborhoods and the shipyard so that parents could drop off their children on the way to and from work.[34]

Kaiserville provided the sort of government support Margaret Benston and other radical activists envisioned. After the war, these facilities disappeared, along with government support. Nor did the government fund child care centers the same way they did schools and libraries, as NOW demanded in its Bill of Rights. As a result, every feminist place provided some sort of arrangement for mothers who should have had other choices. The Los Angeles Feminist Women's Health Center provided child care for staff members, and when Carol Downer was arrested, the clinic offered child care to women who wanted to attend her trial. Comprehensive and affordable child care continues to be the most critical problem for employed mothers.

What Now?

The term *mommy wars* was coined to symbolize the tensions between mothers who are employed while their children are young and those who stay at home. Headlines in 2014 about the rise of "stay-at-home moms" fueled the debate. It is true that the proportion of mothers who did *not* work outside the home rose from a modern-era low of 23 percent in 1999 to 29 percent in 2012, but a growing share say it is because they cannot find jobs. And women in the media spotlight who can choose whether to work—called "opt-out mothers"—are disproportionately white, highly educated, and affluent. In any case, the typical mother who stays at home is married to a husband who works.[35] The physician and author Marcia Angell finds the change in nomenclature from the "housewife" of earlier generations to the contemporary "stay-at-home mom" indicative of the early twenty-first-century obsession with children's priorities. Both denote basically the same role, but with a reorientation toward children rather than the husband.[36] Both ideologies are powerful. Sociologists speculate that the culture of intensive motherhood during the 1990s led to an "egalitarian essentialism" that stalled the continued liberalization of public opinion toward gender roles that began in the 1970s. Attitudes in the early twenty-first century, however, have returned to their previous upward trend toward greater acceptance of women's equality.[37]

Radical activists of the 1970s wanted to be neither housewives nor stay-at-home moms. They directed all their energies outside the home to overthrowing patriarchy, preparing women for new lives in which they could choose motherhood, not be consigned to it.

Threats to voluntary motherhood, however, remain considerable. June 2014 was an especially discouraging month in that regard. With *Burwell v. Hobby Lobby* the US Supreme Court ruled that family-owned businesses whose owners were opposed to birth control on religious grounds could deny female employees insurance coverage for contraception under the 2010 Patient Protection and Affordable Care Act. Dissenting Justice Ruth Bader Ginsburg called it a "decision of startling breadth" that left the door open for firms to deny employees coverage for vaccines or equal pay if those things conflict with the owners' religion.[38] Ginsburg and the two other female dissenting justices recognized that "the ability of women to participate equally in the economic and social life of the nation has been facilitated by their ability to control their reproductive lives."[39]

Just one week earlier, the court unanimously struck down a Massachusetts law requiring no-protest buffer zones around entrances to abortion clinics that had been established to protect patients from harassment by demonstrators seeking to outlaw legal abortion.[40] This court's decisions, despite the historically unprecedented participation of three female justices, have resulted in significant incursions into women's reproductive rights.

In the same month, conservative syndicated columnist George Will trivialized the issue of rape when he declared that "the supposed campus epidemic of rape" was conferring a "coveted status that confers privileges" on victims.[41] (In fact, a 2015 *Washington Post*–Kaiser Family Foundation survey found that 20 percent of young women in college report having been sexually assaulted, considered an understatement of its incidence.[42]) The continued power of religion to control women was illustrated when the Mormon Church excommunicated the activist Kate Kelly for organizing the group Ordain Women. Kelly was not banished for her own beliefs, according to the all-male Quorum of the Twelve Apostles, but for persuading other church members to share her point of view, thus threatening to "erode the faith of others." Kelly responded that she wanted others to "band together and fight against silencing women."[43]

Who today gives voice to concerns about women's rights? NOW and the Women's Equity Action League (WEAL) still play a significant role, as do Planned Parenthood and the National Abortion Rights Action League (NARAL). There is also evidence that some states are liberalizing restrictions pertaining to abortion and contraception. California and Oregon have passed laws allowing women to get birth control pills directly from a pharmacist without a doctor's prescription; in Oregon, women will be able to buy a year-long supply rather than returning to the pharmacy each month.[44] Virginia's attorney general has lifted the requirements imposed in 2011 that abortion clinics adhere to the same building standards as hospitals.[45] And feminists are reclaiming the "A" word. Author Katha Pollitt, in *PRO: Reclaiming Abortion Rights* (2014), argues that choosing an abortion is as moral a decision as choosing to have a child because "caring for children is knowing when it's not a good idea to bring them into the world."[46] Texas State Senator Wendy Davis, who gained national attention for her filibuster against a restrictive abortion bill in 2013, admitted in her memoir that she had had an abortion.[47] A board member of NARAL who wrote a guide to abortion story-telling uses the term abortion deliberately, clarifying that "I didn't have a pro-choice. I had an abortion."[48]

While younger feminists seem to take abortion rights for granted, they still get as angry about sexual harassment and rape as their mothers did. In 2011 women in Toronto organized the first SlutWalk to challenge the idea that provocative dress invites rape. Wearing skimpy clothing, women paraded through the streets chanting: "Don't tell us how to dress. Tell men not to rape." SlutWalks are easily organized through social media and have taken place in more than seventy-five cities around the world. A participant at Stanford University says the parades are "loud, angry, sexy in a way that going to a community activist meeting often isn't." Bypassing mainstream conferences and demonstrations, SlutWalks reignite the anger necessary for social change, cropping up "organically, in city after city, fueled by the raw emotional and political energy of young women."[49] These demonstrations would have horrified nineteenth-century suffragists. Yet they reflect the same passion for equality and liberation that kindled women's demands more than a century ago.

SlutWalks are a product of Third Wave feminism. The term came into use in 1992 with Rebecca Walker's *Ms.* article "Becoming the Third Wave."[50] Walker and other members of the Third Wave opposed the post- or antifeminism represented by Katie Roiphe and Camille Paglia.[51] The Third Wave is loosely defined as the metaphorical daughters of Second Wave feminists; they reject the totalizing identity associated with their mothers' politics (angry and anti-male) in favor of multiple identities (sexy, feminist, and pretty). Making a political statement by flaunting one's sexuality through risqué dress and red lipstick is a rejection of what they perceive as the frumpy feminists of yore. Third Wave activists value personal, intersecting narratives versus a unitary or essentialist definition that pits all women against all men. This includes acknowledging that women of color have different experiences from white women, and that transgender women experience life differently from cisgender women (those whose biological sex and gender identity match). According to Walker, the Third Wave generation is comfortable with ambiguities: they are transgender, biracial, and bisexual.[52] At its most extreme, "[Third Wave] Feminism is something individual to each feminist."[53]

Books about the Third Wave began to appear in 1995 with Rebecca Walker's edited volume, *To Be Real: Telling the Truth and Changing the Future of Feminism.* It was followed by Marcelle Karp and Debbie Stoller, eds., *The BUST Guide to the New Girl Order* (1997), and Merri Lisa Johnson, ed., *Jane Sexes It Up: True Confessions of Feminist Desire* (2002).[54] *BUST* was the original "grrrl zine"[55] in wide publication for the anti-*Glamour*- and anti-*Cosmo*-magazine crowd; the *Guide* was a collection of its best irreverent essays since its inception in 1993. *Jane Sexes It Up* is a collection of "sex-positive" essays by young feminists who enjoy pornography, sadomasochism, and sex toys. Such books are a far cry from *Sisterhood Is Powerful* and *The Feminine Mystique.*[56]

These publications reveal several differences between the Second and Third Waves. First, a younger generation takes for granted earlier gains; for them, feminism is like fluoride in the water—they scarcely notice it. Second, younger feminists want to distance themselves from the image of man-hating humorless prudes they associate with the Second Wave. UCLA undergraduate Savannah Badalich symbolizes the new generation. Silent after being sexually assaulted during her sophomore year, during her junior year, in

2013, Badalich went public and gathered thousands of signatures from students pledging to end sexual assault. The group worked with administrators to toughen policies and sponsor educational programs. In explaining their negotiation techniques, Badalich described herself and others as "totally feminists . . . but we didn't want to be branded as radical or man-hating."[57]

Members of the Third Wave also consider themselves more inclusive, both of differences between women based on race and ethnicity, and of different identities within each individual. Finally, Third Wave activists focus on more than just women's issues; they also participate in struggles for environmental, social, and economic justice. Some of the perceived differences, of course, reflect historical ignorance: plenty of Second Wave feminists enjoyed sex with men; many were lesbians and women of color; and they pursued socialist, antiwar, and civil rights agendas in addition to women's rights.[58]

Whether Third Wave activists have produced new spatial institutions is unclear. They have, however, maintained some of the earlier ones. The executive directors of Boston's Transition House, RESPOND, and the Boston Area Rape Crisis Center are all young women in their thirties. And a new generation of women opened feminist bookstores during the 1990s: Kathryn Welsh's Bluestockings in New York City; Gina Mercurio's People Called Women in Toronto; and co-owners Cheryl Krauth and Lylly Rodriguez's Wild Iris Books in Gainesville, Florida (site of one of the earliest feminist health clinics). These three are among only a dozen feminist bookstores still operating in the United States in 2014 (compared with approximately 120 that existed in the 1990s.)[59]

The Third Wave has intersected with, and benefited from, the gay rights movement that began at the Stonewall Inn in 1969. An early milestone was the election of openly gay candidate Harvey Milk to the San Francisco Board of Supervisors in 1978; his assassination later that year brought the issue of gay rights into the media spotlight. The 1979 National March on Washington for Lesbian and Gay Rights drew approximately seventy-five thousand participants, while in 1993 a similar march drew nearly one million demonstrators. By the beginning of the twenty-first century, several states had begun to recognize same-sex marriages as legitimate. In 2014 President Barack Obama announced federal support for same-sex couples, declaring them eligible for the same spousal benefits granted to heterosexual couples. And in 2015 the Supreme Court legalized gay marriage. The speed with which public attitudes toward gay rights have evolved far outpaces that for either African American or women's rights, on whose victories it has built.[60]

All of these "rights movements" were bound to cause a backlash, and they have. Small groups of younger women are venting their anger against feminists on social media, and even smaller numbers of middle-aged men have joined a "men's rights" movement. Women Against Feminism is a Tumblr page where white millennials (those born in the 1980s and 1990s) have posted photos of themselves holding up signs that finish the sentence "I don't need feminism because . . ." A sampling: "I like when men say compliments about my body!"; "Cooking for my husband is not oppression"; "I can form my own opinions without the influence of other women, politicians, and liberal college professors"; and "I love men and value their rights." The underlying assumption is that feminists hate men, casting women as victims and men as adversaries.[61] The *New York Observer* reporter Nina Burleigh calls their rantings "a compendium of such blinding idiocy and prejudice that [it] defies description," pointing out that feminists enabled their freedom to express such ideas. Burleigh speculates that these women are the brainwashed wives and girlfriends of the growing proportion of low-earning men frustrated by rising income inequalities.[62] These are the same men fueling the men's rights movement.

"Men's rights activists say society has wronged them." This headline appeared in a July 1, 2014, *Washington Post* article covering the First International Conference on Men's Issues held in Detroit, a city chosen because it is an "iconic testimonial to masculinity." The event was originally to be held in the Doubletree Hotel, but organizers claimed the hotel canceled because feminists had issued death threats against the management. The meeting was moved to a suburban Veterans of Foreign Wars (VFW) lodge, a location thought to be even more appropriate because it was more masculine. Attracting about two hundred men, the conference was planned by Paul Elam through his website, A Voice for Men, a site once identified by the Southern Poverty Law Center as overtly misogynistic. Participants talked about being "second-class citizens" compared with "privileged women." Presenter Warren Farrell, a member of NOW before taking up men's rights several decades ago, declared, "I've always said the men's movement is in its embryonic stage. I'm no longer saying that."[63]

What are we to make of this phenomenon? A few hundred disaffected men do not constitute a social movement. But even these beleaguered souls recognized the significance of place. Detroit was the logical city, and a VFW lodge the ideal location. These men did not have to create their own place, though; they simply used one of many preexisting male spaces. Perhaps the main lesson of this small gathering is that the Second and Third Waves have been so effective that certain disempowered men are threatened by feminists—a dubious accomplishment. The entire event, of course, represents what most infuriates Second Wave feminists: men think everything is about them.

Perhaps young women against feminism have yet to experience an unwanted pregnancy, abuse at the hands of a partner (of either sex), or wages less than a man's in the same job. For every man who attended the men's rights conference, there are scores more on corporate boards and in Congress. If the feminist movement had been as effective as these groups claim, there would be far more women—in this country and others—wielding economic and political power. And what about the paucity of recognized women artists, the topic with which I began this book? For eighteen years the Los Angeles Woman's Building proclaimed women's rights to the world of art. When it closed in 1991 it was for financial reasons, not because women had achieved parity with men in exhibiting their art. As recently as 2012, only five percent of art displayed in US museums was produced by women, despite women constituting one-half of all visual artists.[64] Yet the spirit of the Woman's Building lives on in Washington, DC's National Museum of Women in the Arts, opened in 1987 in a refurbished Masonic temple near the White House. Women's accomplishments deserve recognition and validation. Until they achieve that in a masculine world, feminist places will be irreplaceable.[65]

In March 2014 I attended a conference in Boston titled "A Revolutionary Moment: Women's Liberation in the Late 1960s and Early 1970s." Many of the activists I had read or written about for this project were there, including the historian Linda Gordon, formerly of the Bread and Roses collective, and Libby Bouvier and Betsy Warrior of the Cambridge Women's Center. Gilda Bruckman, Carol Downer, and Simone Wallace presented their thoughts on the importance of early feminist places. At that and other events, women reminisced about how important all-female spaces had been to the movement. They were places women could be themselves, where they talked to each other and connected over common interests. They gave women a voice. Feminist places were affirming and creative places where women's knowledge was produced for other women. Most important, women-only spaces had been necessary to gain ground politically. Everyone lamented their disappearance.

I hope this book brings those places back to life, for the people who experienced them and for those who are only just now learning about them. In an ideal world, their example might inspire another wave of constructive feminism to defend women's rights to the city.

Appendix A

Sources of Data for Figure 3

Percentage of All Women in the Labor Force, 1950–2010

Data refer to all women age sixteen and older in the civilian labor force.

1950–1990 data: Daphne Spain and Suzanne M. Bianchi, *Balancing Act: Motherhood, Marriage, and Employment among American Women* (New York: Russell Sage Foundation, 1996), 81.

2000 data: US Bureau of Labor Statistics, "Women in the Labor Force: A Databook," *BLS Reports*, no. 985 (May 2005), accessed Sept. 24, 2012, http://www.bls.gov/cps/wlf-table2-2005.pdf.

2010 data: US Bureau of Labor Statistics, "Women in the Labor Force: A Databook," *BLS Reports*, no. 1026 (Dec. 2010), accessed Sept. 23, 2012, http://www.bls.gov/cps/wlf-databook-2010.pdf.

Percentage of All Mothers in the US Labor Force, 1955–2010

Data refer to mothers of children under age 18 living at home.

Source: US Bureau of Labor Statistics, "Mothers in the Labor Force, 1955–2010," accessed September 23, 2012, http://www.infoplease.com/ipa/A0104670.html.

Note: Before 2000 data were collected using a survey that underwent major revisions in 1994, making it difficult to compare them with data collected in 2000 and 2010.

Number of US McDonald's Restaurants, 1955–2011

Data for 1955, 1959, 1963, and 1965: McDonald's History, accessed August 3, 2012, http://www.aboutmcdonalds.com/mcd/our_company/mcdonalds_history_timeline.html.

Data for 1960, 1973, and 1978–88: Robert L. Emerson, *The New Economics of Fast Food* (New York: Van Nostrand Reinhold, 1990), 59, 111.

Data for 1968: Eric Schlosser, *Fast Food Nation: What the All-American Meal Is Doing to the World* (New York: Penguin Books, 2002), 4.

Data for 1970: Stan Luxenberg, *Roadside Empires: How the Chains Franchised America* (New York: Penguin Books, 1985), 5.

Data for 1975: John A. Jakle and Keith A. Sculle, *Fast Food: Roadside Restaurants in the Automobile Age* (Baltimore: Johns Hopkins University Press, 1999), 58.

Data for 1992–2001: *2002 McDonald's Corporation Summary Annual Report*, accessed October 5, 2012, http://www.aboutmcdonalds.com/content/dam/AboutMcDonalds/Investors/C-%5Cfakepath%5Cinvestors-2002-annual-report.pdf.

Data for 2006 and 2010: McDonald's Corporation, *2011 Annual Report*, accessed October 5, 2012, http://www.aboutmcdonalds.com/content/dam/AboutMcDonalds/Investors/Investors%202012/2011%20Annual%20Report%20Final.pdf.

Number of Businesses Providing Child-Care Services in the United States, 1977–2010

Carolyn Hronis and Martin O'Connell, "Child Care Establishment Types: 2002," *US Census Bureau, Census of Service Industries Working Paper*, paper presented at the Annual Population Association of America Conference, April 2006.

Grace O'Neill and Martin O'Connell, "State Estimates of Child Care Establishments 1977–1997," Population Division Working Paper Series No. 55, April 2001. U.S. Census Bureau, accessed July 18, 2007, http://www.census.gov/population/www/documentation/twps0055.html.

Lynne Casper and Martin O'Connell, "State Estimates of Organized Child Care Facilities," Population Division Working Paper No. 21, March 1998, accessed July 18, 2012, http://www.census.gov/hhes/childcare/data/service/index.html.

US Census Bureau, Health Care and Social Assistance, "County Business Patterns: Child Day Care Services 2003–2010," accessed November 1, 2012, http://censtats.census.gov/cgi-bin/cbpnaic/cbpdetl.pl.

Number of Adult Day Service Centers in the United States, 1974–2010

William G. Weissert, "Adult Day Care Programs in the United States: Current Research Projects and a Survey of 10 Centers," *Public Health Reports* 92, no. 1 (January–February 1977), 49–56.

Ruth Von Behren, "Adult Day Care: A Decade of Growth," *Perspectives on Aging* 18, no. 4 (1989), 14–19.

"Adult Day Care Programs," hearing before the Subcommittee on Health and Long-Term Care of the Select Committee on Aging, House of Representatives, Ninety-Sixth Congress, April 23, 1980 (Washington, DC: US Government Printing Office, 1980). Data for 1989–2010 are from The MetLife Mature Market Institute, "The MetLife National Study of Adult Day Services," October 2010, accessed July 25, 2012, http://www.tn.gov/humanserv/adfam/ADS_Study.pdf.

Lynda Laughlin, "Who's Minding the Kids? Child Care Arrangements: Spring 2011," Household Economic Studies P70-135, US Census Bureau, 2013, accessed July 24, 2015, http://www.census.gov.

APPENDIX B

Women's Centers in the United States, 1973

STATE	NAME	FIGURE 4 MAP ID	ADDRESS	CITY
Alaska	Anchorage Women's Liberation Center	none	732 O Street, A-3	Anchorage
Arizona	Women's Center	2	1414 S. McAllister	Tempe
California	Advocates for Women	3	564 Market Street, Suite 218	San Francisco
	American Indian Women's Center	4	227 Valencia	San Francisco
	Center for Women's Studies and Services (CWSS)	5	908 F Street	San Diego
	Center for Women's Studies and Services (CWSS) Storefront	6	805 Ninth Avenue	San Diego
	Chicana Service Center	7	435 S. Boyle Avenue	Los Angeles
	Davis Women's Center	8	University of California, Davis	Davis
	Feminist Women's Health Center	9	746 S. Crenshaw Boulevard	Los Angeles
	Gay Community Services Center	10	1614 Wilshire Boulevard	Los Angeles
	Harbor Free Clinic/ Women's Night	11	112 W. Seventh Street	San Pedro
	Isla Vista Women's Center, Santa Barbara	12	6504 Pardell	Isla Vista

	Marin Women's Center	13	1618 Mission Avenue	San Rafael
	Sacramento Women's Center and Bookstore	14	1221 Twentieth Street	Sacramento
	San Diego Women's Center, YWCA	15	Tenth and C Streets	San Diego
	San Francisco Women's Switchboard	16	620 Sutton Street	San Francisco
	San José Community Women's Center	17	Ninth and San Carlos	San José
	Santa Cruz Women's Center	18	314B Laurel	Santa Cruz
	Stan. NOW Women's Center	19	631 Fifteenth Street	Modesto
	Stanford Women's Center	20	Stanford University	Stanford
	The Women's Center	21	1027 S. Crenshaw Boulevard	Los Angeles
	Well Woman Clinic	22	1050 Garnet Street	Pacific Beach
	Women Together	23	422 S. Murphy	Sunnyvale
	Women's Center	24	Fifty-Ninth and E. San Carlos	San José
	Women's Center	25	218 Venice Boulevard	Venice
	Women's Center, Santa Barbara Community Union	26	1421 State Street	Santa Barbara
	Women's Opportunity Center	27	University of California, Irvine	Irvine
	Women's Re-entry Educational Program De Anza College	28	21250 Stevens Creek Boulevard	Cupertino
Colorado	The Boulder Women's Center	29	Ninth and Arapahoe	Boulder
	Virginia Neal Blue Resource Centers: Administrative Headquarters	30	Colorado Women's College	Denver
	Virginia Neal Blue Resource Centers: Colorado Springs Branch	31	420 N. Nevada Avenue	Colorado Springs
	Virginia Neal Blue Resource Centers: Denver Branch, YWCA	32	1545 Tremont Place	Denver
	Virginia Neal Blue Resource Centers: Grand Junction Branch	33	Mesa Junior College	Grand Junction
	Virginia Neal Blue Resource Centers: Pueblo Branch	34	Southern Colorado State College	Pueblo
	Virginia Neal Blue Resource Centers: San Luis Valley Branch	35	Adams State College	Alamosa
	Virginia Neal Blue Resource Centers: South Suburban Branch	36	Arapahoe Community College	Littleton
	Women in Transition House	37	1895 Lafayette Street	Denver
	Women's Center	38	University of Colorado	Boulder

Connecticut	Information and Counseling Service for Women	39	215 Park Street	New Haven
	Women's Center	40	11 N. Main Street	South Norwalk
Delaware	Women's Resource Center	41	317 W. Nineteenth Street	Wilmington
District of Columbia	Washington Area Women's Center	42	1736 R Street NW	Washington
Florida	Women's Center, Inc.	43	405 Grand Central Avenue	Tampa
	Women's Information Center	44	6255 SW Sixty-Ninth Street	South Miami
Georgia	A Woman's Place	45	140 Marion Drive	Athens
Hawaii	Women's Center—Hawaii	none	University of Hawaii	Honolulu
Idaho	Women's Center	47	3309 Crescent Rim Drive	Boise
Illinois	A Woman's Place	48	401 W. California Avenue	Urbana
	Chicago Women's Liberation Union	49	600 W. Fullerton	Chicago
	Counseling Center for Women	50	Mundelein College	Chicago
	Prelude	51	Knox College	Galesburg
Iowa	Women's Center	52	3 E. Market	Iowa City
Kansas	Women's Center	53	615 Fairchild Terrace	Manhattan
Maryland	Baltimore Women's Liberation	54	101 E. Twenty-Fifth Street	Baltimore
	Women's Center	55	Goucher College	Towson
Massachusetts	Birth Control Information Center	56	45 Eagle Street	North Adams
	Boston University Women's Center	57	185 Bay State Road	Boston
	Boston Women's Collective, Inc.	58	651 Concord Avenue	Cambridge
	Cambridge Women's Center	59	46 Pleasant Street	Cambridge
	Community Women's Center	60	308 Main Street	Greenfield
	Everywoman's Center	61	University of Massachusetts	Amherst
	Springfield Women's Center	62	115 State Street	Springfield
	Valley Women's Center	63	200 Main Street	Northampton
	WINNERS	64	48 Rutland Street	Boston
	Woman's Place	65	49 Parker Street	Watertown
	Women's Center	66	347 County Street	New Bedford
	Women's Center	67	Salem State College	Salem
	Women's Center	68	51 Downing Street	Worcester

	Women's Opportunity Research Center	69	Middlesex Community College	Bedford
	Women's Resource Center, West Suburban Branch, YWCA	70	105 Hartford Street	Natick
Michigan	Women's Center	71	Oakland University	Rochester
	Kalamazoo Women's Center	72	211 S. Rose Street	Kalamazoo
	Woman's Crisis Center	73	306 N. Division Street	Ann Arbor
	Feminist House	74	818 Church Street	Ann Arbor
	Women's Health and Information Project (WHIP)	75	Central Michigan University	Mount Pleasant
Minnesota	Grace High School Women's Center	76	1350 Gardena Avenue NE	Fridley
	Minnesota Women's Center	77	University of Minnesota	Minneapolis
	Rape Counseling Center, Neighborhood Involvement Program	78	2617 Hinnepin [sic] Avenue	Minneapolis
	Women's Advocates	79	728 Osceola	St. Paul
	Women's Resource Center, YWCA	80	130 Nicollet	Minneapolis
Missouri	Columbia Women's Center	81	501 Rollins	Columbia
	Kansas City Women's Liberation Union	82	3800 McGee	Kansas City
	Women's Center	83	University of Missouri	St. Louis
Montana	Women's Action Center	84	University of Montana	Missoula
Nebraska	YWCA Women's Resource Center	85	1432 N Street	Lincoln
Nevada	Women Associates	86	325 Flint Street	Reno
New Jersey	The Women's Place	87	PO Box 474	Red Bank
	The YWCA Women's Center of the Oranges	88	395 Main Street	Orange
	Women's Center	89	15 W. Main Street	Moorestown
	Women's Center at Douglass	90	Douglass College	New Brunswick
	YWCA Women's Center	91	Upsala College	East Orange
New Mexico	Women's Center	92	University of New Mexico	Albuquerque
New York	Astoria Women's Center	93	44–03 Twenty-Eighth Avenue	Astoria
	Barnard Women's Center	94	Barnard College	New York
	Bronx Women's Center	95	1945 Loring Place	New York
	Buffalo Women's Center	96	564 Franklin Street,	Buffalo
	Community of Women	97	359 E. Sixty-Eighth Street	New York
	Nassau Women's Center	98	14 W. Columbia Street	Hempstead
	New York Women's Liberation Firehouse	99	243 W. Twentieth Street	New York

	Northport Women's Center	100	144 Bayview Avenue	Northport
	Queens Women's Center	101	153–11 Sixty-First Road	Flushing
	Richmond College Free Clinic and Women's Center	102	130 Stuyvesant Place	New York
	Rochester Women's Liberation c/o Womansplace	103	PO Box 1198	Rochester
	Rockland City Women's Center	104	St. Stephen's Episcopal Church	Pearl River
			Pierce Parkway and Ehrhardt Road	
	Staten Island College Women's Center	105	Staten Island College	New York
	Union Center for Women	106	8101 Ridge Boulevard	New York
	Westchester Women's Center, YWCA	107	69 N. Broadway	White Plains
	Women's Center	108	State University College at Brockport	Brockport
	Women's Center	109	140 W. State Street	Ithaca
	Women's Center	110	104 Avondale Place	Syracuse
	Women's Center of Brooklyn, YWCA	111	30 Third Avenue	New York
	Women's Counseling Project	112	Broadway and 117th Street	New York
	Women's Resource Center, YWCA	113	600 Lexington Avenue	New York
	Women's Studies Board; United Students' Government,	114	State University College at Buffalo	Buffalo
North Carolina	Durham Women's Center, YWCA	115	515 W. Chapel Hill Street	Durham
	Women's Center	116	Lyndhurst Avenue	Charlotte
Ohio	Dayton Free Clinic and Counseling Center, Inc.	117	1007 N. Main Street	Dayton
	Miami University Women's Information Center	118	Miami University	Oxford
	Oberlin Women's Service Center	119	229 W. College Street	Oberlin
	The Women's Center	120	Antioch College	Yellow Springs
	Women's Center	121	University of Cincinnati	Cincinnati
	Women's Center	122	Cleveland State University	Cleveland
	Women's Center	123	University of Dayton	Dayton
Oregon	Portland Women's Center	124	6367 N. Moore	Portland
Pennsylvania	Germantown Women's Center, c/o YWCA	125	5820 Cheltenham Avenue	Philadelphia
	Kensington Women's Center, YWCA	126	174 W. Allegheny	Philadelphia
	Lancaster Women's Center	127	230 W. Chestnut Street	Lancaster

	Philadelphia Women's Liberation	128	4634 Chester Avenue	Philadelphia
	Women in Transition, Inc.	129	4634 Chester Avenue	Philadelphia
	Women's Center	130	Bucks County Community College	Newton
	YWCA of Greater Pittsburgh	131	Fourth and Wood Street	Pittsburgh
Rhode Island	Higher Education Resource Service (HERS)	132	Brown University	Providence
	YWCA	133	62 Jackson Street	Providence
	YWCA Women's Center	134	324 Broad Street	Central Falls
Tennessee	Nashville Women's Center	135	1112 Nineteenth Avenue South	Nashville
Texas	Austin Women's Center	136	1208 Baylor Street	West Austin
	Women for Change Center	137	3000 Diamond Park	Dallas
Virginia	Roanoke Valley Women's Coalition	138	702 Shenandoah Avenue NW	Roanoke
Washington	Metropolitan YWCA	139	Fifth and Seneca	Seattle
	University YWCA	140	University of Washington	Seattle
Wisconsin	Westside Women's Center	141	2110 W. Wells Street	Milwaukee
	Women's Center	142	836 E. Johnson	Madison
	Women's Center	143	Route 1	Green Bay
	YWCA Women's Center	144	306 N. Brooks Street	Madison

Source: Carol Shapiro, "How to Organize a Multi-Service Women's Center," Women's Action Alliance, Inc., New York, New York, 1973, Cambridge Women's Educational Center, Inc., 46 Pleasant Street, Cambridge, MA.

Note: Some of these places are health clinics, and there is one duplication (Philadelphia Women's Liberation and Women in Transition, Inc., are listed at the same address); they were all separate entries in the guide. Women's centers affiliated with colleges and universities are listed by institution only.

Appendix C

Feminist Bookstores in the United States, ca. 1980

STATE	NAME	FIGURE 7 MAP ID	ADDRESS	CITY
Alabama	The Book Legger	1	522 Jordan Lane	Huntsville
Alaska	Ships, Shoes and Sealing Wax	none	513 W. Seventh Avenue, #4	Anchorage
Arizona	Antigone Books	3	403 E. Fifth Street	Tucson
	Arcadia	4	McMillan Building 116 W. Cottage	Flagstaff
	Womansplace Bookstore	5	2401 N. 32nd Street	Phoenix
California	Califia, Inc.	6	3415 Highland Avenue	Manhattan Beach
	Charmed Circle Feminist Books	7	4603 Park Boulevard	San Diego
	Davis Women's Books	8	217 K Street	Davis
	Everywoman's Bookstore	9	715 Sir Francis Drake	San Anselmo
	Feminist Horizons	10	10586½ Pico Boulevard	Los Angeles
	Feminist Wicca	11	422 Lincoln Boulevard	Venice
	Full Moon	12	4416 18th Street	San Francisco
	ICI: A Woman's Place	13	4015 Broadway	Oakland
	Lioness Books	14	2104 Capitol Avenue	Sacramento
	Motherright	15	530 Seabright Avenue	Santa Cruz
	Ms Atlas Press and Bookstore	16	330 S. Third Street	San José

	Old Wives' Tales	17	1009 Valencia Street	San Francisco
	Outrageous Woman Enterprises	18	PO Box 1985	San Francisco
	Page One	19	453 E. Colorado Boulevard	Pasadena
	Rising Woman Books	20	600 Wilson	Santa Rosa
	River Queen Women's Center Bookstore	21	17140 River Road	Guernewood Park
	Sacramento Women's Center	22	1230 H Street	Sacramento
	Sisterhood Bookstore	23	1351 Westwood Boulevard	Los Angeles
	Sojourner Bookstore	24	538 Redondo Avenue	Long Beach
	The Magic Speller Bookstore	25	506 31st Street	Pacific Beach
	The Oracle	26	22640 Main Street	Hayward
	Womankind Bookstore	27	6551 Trigo Road	Isla Vista
Colorado	Lilith: Womyn's Bookstore	28	1743 Walnut	Boulder
	Woman to Woman Bookcenter	29	2023 E. Colfax	Denver
Connecticut	Bloodroot Restaurant/ Bookstore	30	85 Ferris Street	Bridgeport
	Sonya Wetstone's Book and Cheese	31	529 Farmington Avenue	Hartford
District of Columbia	Lammas Women's Shop	32	312 Seventh Street SE	Washington
Florida	Feminist Connection	33	1202 W. Platt	Tampa
	Herstore, Inc.	34	112 E. Call Street	Tallahassee
	Our Place	35	12315 N. Nebraska Avenue	Tampa
Georgia	Charis Books and More	36	419 Moreland Avenue NE	Atlanta
Hawaii	Women's Word Bookstore	none	1820 University Avenue	Honolulu
Illinois	Booklovers and Co.	38	8 W. Burlington	Westmont
	Jane Addams Bookstore and Bakery	39	5 S. Wabash Avenue	Chicago
	Lesbian Feminist Center Bookstore	40	707 W. Wrightwood	Chicago
	Small Changes Bookstore	41	409A N. Main Street	Bloomington
	Sojourner Book Center	42	203 E. Locust	DeKalb
	Women and Children First	43	926 Armitage Street	Chicago
Indiana	A Room of One's Own	44	101½ W. Kirkwood	Bloomington
	Dreams and Swords	45	116 N. Grant	Bloomington
	Dreams and Swords	46	3711 N. Sherman Drive	Indianapolis
	Sisterspace	47	1414 N. Broadway	Fort Wayne

Iowa	A Mind of Your Own	48	1171 Twenty-Fifth Street	Des Moines
	Plains Woman Bookstore★	49	PO Box 1935	Iowa City
	Plains Woman Bookstore★	50	114 E. College	Iowa City
Kansas	Spinsters Books	51	1101½ Massachusetts Street	Lawrence
Maryland	A Room of One's Own	52	12 Frances Street	Annapolis
	A Woman's Bookstore	53	12 W. Twenty-Fifth Street	Baltimore
	Thirty First Street Bookstore	54	425 E. Thirty-First Street	Baltimore
Massachusetts	Isis	55	146 Commercial Street	Provincetown
	Lesbian Gardens	56	200 Main Street	Northampton
	New Words	57	186 Hampshire Street	Cambridge
	Organizer's Book Center	58	44 N. Prospect Street	Amherst
	The Women's Bookstore	59	78 May Street	Worcester
	Womancrafts	60	373 Commercial Street	Provincetown
	Womonfyre Books	61	68 Masonic Street	Northampton
Michigan	Book Co-op	62	201½ Grand River	East Lansing
	Hershelf	63	2 Highland	Highland Park
	Les Tresors de la Femme, Wimmin's Emporium Co-op	64	950 E. Fulton Street	Grand Rapids
	Pandora	65	505 Davis Street	Kalamazoo
Minnesota	Amazon Bookstore	66	2607 Hennepin Avenue South	Minneapolis
Missouri	New Earth Bookstore	67	2 W. Thirty-Ninth Street	Kansas City
	The Woman's Eye	68	6344 S. Rosebury Street	St. Louis
Nebraska	The Book End, Inc.	69	7641 Pacific Street	Omaha
New Hampshire	Women's Concern Center	70	20 Main Street	Littleton
New Jersey	Herizon Books	71	92½ Elm Street	Morristown
	My Sister's Place	72	100 Main Street	Fort Lee
New Mexico	A Woman's Gallery	73	302 Rio Grande Boulevard	Albuquerque
	Full Circle Books	74	2205 Silver SE	Albuquerque
New York	Alternatives Corner	75	374 Woodfield Road	West Hemstead
	Djuna Books	76	154 W. Tenth Street	New York
	Earth's Daughters	77	944 Kensington Avenue	Buffalo
	Emma, The Buffalo Women's Bookstore	78	2474 Main Street	Buffalo
	Eve's Garden	79	119 W. Fifty-Seventh Street	New York

	Kay's Book Studio	80	86 Front Street	Birmingham
	La Papaya	81	331 Flatbush Avenue	New York
	Shameless Hussy	82	9 Prospect Street	Nanuet
	Sister Bear Books	83	401 First Street	Liverpool
	Smedley's Bookshop	84	119 E. Buffalo Street	Ithaca
	Womanbooks	85	201 W. Ninety-Second Street	New York
	Womankind Books, Inc.	86	1899 New York Avenue	Huntington
North Carolina	New Leaf	87	223 N. Bloodworth Street	Raleigh
Ohio	Coventry Books	88	1824 Coventry Road	Cleveland Heights
	Fan the Flames Feminist Book Collective	89	127 E. Woodruff Avenue	Columbus
	The Crazy Ladies Bookstore	90	4168 Hamilton Avenue	Cincinnati
Oklahoma	A Room of Her Own	91	3305 S. Peoria	Tulsa
Oregon	A Woman's Place Bookstore★	92	2349 SE Ankeney	Portland
	A Woman's Place Bookstore★	93	1300 SW Washington	Portland
	Book and Tea Shop	94	1646 E. Nineteenth Avenue	Eugene
	Mother Kali's Books	95	541 Blair Boulevard	Eugene
Pennsylvania	Alternative Booksellers	96	10 N. Fourth Street	Reading
	Birmingham Booksellers	97	2222 E. Carson Street	Pittsburgh
	Bookstore	98	742 N. Beatty Street	Pittsburgh
	Penn Woman's Center Bookstore, Women's Cultural Trust	99	3601 Locust Walk	Philadelphia
Tennessee	Womankind Books	100	2011 Belmont Boulevard	Nashville
Texas	Bookwomen	101	324 E. Sixth Street	Austin
	Common Woman Bookstore	102	1510 San Antonio	Austin
	Las Mujeres Women's Bookstore	103	802 E. Mistletoe	San Antonio
	The Bookstore	104	1728 Bissonet	Houston
Utah	20 Rue Jacob	105	232 E. Eighth South	Salt Lake City
	The Open Book	106	1025 Second Avenue	Salt Lake City
Vermont	Tigris-Euphrates, A Feminist Bookstore	107	PO Box 6	Plainfield
Washington	It's About Time	108	5241 University Way NE	Seattle

Wisconsin	A Room of One's Own	109	315 W. Gorham Street	Madison
	Kaleidoscope Books	110	11 Merritt	Oshkosh
	Mother Courage	111	224 State Street	Racine
	Sistermoon Feminist Bookstore and Art Gallery★	112	1625 E. Irving Place	Milwaukee
	Sistermoon Feminist Bookstore and Art Gallery★	113	2128 E. Locust	Milwaukee
	Something Ventured	114	524 S. Monroe Street	Green Bay

★ Names with an asterisk indicate the same bookstore at two different locations.

I compiled this list by combining two sources. The first was from a list circulated by Womansplace Bookstore, Phoenix, Arizona, January 1982. Records of New Words, Schlesinger Library, Radcliffe Institute, Harvard University, 2002-M130, carton 1. The second was an undated list from New Words that was compiled between the store's opening in 1974 and sometime in 1979. I am relatively certain of the time frame because one of the most famous feminist bookstores, Chicago's Women and Children First (established in 1979), was missing from the undated list. "Bookstores," Records of New Words, Schlesinger Library, Radcliffe Institute, Harvard University, 2002-M130, carton 1.

Feminist Health Clinics in the United States, 1975

STATE	NAME	ADDRESS	CITY
California	Berkeley Women's Health Collective	2214 Grove Street	Berkeley
	Chico Feminist Women's Health Center	PO Box 3467	Chico
	Feminist Women's Health Center	746 S. Crenshaw Boulevard	Los Angeles
		429 S. Sycamore Street	Santa Ana
		2930 McClure	Oakland
	Womancare	1050 Garnet	San Diego
	Santa Cruz Women's Health Center	250 Locust Street	Santa Cruz
Colorado	Women's Health Service of Colorado Springs	730 N. Tejon Street	Colorado Springs
	Ft. Collins Self-Help Clinic for Women	629 S. Hawes	Fort Collins
Connecticut	Women's Health Services, Inc.	40 Foster Street	New Haven
Florida	Gainesville Women's Health Center, Inc.	805 SE Fourth Street	Gainesville
	Tampa Women's Health Center	PO Box 7350	Tampa
	Feminist Women's Health Center	2411-12 Jackson Bluffs Road	Tallahassee
		1126 Lee Avenue	Tallahassee
Illinois	Chicago Women's Liberation Union	2748 N. Lincoln	Chicago
	The Emma Goldman Women's Health Center	1317 W. Loyola	Chicago

Indiana	Indianapolis Women's Health Center	5656 E. Sixteenth Street	Indianapolis
Iowa	Feminist Women's Health Center	129½ N. Sheldon	Ames
	Emma Goldman Clinic for Women	715 N. Dodge	Iowa City
Louisiana	Delta Women's Clinic	1406 St. Charles Avenue	New Orleans
Maine	Maine Feminist Health Project	105 Dresden Avenue	Gardiner
Massachusetts	Women's Community Health Center	137 Hampshire Street	Cambridge
	New Bedford Women's Clinic	347 County Street	New Bedford
	Somerville Women's Health Project	326 Somerville Avenue	Somerville
Michigan	Community Women's Clinic	306 N. Division Street	Ann Arbor
	Feminist Women's Health Center	2445 W. 8 Mile	Detroit
Minnesota	Elizabeth Blackwell Women's Health Center	200 S. Fifth Street	Minneapolis
New Mexico	Women's Health Services		Santa Fe
New York	Buffalo Women's Self-Help Clinic	499 Franklin Street	Buffalo
	Eastern Women's Center	14 E. Sixtieth Street	New York
	St. Marks Clinic	44 St. Marks Place	New York
Oregon	Women's Clinic	341 E. Twelfth Street	Eugene
	Women's Clinic	4160 SE Division	Portland
Pennsylvania	Elizabeth Blackwell Health Center for Women	112 S. Sixteenth Street	Philadelphia
	Philadelphia Women's Health Collective	5030 Newhall Street	Philadelphia
	Women's Health Services, Inc.	1209 Allegheny Tower	Pittsburgh
		625 Stanwix Street	Pittsburgh
	Williamsport Women's Clinic	Clancy's Candleshop	South Williamsport
Utah	Feminist Women's Health Center	368 E. Sixth Street	Salt Lake City
Vermont	Vermont Women's Health Center	PO Box 29	Burlington
Washington	Aradia Clinic	4224 University Way NE	Seattle
	Country Doctor Women's Clinic	402 Fifteenth Avenue East	Seattle
	Open Door Women's Clinic	5012 Roosevelt Way NW	Seattle

Based on a list in Kirsten Grimstad and Susan Rennie, eds., *The New Woman's Survival Sourcebook* (New York: Alfred A. Knopf, 1975), 35–36.

NOTES

Preface

1. *Constructive Feminism: Reconstruction of the Woman's Building*, directed by Sheila Ruth, produced by Sheila Ruth, Diana Johnson, and Annette Hunt (Los Angeles: Getty Research Institute Research Library, 1975), http://.library.getty.edu/cgi-bin/Pwebrecon.cgi?BBID=705169. Sheila Ruth is deceased. I obtained permission from Annette Hunt to use the title of their video.

2. Terry Wolverton, *Insurgent Muse: Life and Art at the Woman's Building* (San Francisco: City Lights, 2002), xv. Nineteenth-century suffragists used the word "woman" as a universal designation, hence the Woman's Building for women's arts.

3. Author's interview with Sue Maberry, Director of Library and Instructional Design, Otis College of Art and Design, Los Angeles, March 12, 2010.

4. Wolverton, *Insurgent Muse*, 6.

5. Second Wave feminism of the 1960s and 1970s drew its inspiration from the nineteenth century's First Wave of suffragists who won women's right to vote in 1920.

6. Dolores Hayden, *The Grand Domestic Revolution: A History of Feminist Designs for American Homes, Neighborhoods, and Cities* (Cambridge, MA: MIT Press, 1981).

7. Sarah Deutsch, *Women and the City: Gender, Space, and Power in Boston, 1870–1940* (New York: Oxford University Press, 2000); Elizabeth York Enstam, *Women and the Creation of Urban Life: Dallas, Texas, 1843–1920* (College Station: Texas A&M University Press, 1998); Maureen Flanagan, *Seeing with their Hearts: Chicago Women and the Vision of the Good City, 1871–1933* (Princeton, NJ: Princeton University Press, 2002); Marta Gutman, *A City for Children: Women, Architecture, and the Charitable Landscapes of Oakland, 1850–1950* (Chicago and London: The University of Chicago Press, 2014); Jessica Ellen Sewell, *Women and the Everyday City: Public Space in San Francisco, 1890–1915* (Minneapolis: University of Minnesota Press, 2011); Despina Stratigakos, *A Women's Berlin: Building the Modern City* (Minneapolis: University of Minnesota Press, 2008).

8. Ruth Lister, *Citizenship: Feminist Perspectives*, 2nd ed. (New York: New York University Press, 2003); Mary Ryan, *Women in Public: Between Banners and Ballots, 1825–1880* (Baltimore: Johns Hopkins University Press, 1990); Marilyn Friedman, ed., *Women and Citizenship* (Oxford: Oxford University Press, 2005).

9. Elisabeth Armstrong, *The Retreat from Organization: U.S. Feminism Reconceptualized* (Albany: State University of New York Press, 2002); Sara Evans, "Re-Viewing the Second Wave," *Feminist Studies* 28, no. 2 (2002): 259–67; Kathleen Laughlin and Jacqueline Castledine, eds., *Breaking the Wave: Women, Their Organizations, and Feminism, 1945–1985* (New York: Routledge, 2011); Linda J. Nicholson, ed., *The Second*

Wave: A Reader in Feminist Theory (New York: Routledge, 1997); Brian Norman, "The Consciousness-Raising Document, Feminist Anthologies, and Black Women in *Sisterhood Is Powerful*," *Frontiers: A Journal of Women Studies* 27, no. 3 (2006): 38–64.

10. Anne Enke, *Finding the Movement: Sexuality, Contested Space, and Feminist Activism* (Durham, NC: Duke University Press, 2007).

11. Abigail Van Slyck, *Free to All: Carnegie Libraries and American Culture, 1890–1920* (Chicago: University of Chicago Press, 1995), xxi; see also Sewell, *Women and the Everyday City.*

12. Rosalyn Baxandall and Linda Gordon, eds., *Dear Sisters* (New York: Basic Books, 2000); Steven M. Buechler, *Women's Movements in the United States* (New Brunswick, NJ: Rutgers University Press, 1990); Myra Marx Ferree and Patricia Yancey Martin, eds., *Feminist Organizations: Harvest of the New Women's Movement* (Philadelphia: Temple University Press, 1995); Eleanor Flexner and Ellen Fitzpatrick, *Century of Struggle: The Woman's Rights Movement in the United States* (Cambridge, MA: Harvard University Press, 1959).

13. Kirsten Grimstad and Susan Rennie, eds., *The New Woman's Survival Catalog: A Woman-Made Book* (New York: Coward, McCann, and Geoghegan, 1973) and *The New Woman's Survival Sourcebook: Another Woman-made Book* (New York: Alfred A. Knopf, 1975).

14. Barbara Love, ed., *Feminists Who Changed America, 1963–1975* (Urbana: University of Illinois Press, 2006).

15. My interviewing technique relied on case study logic. In contrast to the sampling logic applied in surveys to ensure random selection, in case study logic interviews occur sequentially based on information gained in the previous interview. The selection of respondents is not random, and the number of interviews is unknown until the study is finished. Similarly to snowball sampling, each person is selected based on referrals from another respondent, for whom the questions may have been slightly different. The first interview yields findings and generates questions that inform the next interview. Sampling logic is more appropriate when asking descriptive questions about a population, while case study logic is more effective when asking about previously unknown processes and connections. See Robert K. Yin, *Case Study Research: Design and Methods* (Thousand Oaks, CA: Sage, 1994); Mario Luis Small, "How Many Cases Do I Need? On Science and the Logic of Case Selection in Field-Based Research," *Ethnography* 10, no. 1 (2009): 25.

16. In order to minimize errors of interpretation, I asked Carol Downer to read a draft of the chapter on health clinics and Simone Wallace and Carol Seajay to read a draft of the chapter on bookstores; their edits significantly improved the accuracy of their stories.

17. Robin Morgan, ed., *Sisterhood Is Powerful: An Anthology of Writings from the Women's Liberation Movement* (New York: Random House, 1970), 589, 591.

18. Maren Lockwood Carden, *The New Feminist Movement* (New York: Russell Sage Foundation, 1974), 64–65.

19. "Who We Are: Descriptions of Women's Liberation Groups," notes from the Sandy Spring conference, ca. November 1968, Irene Peslikis Papers, David M. Rubenstein Rare Book and Manuscript Library, Duke University, correspondence, box 24, http://library.duke.edu/rubenstein/findingaids/peslikisirene/.

20. Susan Brownmiller, *In Our Time: Memoir of a Revolution* (New York: Dial, 1999), 28–30, 62–64.

21. Author's interview with Jeanne Córdova, Los Angeles, March 17, 2010. Susan Brownmiller remembers that in Boston, "Theory was taking precedence over action in other cities." Brownmiller, *In Our Time*, 50.

22. Thomas J. Schlereth, *Artifacts and the American Past* (Nashville, TN: American Association for State and Local History, 1980), chap. 9.

23. Adam Liptak, "Supreme Court Rejects Contraceptives Mandate for Some Corporations," *New York Times*, June 30, 2014.

24. Adam Liptak, "Justices' Rulings Advance Gays; Women Less So," *New York Times*, August 4, 2014. According to the Centers for Disease Control and Prevention, less than 3 percent of the US population identify themselves as gay, lesbian, or bisexual. Sandhya Somashekhar, "Health Survey Gives Government its First Large-Scale Data on Gay, Bisexual Population," *The Washington Post*, July 15, 2014. Women, in contrast, make up 50 percent of the population.

25. Jill Lepore, "To Have and to Hold," *The New Yorker* (May 25, 2015): 34–39.

26. Redstockings, "Women's Liberation Movement Archives for Action," http://www.redstockings.org/index.php?option=com_content&view=article&id=60&Itemid=76.

Acknowledgments

27. Daphne Spain, "Gendered Spaces in 1970s Boston," *Frontiers: A Journal of Women Studies* 32, no. 1 (2011): 152–78.

Introduction

1. African American women have always had higher labor force participation rates than white women, both before and after World War II.

2. Susan Saegert, "Masculine Cities and Feminine Suburbs: Polarized Ideas, Contradictory Realities," in *Women and the American City*, ed. Catharine R. Stimpson, Elsa Dixler, Martha J. Nelson, and Kathryn B. Yatrakis (Chicago: The University of Chicago Press, 1980), 93–108.

3. Suzanne M. Bianchi and Daphne Spain, *American Women in Transition* (New York: Russell Sage Foundation, 1986), 141.

4. Although the Second Wave arose partly out of the anti–Vietnam-war activism of the 1960s, it was not a direct result of men's engagement in that war.

5. Elizabeth Siegel Watkins, *On the Pill: A Social History of Oral Contraceptives* (Baltimore: Johns Hopkins University Press, 1998), 12.

6. Margaret Benston, "The Political Economy of Women's Liberation," *Monthly Review* 21, no. 4 (September 1969).

7. Ibid., 9–10.

8. Bianchi and Spain, *American Women*, 141.

9. "Women in the Labor Force: A Databook," *BLS Reports*, no. 1040 (February 2013): 18–23, http://www.bls.gov/cps/wlf-databook-2012.pdf.

10. Between 1965 and 1995, the average number of hours of housework performed weekly by women declined (from 30 to 18) while it increased for men

(from 5 to 10). Lynne M. Casper and Suzanne M. Bianchi, *Continuity and Change in the American Family* (Thousand Oaks, CA: Sage, 2002), 297. The female-to-male ratio of housework was similar in the 1990s for married women and men. Suzanne M. Bianchi, Melissa A. Milkie, Liana C. Sayer, and John P. Robinson, "Is Anyone Doing the Housework? Trends in the Gender Division of Household Labor," *Social Forces* 79, no. 1: 191–228. Time diary studies for 2000 reveal that women continued to perform approximately twice as much housework as men. Suzanne M. Bianchi, John P. Robinson, and Melissa A. Milkie, *Changing Rhythms of American Family Life* (New York: Russell Sage Foundation, 2006), 116.

11. Dolores Hayden recognized the connection between women's increasing labor force participation and the need for commercial services soon after 1980. See Dolores Hayden, *Redesigning the American Dream: The Future of Housing, Work, and Family Life* (New York: W. W. Norton, 1984), 78–79.

12. Scott Coltrane and Justin Galt, "The History of Men's Caring," in *Care Work: Gender, Labor, and the Welfare State*, ed. Madonna Harrington Meyer (New York: Routledge, 2000), 15–36.

13. Ruth Schwartz Cowan, *More Work for Mother: The Ironies of Household Technology from the Open Hearth to the Microwave* (New York: Basic Books, 1983); Susan Strasser, *Never Done: A History of American Housework* (New York: Henry Holt, 1982).

14. International expansion has also made McDonald's the largest owner of retail property in the world. See Eric Schlosser, *Fast Food Nation: What the All-American Meal Is Doing to the World* (New York: Penguin Books, 2002), 4; Robert L. Emerson, *The New Economics of Fast Food* (New York: Van Nostrand Reinhold, 1990).

15. Emerson, *New Economics*, 19, 23, 47.

16. Ibid., 42.

17. Ray Kroc, *Grinding It Out: The Making of McDonald's* (New York: St. Martin's Press, 1977), 9–10.

18. Harvey Levenstein, *Paradox of Plenty: A Social History of Eating in Modern America* (Berkeley: University of California Press, 2003), 229.

19. Schlosser, *Fast Food Nation*, 4; McDonald's Corporation, "McDonald's History," http://www.aboutmcdonalds.com/mcd/our_company/mcdonalds_history_timeline.html.

20. Kroc, *Grinding It Out*, 160.

21. Ibid., 208.

22. John Love, *McDonald's: Behind the Arches* (New York: Bantam Books, 1995), 164–65.

23. John A. Jakle and Keith A. Sculle, *Fast Food: Roadside Restaurants in the Automobile Age* (Baltimore: Johns Hopkins University Press, 1999), 150.

24. Schlosser, *Fast Food Nation*, 96.

25. Jakle and Sculle, *Fast Food*, 151.

26. Love, *McDonald's*, 152–59; Emerson, *New Economics*, 9, 60.

27. KinderCare Learning Centers, Inc., "Company History," http://www.fundinguniverse.com/company-histories/kindercare-learning-centers-inc-history/.

28. Elizabeth Waldman, "Labor Force Statistics from a Family Perspective," *Monthly Labor Review* (December 1983): 16–20, http://www.bls.gov/opub/mlr/1983/12/art2full.pdf.

29. Bianchi and Spain, *American Women*, 227. Data for 1965 were for children of ever-married mothers working full time; data after 1982 were for all mothers of any marital status.

30. US Census Bureau, "Who's Minding the Kids? Child Care Arrangements: Spring 2010," http://www.census.gov/hhes/childcare/data/sipp/2010/tables.html. Between 1977 and 2010 the percentage of children being cared for in their own homes by a nonrelative, i.e., a nanny, never exceeded 6 percent of all children of employed mothers. David M. Blau, *The Child Care Problem: An Economic Analysis* (New York: Russell Sage Foundation, 2001), 20; US Census Bureau, "Who's Minding the Kids? Child Care Arrangements: Winter 2002," http://www.census.gov/hhes/childcare/data/sipp/2002/tables.html.

31. Roger Neugebauer, "For Profit Child Care: Four Decades of Growth," *Exchange* (January/February 2006), http://www.childcareexchange.com/library/5016722.pdf.

32. Bob Benson, "A Capsule History of For-Profit Child Care," *Child Care Information Exchange* 108 (March/April 1996): 67–68, http://www.childcareexchange.com/catalog/product/a-capsule-history-of-for-profit-child-care/5010867/.

33. "15,000 Books . . . Ten States . . . and Seven Countries: KinderCare 'Read, Share, Give' Campaign Promotes Early Reading," accessed April 18, 2014, http://www.kindercare.com/about-us/press-releases/.

34. Roger Neugebauer, "Looking Back: Events That Have Shaped Our Current Child Care Delivery System," *Child Care Information Exchange* 135 (September/October 2000): 35–38, http://www.childcareexchange.com/catal og/product/looking-back-events-that-have-shaped-our-current-child-care-delivery-system/5013535/.

35. Suzanne M. Bianchi et al., "Intergenerational Ties: Theories, Trends, and Challenges," in *Intergenerational Caregiving*, ed. Alan Booth et al. (Washington, DC: Urban Institute Press, 2008), 3–43.

36. Ruth Von Behren, "Adult Day Care: A Decade of Growth," *Perspectives on Aging* 18 (1989): 14–19.

37. The MetLife Mature Market Institute, "The MetLife National Study of Adult Day Services, October 2010," pp. 14, 15, http://www.tn.gov/human serv/adfam/ADS_Study.pdf; Centers for Disease Control and Prevention, "Long-Term Care Services in the United States: 2013 Overview," series 3, no. 37, http://cdc.gov.

38. MetLife, 4.

39. Ibid., 22.

40. Andrew Scharlach and Sandra Boyd, "Caregiving and Employment: Results of an Employee Survey," *Gerontologist* 29 (1989): 382–87; for similar strains on women caring for people with Alzheimer's, see Clifton Barber and B. Kay Pasley, "Family Care of Alzheimer's Patients: The Role of Gender and Generational Relationship on Caregiver Outcomes," *Journal of Applied Gerontology* 14 (June 1995): 172–92.

41. Robyn Stone, Gail Lee Cafferata, and Judith Sangl, "Caregivers of the Frail Elderly: A National Profile," *Gerontologist* 27 (1987): 616–26.

42. Eleanor Palo Stoller, "Parental Caregiving by Adult Children," *Journal of Marriage and the Family* 45, no. 4 (November 1983): 851–58.

43. Laura Gitlin et al., "Enhancing Quality of Life of Families Who Use Adult Day Services: Short- and Long-Term Effects of the Adult Day Services Plus Program," *Gerontologist* 46 (2006): 630–39.

44. Ibid.; Marina Bastawrous, Monique A. Gignic, Moira K. Kapral, and Jill I. Cameron, "Adult Daughters Providing Post-Stroke Care to a Parent: A Qualitative Study of the Impact that Role Overload has on Lifestyle, Participation, and Family Relationships," *Clinical Rehabilitation* 29, no. 6 (June 2015): 592–600; Shannon Jarrott et al., "Effects of Adult Day Service Programs on Time Usage by Employed and Non-Employed Caregivers," *Journal of Applied Gerontology* 19 (2000): 371–88; Evanne Juratovac and Jaclene A. Zauszniewski, "Full-Time Employed and a Family Caregiver: A Profile of Women's Workload, Effort, and Health," *Women's Health Issues* 24, no. 2 (March-April 2014): e187–e196; Steven Zarit et al., "Stress Reduction for Family Caregivers: Effects of Adult Day Care Use," *Journal of Gerontology* 53B, no. 5 (1998): S267–S277; see also the National Adult Day Services Association, http://www.nasda.org.

45. MetLife, 11.

46. "History of Hospice Care," National Hospice and Palliative Care Organization, http://www.nhpco.org/history-hospice-care.

47. Cathy Siebold, *The Hospice Movement: Easing Death's Pains* (New York: Twayne, 1992).

48. "About NHPCO," National Hospice and Palliative Care Organization, http://www.nhpco.org/about-nhpco.

49. The data for hospice providers do not indicate whether the care is delivered in a patient's home or at a facility; therefore I have not included hospices in the graph in fig. 3. National Hospice and Palliative Care Organization, "NHPCO's Facts and Figures: Hospice Care in America, 2013 Edition," http://www.nhpco. org/sites/default/files/public/Statistics_Research/2013_Facts_Figures.pdf; Centers for Disease Control and Prevention, "Long Term Care Services," http://www.cdc. gov/nchs/data/nsltcp/long_term_care_services_2013.pdf.

50. Daphne Spain, *How Women Saved the City* (Minneapolis: University of Minnesota Press, 2001), chap. 4.

51. Jo Freeman, "The Women's Liberation Movement: Its Origins, Structures, and Ideals," 1971, Documents from the Women's Liberation Movement, Special Collections Library, Duke University, http://library.duke.edu/rubenstein/scriptorium/ wlm/womlib.

52. Author's interview with Simone Wallace, Los Angeles, February 12, 2010.

53. More than one hundred women's centers existed by 1973. Carol Shapiro, *How to Organize a Multi-Service Women's Center* (New York: Women's Action Alliance, 1973), 49–60.

54. Verta Taylor and Nancy Whittier, "Collective Identity in Social Movement Communities: Lesbian Feminist Mobilization," in *Frontiers in Social Movement Theory*, ed. Aldon Morris and Carol McClurg Mueller (New Haven, CT: Yale University Press, 1992), 104–29.

55. Sara M. Evans and Harry C. Boyte, *Free Spaces: The Sources of Democratic Change in America* (Chicago: University of Chicago Press, 1992), 17.

56. Margaret Kohn, *Radical Space: Building the House of the People* (Ithaca, NY: Cornell University Press, 2003), 7–8.

57. David M. Smith, "Moral Aspects of Place," *Planning Theory* 6 (2007): 7–15.

58. Robert D. Sack, *A Geographical Guide to the Real and the Good* (London: Routledge, 2003), ix.

59. For a comprehensive summary of successful efforts to incorporate women into historic preservation, see Gail Lee Dubrow and Jennifer B. Goodman, eds., *Restoring Women's History through Historic Preservation* (Baltimore: Johns Hopkins University Press, 2003). See also Laura Pulido, Laura Barraclough, and Wendy Cheng, *A People's Guide to Los Angeles* (Berkeley: University of California Press, 2012), which discusses Sisterhood Bookstore on p. 212.

60. Henri Lefebvre, *Writings on Cities*, trans. Eleonore Kofman and Elizabeth Lebas (Oxford: Blackwell, 1996), 147–59.

61. Denise Lawrence and Setha Low, "The Built Environment and Spatial Form," *Annual Reviews in Anthropology* 19 (1990): 453–505; Margaret Rodman, "Empowering Place: Multilocality and Multivocality," *American Anthropologist* 94 (1992): 640–56; Michel de Certeau, *The Practice of Everyday Life*, trans. Steven F. Rendall (Berkeley: University of California Press, 1984).

62. Thomas F. Gieryn, "A Space for Place in Sociology," *Annual Review of Sociology* 26 (2000): 463–96.

63. "Anti-abortion Violence Dots Florida's Past," *Ocala Star Banner*, April 16, 1989, NOW Archives, Schlesinger Library, Radcliffe Institute, Harvard University, Collection MC 496, carton 214, folder 4 (hereafter cited as NOW archives).

64. "Clinics Vow to Survive Operation Rescue Siege," *USA Today*, October 7, 1988, NOW Archives, collection MC 496, carton 214, folder 4.

65. "Abortion Foes' Headquarters Shut," *USA Today*, February 1, 1990, NOW Archives, collection MC 496, carton 214, folder 6.

66. Joe Stumpe and Monica Davey, "Abortion Doctor Slain by Gunman in Kansas Church," *New York Times*, June 1, 2009.

67. Monica Davey, "Kansas Abortion Clinic Operated by Doctor Who Was Killed Closes Permanently," *New York Times*, June 11, 2009.

68. Jill Filipovic, "How A New Generation of Activists Is Trying to Make Abortion Moral," *The Washington Post* (June 12, 2015), https://www.washington post.com/opinions/reclaiming-abortion/2015/06/12/310b2204-0f8e-11e5-a0dc-2b6f404ff5cf_story.html.

69. "States Enact Record Number of Abortion Restrictions in First Half of 2011," Guttmacher Institute, July 13, 2011, www.guttmacher.org/media/inthe news/2011/07/13/index.html.

70. National Abortion Rights Action League, accessed May 30, 2012, http://www.prochoiceamerica.org.

71. "State Policy Trends: Abortion and Contraception in the Crosshairs," Guttmacher Institute, April 13, 2012, http://www.guttmacher.org/media/inthe news/2011/07/13/index.html.

72. Tara Culp-Ressler, "Radical Personhood Initiatives Fail in States Across the Country," *ThinkProgress*, July 5, 2012, http://thinkprogress.org/health/2012/07/05/511421/radical-personhood-initiatives-fail-in-states-across-the-country/; Editorial, "The 'Personhood' Initiative," *The New York Times*, October 27, 2011, http://www.nytimes.com/2011/10/28/opinion/the-personhood-initiative.html?_r=0; Jason Millman, "North Dakota Could Approve the Country's First Embryonic Personhood Law Today," *The Washington Post*, November 4, 2014, http://www.washingtonpost

.com/blogs/wonkblog/wp/2014/11/04/north-dakota-could-approve-the-countrys-first-embryonic-personhood-law-today/.

73. Lori Moore, "Rep. Todd Akin: The Statement and the Reaction," *New York Times*, August 20, 2012, http://www.nytimes.com/2012/08/21/us/politics/rep-todd-akin-legitimate-rape-statement-and-reaction.html?_r=1&ref=sexcrimes.

74. Rosalind Helderman, "On Abortion, GOP Platform Omits Details," *Washington Post*, August 22, 2012: A6.

75. "Trends in Abortion in the United States, 1973–2008," Guttmacher Institute, January 2011, http://www.guttmacher.org/presentations/trends.pdf; "Fact Sheet: Induced Abortion in the United States," Guttmacher Institute, July 2014, http://www.guttmacher.org/pubs/fb_induced_abortion.html.

76. On the right to the city, see Henri Lefebvre, *Writings on Cities*, 147–59; and Don Mitchell, *The Right to the City: Social Justice and the Fight for Public Space* (New York: Guilford Press, 2003).

77. Mitchell, *Right to the City*, 29, 148.

78. Lefebvre, *Writings on Cities*, 147–59; see also Mark Purcell, "Excavating Lefebvre: The Right to the City and Its Urban Politics of the Inhabitant," *Geo-Journal* 58 (2002): 99–108. For examples of another minority group asserting its right to the city, see Christina M. Jimenez, "Performing Their Right to the City: Political Uses of Public Space in a Mexican City, 1880–1910s," *Urban History* 33 (2006): 435–56.

79. Tovi Fenster, "The Right to the Gendered City: Different Formations of Belonging in Everyday Life," *Journal of Gender Studies* 14 (November 2005): 217–31; see also Elizabeth Wilson, *The Sphinx in the City: Urban Life, the Control of Disorder, and Women* (Berkeley: University of California Press, 1991).

80. Thomas Bender, "Cities and Citizenship," in *The Unfinished City: New York and the Metropolitan Idea*, ed. Thomas Bender (New York: New Press, 2002), 199–217.

81. Gerda R. Wekerle, "Women's Rights to the City: Feminist Spaces of a Pluralistic Citizenship," in *Democracy, Citizenship, and the Global City*, ed. Engin F. Isin (London: Routledge, 2000), 203.

82. Leonore Davidoff, "Regarding Some 'Old Husbands' Tales': Public and Private in Feminist History," in *Feminism: The Public and the Private*, ed. Joan B. Landes (New York: Oxford University Press, 1998), 165.

83. T. H. Marshall, *Citizenship and Social Class* (Cambridge: Cambridge University Press, 1950), 10–11, 15.

84. Author's telephone interview with Gilda Bruckman, September 18, 2013.

85. Evans and Boyte, *Free Space*, 69.

86. Martha Nussbaum, "Promoting Women's Capabilities," in *Global Tensions: Challenges and Opportunities in the World Economy*, ed. Lourdes Benería and S. Bisnath (New York: Routledge, 2003), 241–56; Amartya Sen, *Development as Freedom* (New York: Knopf, 1999).

87. Ruth Lister, *Citizenship: Feminist Perspectives*, 2nd ed. (New York: New York University Press, 2003), 5.

88. Lister, *Citizenship*, 113.

89. Young identifies oppressed groups as those that experience exploitation, marginalization, powerlessness, cultural imperialism, and violence. Iris Marion Young,

Justice and the Politics of Difference (Princeton, NJ: Princeton University Press, 1990), 48–63, 161, 162.

90. Nancy Fraser, "Rethinking the Public Sphere: A Contribution to the Critique of Actually Existing Democracy," in *The Phantom Public Sphere*, ed. Bruce Robbins (Minneapolis: University of Minnesota Press, 1993), 14–15; Nancy Fraser, *Unruly Practices: Power, Discourse, and Gender in Contemporary Social Theory* (Minneapolis: University of Minnesota Press, 1989), 113–43.

91. Carole Pateman, "The Patriarchal Welfare State," in *Democracy and the Welfare State*, ed. A. Gutmann (Princeton, NJ: Princeton University Press, 1988), 238–239, quoted in Ann Shola Orloff, "Gender and the Social Rights of Citizenship: The Comparative Analysis of Gender Relations and Welfare States," *American Sociological Review* 58 (June 1993): 308. See also Lynn A. Staeheli and Susan E. Clarke, "Gender, Place, and Citizenship," in *Gender in Urban Research*, ed. Judith A. Garber and Robyne S. Turner (Thousand Oaks, CA: Sage Publications, 1995), 16–17; Lister, *Citizenship*, 138–41.

92. Orloff, "Gender and the Social Rights of Citizenship," 315.

93. Ruth Lister, "Women, Economic Dependency, and Citizenship," *Journal of Social Policy* 19 (October 1990): 464.

94. Rannveig Traustadóttir, "Disability Reform and Women's Caring Work" in *Care Work: Gender, Labor, and the Welfare State*, ed. Madonna Harrington Meyer (New York: Routledge, 2000), 269.

95. Evelyn Nakano Glenn, "Creating a Caring Society," *Contemporary Sociology* 29 (January 2000): 84–94.

96. Joan Tronto, "Care as the Work of Citizens: A Modest Proposal," in *Women and Citizenship*, ed. Marilyn Friedman (Oxford: Oxford University Press, 2005), 142.

97. Glenn, "Creating a Caring Society," 84–94.

98. Deborah Stone, "Why We Need a CARE movement," *Nation*, March 13, 2000, 15; see also Nancy Folbre and Julie A. Nelson, "For Love or Money—or Both?" *Journal of Economic Perspectives* 14 (Fall 2000): 123–40.

99. Bryan S. Turner, *Citizenship and Capitalism: The Debate over Reformism* (London: Allen & Unwin, 1986), chap. 4.

100. Occupy Wall Street, accessed April 26, 2014, http://www.occupywallst.org/.

101. Amy Goodman, "Cornel West on Occupy Wall Street: It's the Makings of a U.S. Autumn Responding to the Arab Spring," September 29, 2011, http://www.democracynow.org/blog/2011/9/29/cornel_west_on_occupy_wall_street.

102. Mattathias Schwartz, "Map: How Occupy Wall Street Chose Zuccotti Park," November 21, 2011, http://www.newyorker.com/online/blogs/newsdesk/2011/11/occupy-wall-street-map.html.

103. Harold Wickliffe Rose, *The Colonial Houses of Worship in America* (New York: Hastings House, 1963).

104. Cheryl Janifer LaRoche, *Free Black Communities and the Underground Railroad* (Urbana: University of Illinois Press, 2014).

105. Judith Wellman, *The Road to Seneca Falls: Elizabeth Cady Stanton and the First Woman's Rights Conference* (Urbana: University of Illinois Press, 2004), 189.

106. Ruth Bordin, *Woman and Temperance: The Quest for Power and Liberty, 1873–1900* (New Brunswick, NJ: Rutgers University Press, 1990), 4, 15–20.

107. Jean Bethke Elshtain, *Jane Addams and the Dream of American Democracy* (New York: Basic Books, 2002), 72.

108. Daphne Spain, *How Women Saved the City*.

109. Norman I. Fainstein and Susan S. Fainstein, *Urban Political Movements: The Search for Power by Minority Groups in American Cities* (Englewood Cliffs, NJ: Prentice-Hall, 1974); Sara Evans, *Personal Politics: The Roots of Women's Liberation in the Civil Rights Movement and the New Left* (New York: Random House, 1979).

110. Brownmiller, *In Our Time*, 30.

111. Jo Freeman, "The Women's Liberation Movement: Its Origin, Structures, and Ideals," http://library.duke.edu/rubenstein/scriptorium/wlm/womlib/.

112. Herbert Aptheker, *Abolitionism: A Revolutionary Movement* (Boston: Twayne, 1989), 77–93.

113. Bordin, *Woman and Temperance*; Raymond Calkins, *Substitutes for the Saloon: An Investigation Originally Made for the Committee of Fifty*, 2nd ed. (Boston: Houghton Mifflin, 1919; Kessinger Publishing Reprint); Janet Zollinger Giele, *Two Paths to Women's Equality: Temperance, Suffrage, and the Origins of Modern Feminism* (New York: Twayne, 1995).

114. In 1973 Joanne Parrent and Valerie Angers founded the first Feminist Federal Credit Union (FFCU) in Detroit. The credit union started in their home and eventually moved into larger quarters downtown in the Women's City Club of Detroit. The Detroit FFCU became the model for feminist credit unions in Boston, Dallas, Los Angeles, New Haven, and San Diego. Interview with Joanne Parrent, Los Angeles, March 26, 2010. The Woman's Building in Los Angeles and New York City's Artists in Residence (A.I.R.) Gallery were models for feminist art collectives in Philadelphia, Chapel Hill, Chicago, Boulder, and Minneapolis. Between 1972 and 1977 at least twelve major women's cooperative galleries were operating. See Joanna Inglot, *WARM: A Feminist Art Collective in Minnesota* (Minneapolis: University of Minnesota Press for Weisman Art Museum, 2007), 6–13.

115. Maureen Flanagan, *Seeing With Their Hearts: Chicago Women and the Vision of the Good City, 1871–1933* (Princeton, NJ: Princeton University Press, 2002); Spain, *How Women Saved the City*.

116. David Cotter, Joan M. Hermsen, and Reeve Vanneman, "The End of the Gender Revolution? Gender Role Attitudes from 1977 to 2008," *American Journal of Sociology* 117, no. 1 (July 2011): 259–89.

117. Lister, *Citizenship*, 74–75.

118. *Monthly Extract: An Irregular Periodical* 1, no. 2 (October–November 1972): 2, Southern California Library, Los Angeles, Los Angeles Women's Liberation Collection, 1970–76, MSS 023, carton 1, folder 8.

119. Kay Anderson, "Engendering Race Research: Unsettling the Self-Other Dichotomy," in *Bodyspace: Destabilizing Geographies of Gender and Sexuality*, ed. Nancy Duncan (London: Routledge, 1996); Winifred Breines, *The Trouble between Us: An Uneasy History of White and Black Women in the Feminist Movement* (Oxford: Oxford University Press, 2006); Elsa Barkley Brown, "What Has Happened Here: The Politics of Difference in Women's History and Feminist Politics," in *The Second Wave: A Reader in Feminist Theory*, ed. Linda Nicholson (New York: Routledge, 1997). For a history of class relations, see Dorothy Sue Cobble, "Recapturing Working-Class Feminism: Union Women in the Postwar Era" in *Not June Cleaver: Women and Gender in Postwar America, 1945–1960*, ed. Joanne Meyerowitz (Philadelphia: Temple University Press, 1994).

120. Roth, *Separate Roads*, chaps. 3 and 4; Becky Thompson, "Multiracial Feminism: Recasting the Chronology of Second Wave Feminism," *Feminist Studies* 28 (Summer 2002): 337–60.

121. Author's interview with Sandra Serrano Sewell, Los Angeles, February 23, 2010.

122. Rosalyn Baxandall, "Re-visioning the Women's Liberation Movement's Narrative: Early Second Wave African American Feminists," *Feminist Studies* 27 (2001): 225–45; Roth, *Separate Roads*.

123. See Sarah J. Hautzinger, *Violence in the City of Women: Police and Batterers in Bahia, Brazil* (Berkeley: University of California Press, 2007), for a discussion of women's police stations in Brazil and India established to address the high incidence of wife battering in those countries. See also "Violence against Women," chap. 6 in United Nations, *The World's Women 2010: Trends and Statistics*, http://unstats.un.org/unsd/demographic/products/Worldswomen/WW2010pub.htm.

1. Feminist Practice

1. Herbert Blumer, "Collective Behavior" in *New Outline of the Principles of Sociology*, ed. Alfred McClung Lee (New York: Barnes and Noble, 1951), 165–220; Neil J. Smelser, *Theory of Collective Behavior* (New York: Free Press, 1962); Ralph H. Turner and Lewis M. Killian, *Collective Behavior* (Englewood Cliffs, NJ: Prentice-Hall, 1959).

2. Hank Johnston, Enrique Larana, and Joseph R. Gusfield, "Identities, Grievances, and New Social Movements" in *New Social Movements: From Ideology to Identity*, ed. Hank Johnston, Enrique Larana, and Joseph R. Gusfield (Philadelphia: Temple University Press, 1994), 3–35.

3. Margaret Benson, "The Political Economy of Women's Liberation," *Monthly Review* 21, no. 4 (September 1969), reprinted by New England Free Press, Somerville, MA.

4. Verta Taylor and Nancy E. Whittier, "Collective Identity in Social Movement Communities" in *Frontiers in Social Movement Theory*, ed. Aldon Morris and Carol McClurg Mueller (New Haven, CT: Yale University Press, 1992), 111.

5. Johnston, Larana, and Gusfield, "Identities," 7–8.

6. Jo Freeman, "No More Miss America! (1968–69)," http://www.jofreeman.com/photos/MissAm1969.html.

7. Frances Fox Piven and Richard A. Cloward, *Poor People's Movements: Why They Succeed, How They Fail* (New York: Vintage Books, 1977), xix–40.

8. Rita J. Simon and Jean M. Landis, "The Polls—A Report: Women's and Men's Attitudes about a Woman's Place and Role," *Public Opinion Quarterly* 53 (Summer 1989): 265–76.

9. Ibid. As it turned out, public opinion became swiftly more egalitarian in the 1970s and 1980s, then stagnated in the 1990s before returning to an increase in the early twenty-first century. In 2008, a little more than one-third of the population believed that women should take sole responsibility for the home and family. David Cotter, Joan M. Hermsen, Reeve Vanneman, "The End of the Gender Revolution? Gender Role Attitudes from 1977 to 2008," *American Journal of Sociology* 117, no. 1 (July 2011): 259–89. Using General Social Survey data, the authors find that gender role attitudes have changed less since the mid-1990s than during the 1970s and 1980s.

10. Scott Nesbit, Robert K. Nelson, Maurie McInnis, "Visualizing the Richmond Slave Trade," http://dsl.richmond.edu/civilwar/slavemarket.html.

11. Cheryl Janifer LaRoche, *Free Black Communities and the Underground Railroad* (Urbana: University of Illinois Press, 2014), 133.

12. Ibid., 32, 133–36.

13. Reynolds Farley and Walter R. Allen, *The Color Line and the Quality of Life in America* (New York: Russell Sage Foundation, 1987), 104–16. The Pulitzer Prize–winning journalist Isabel Wilkerson reveals the compelling stories of those who left, and the lives they created, in *The Warmth of Other Suns: The Epic Story of America's Great Migration* (New York: Random House, 2010).

14. Herbert Aptheker, *Abolitionism: A Revolutionary Movement* (Boston: Twayne, 1989).

15. Alice Rossi, ed., *The Feminist Papers: From Adams to De Beauvoir* (New York: Columbia University Press, 1973), 241–42.

16. Judith Wellman, *The Road to Seneca Falls: Elizabeth Cady Stanton and the First Woman's Rights Convention* (Urbana: University of Illinois Press, 2004), 189.

17. Rossi, *The Feminist Papers*, 247.

18. Ibid., 249.

19. Sheridan Harvey, "Marching for the Vote: Remembering the Woman Suffrage Parade of 1913," *The Women's History Resource Guide* (Washington, DC: Library of Congress), http://www.loc.gov/loc/lcib/9803/suffrage.html.

20. Ruth Bordin, *Woman and Temperance: The Quest for Power and Liberty, 1873–1900* (New Brunswick, NJ: Rutgers University Press, 1990), xv.

21. Norman H. Clark, *Deliver Us from Evil: An Interpretation of American Prohibition* (New York: W. W. Norton & Company, 1976); Joseph R. Gusfield, *Symbolic Crusade: Status Politics and the American Temperance Movement* (Urbana: University of Illinois Press, 1963); W. J. Rorabaugh, *The Alcoholic Republic: An American Tradition* (Oxford: Oxford University Press, 1979).

22. Gusfield, *Symbolic Crusade*, 41, 48.

23. Bordin, *Woman and Temperance*, 3; Frances Elizabeth Willard, *Woman and Temperance: Or, the Work and Workers of the Woman's Christian Temperance Union*, 4th ed. (Hartford, CT: Park Publishing Co., 1883).

24. Women in Ohio improvised the first marching prayer vigils from churches to establishments selling alcohol in 1873. Willard, *Woman and Temperance*, 53–64.

25. Raymond Calkins and Francis G. Peabody, *Substitutes for the Saloon*, 2nd ed. (Boston: Houghton Mifflin, 1919), 1–24, Kessinger Publishing Legacy Reprints.

26. Willard, *Woman and Temperance*, 65.

27. Ibid., 644.

28. Bordin, *Woman and Temperance*, xiv.

29. Jane Addams, *Twenty Years at Hull-House* (New York: Signet Books, 1961; originally published 1910), 77–78.

30. Robert A. Woods and Albert J. Kennedy, eds., *Handbook of Settlements* (New York: Arno Press, 1970; originally published 1911).

31. Daphne Spain, *How Women Saved the City* (Minneapolis: University of Minnesota Press, 2001), 70.

32. Jean Bethke Elshtain, *The Jane Addams Reader* (New York: Basic Books, 2002), xix.

33. Addams, *Twenty Years*, 114.

34. Spain, *How Women Saved the City*.

35. Carol Downer, e-mail message to author, March 19, 2014.

36. Aldon D. Morris, *The Origins of the Civil Rights Movement: Black Communities Organizing for Change* (New York: Free Press, 1984), 88.

37. Ibid., 1–11, 87, 137.

38. Jeff Wiltse, *Contested Waters: A Social History of Swimming Pools in America* (Chapel Hill: University of North Carolina Press, 2007).

39. Rhoda Lois Blumberg, *Civil Rights: The 1960s Freedom Struggle* (Boston: Twayne, 1984), xvii–xxiii.

40. Ibid., 106.

41. Charles Connerly, *The Most Segregated City in America: City Planning and Civil Rights in Birmingham, 1920–1980* (Charlottesville: University of Virginia Press, 2005); David M. P. Freund, *Colored Property: State Policy and White Racial Politics in Suburban America* (Chicago: University of Chicago Press, 2007).

42. Blumberg, *Civil Rights*; Robert Weisbrot, *Freedom Bound: A History of America's Civil Rights Movement* (New York: Norton, 1990); Morris, *The Origins*; Connerly, *The Most Segregated City*. In June 2013, the Supreme Court overturned a key provision of the Voting Rights Act that required federal oversight of states wishing to change voting rules if those states had a history of discriminating against minority voters. Adam Liptak, "Supreme Court Invalidates Key Part of Voting Rights Act," *New York Times*, June 25, 2013, http://www.nytimes.com/2013/06/26/us/supreme-court-ruling.html?pagewanted%253Dall&_r=0.

43. *Report of the National Advisory Commission on Civil Disorders* (New York: New York Times Company, 1968), 1.

44. Sara Evans, *Personal Politics: The Roots of Women's Liberation in the Civil Rights Movement and the New Left* (New York: Random House, 1979).

45. Transcript of the NOW "Herstory" session at the January 1992 NOW Global Feminist Conference, p. 13, Betty Friedan Papers, Schlesinger Library, Radcliffe Institute, Harvard University. Collection MC577, carton 1, file 8.

46. Suzanne M. Bianchi and Daphne Spain, *American Women in Transition* (New York: Russell Sage Foundation, 1986), 141. Data for this time period were for married mothers only. Elizabeth Waldman, "Labor Force Statistics from a Family Perspective," *Monthly Labor Review* (December 1983): 16–20, http://www.bls.gov/opub/mlr/1983/12/art2full.pdf.

47. Stephanie Coontz, *A Strange Stirring: The Feminine Mystique and American Women at the Dawn of the 1960s* (New York: Basic Books, 2011), xv.

48. Linda Jean Carpenter and R. Vivian Acosta, "Title IX—Two for One: A Starter Kit of the Law and a Snapshot of Title IX's Impact," *Cleveland State Law Review* 55 (2007): 503–12.

49. Bernice Resnick Sandler, "Title IX: How We Got It and What a Difference It Made," *Cleveland State Law Review* 55 (2007): 473–89.

50. Richard Pérez-Peña, "College Groups Connect to Fight Sexual Assault," *The New York Times*, March 19, 2013; Richard Pérez-Peña and Kate Taylor, "Fight Against Sexual Assaults Holds Colleges to Account," *The New York Times*, May 3, 2014.

51. Maren Lockwood Carden, *The New Feminist Movement* (New York: Russell Sage Foundation, 1974); Jo Freeman, *The Politics of Women's Liberation: A Case Study*

of an Emerging Social Movement and Its Relation to the Policy Process (New York: Longman, 1975).

52. Jo Freeman, "The Women's Liberation Movement: Its Origins, Structures, and Ideals," http://library.duke.edu/rubenstein/scriptorium/wlm/womlib/.

53. Transcript of the NOW "Herstory" session.

54. Carden, *The New Feminist Movement*, 104.

55. National Organization for Women Statement of Purpose, in Toni Carabillo, Judith Meuli, and June Bundy Csida, *Feminist Chronicles 1953–1993* (Los Angeles: Women's Graphics, 1993), 161.

56. Carabillo, Meuli, and Csida, "Task Force on the Family," *Feminist Chronicles*, 201–4.

57. Robin Morgan, ed., *Sisterhood Is Powerful: An Anthology of Writings from the Women's Liberation Movement* (New York: Vintage, 1970), 512.

58. http://www.equalrightsamendment.org.

59. Barbara Miller Solomon, *In the Company of Educated Women: A History of Women and Higher Education in America* (New Haven, CT: Yale University Press, 1985), 44.

60. Georgina Hickey, "Barred from the Barroom: Second Wave Feminists and Public Accommodations in U.S. Cities," *Feminist Studies* 34 (Fall 2008): 382–408.

61. Baxandall and Gordon, *Dear Sisters*, 11.

62. "Court Rejects Want Ad Appeal," *Pittsburgh Press*, October 9, 1973.

63. Jo Anne Levine, "Landmark Bias Case Settlement," *Washington Post*, September 9, 1973.

64. Carden, *The New Feminist Movement*, 105.

65. Minutes of the First Meeting, Southern California Chapter, National Organization of [*sic*] Women, December 5, 1967, NOW archives, Schlesinger Library, Radcliffe Institute, Harvard University, collection MC496, box 169, file 38 (hereafter cited as NOW Archives).

66. Blue Chip stamps, like S & H Green Stamps, were distributed by gas stations and grocery stores in proportion to the amount of the sale. Customers would paste the stamps into books and redeem the books for a variety of items. As a fund-raising venture, it was about as effective as a bake sale. Minutes of the Southern California Chapter, National Organization for Women, General Membership Meeting, April 1, 1967 and April 8, 1969, NOW Archives, collection MC496, box 169, file 38.

67. Boston NOW, Highlights of Accomplishments, n.d., NOW Archives, collection MC496, box 170, file 6.

68. U.S. Department of Health, Education, and Welfare, "Abortion Surveillance Report Annual Summary 1970," table 21.

69. Dear NOW member, from fundraising chairman Joan B. Mattuck, August 12, 1970, NOW Archives, collection MC496, box 170, file 6.

70. Carol Mueller, "Conflict Networks and the Origins of Women's Liberation," in Johnston, Larana, and Gusfield, *New Social Movements: From Ideology to Identity*, 234–63.

71. David A. Snow and Robert D. Benford, "Ideology, Frame Resonance, and Participant Mobilization" in *From Structure to Action: Comparing Social Movement Research across Cultures*, ed. Bert Klandermans, Hanspeter Kriesi, and Sidney Tarrow (Greenwich, CT: JAI Press, 1988), 197–217.

72. Johnston, Larana, and Gusfield, "Identities," 18–19.

73. Roberta Salper, "U.S. Government Surveillance and the Women's Liberation Movement, 1968–1973: A Case Study," *Feminist Studies* 34 (Fall 2008): 445.

74. Baxandall and Gordon, *Dear Sisters*, 12. For a comprehensive analysis of the multiple origins of the women's movement written during that era, see Jo Freeman, *The Politics of Women's Liberation*.

75. "Dear Sisters," letter, January 22, 1970, National Abortion Rights Action League Papers, Schlesinger Library, Radcliffe Institute, Harvard University, collection MC313, carton 3.

76. Bread and Roses, Outreach Leaflet, in Baxandall and Gordon, *Dear Sisters*, 35.

77. Ann Hunter Popkin, "Bread and Roses: An Early Movement in the Development of Socialist-Feminism" (Ph.D. diss., Brandeis University, 1978), 92, 93, 129, 130.

78. Author's telephone conversation with Gilda Bruckman, September 18, 2013.

79. Popkin, "Bread and Roses."

80. Suzanne Staggenborg, "Can Feminist Organizations Be Effective?" in *Feminist Organizations: Harvest of the New Women's Movement*, ed. Myra Marx Ferree and Patricia Yancey Martin (Philadelphia: Temple University Press, 1995), 339–55; Jo Freeman, "Trashing: The Dark Side of Sisterhood," 1976, Chicago Women's Liberation Union archives, http://www.cwluherstory.com/trashing-the-dark-side-of-sisterhood.html.

81. Popkin, "Bread and Roses," 136–38.

82. Jo Freeman, "The Tyranny," 75.

83. *The Monthly Extract: An Irregular Periodical* 1, no. 2 (October–November 1972): 1, Southern California Library, Los Angeles Women's Liberation Collection 1970–1976, MSS023, box 1, file 8.

84. "NOW's Child Care Accomplishments," n.d., NOW Archives, MS Collection MC496, carton 201, file 52.

85. Carol Shapiro, "How to Organize a Child Care Center" (New York: Women's Action Alliance, 1973). Obtained from the library of the Cambridge Women's Center, Cambridge, MA.

86. The Women's Union Child Care Collective, "Notes on Child Care," n.d., Papers of Winifred Breines, Schlesinger Library, Radcliffe Institute, Harvard University, collection 89-M17, carton 1.

87. Louise Gross and Phyllis MacEwan, "On Day Care," *Women: A Journal of Liberation* (Winter 1970), 26–29, Papers of Winifred Breines, Schlesinger Library, Radcliffe Institute, Harvard University, collection 2007-M114, carton 1.

88. Kirsten Grimstad and Susan Rennie, *The New Woman's Survival Catalog* (New York: Coward, McCann, and Geoghegan, 1973), 95.

89. Author's interview with Kit Kollenberg, February 25, 2010, Los Angeles.

90. Grimstad and Rennie, *The New Woman's Survival Catalog*, 95.

91. Playgroup History, http://www.ourplaygroup.org/about.html.

92. Winifred Breines, *The Trouble Between Us: An Uneasy History of White and Black Women in the Feminist Movement* (New York: Oxford University Press, 2006). Brian Norman argues that the tensions between white and black feminists did not necessarily mean that their goals were in opposition. See Brian Norman, "The Consciousness-Raising Document, Feminist Anthologies, and Black Women in *Sisterhood Is Powerful*," *Frontiers: A Journal of Women Studies* 27 (2006): 9

93. Rosalyn Baxandall, "Re-Visioning the Women's Liberation Movement's Narrative: Early Second Wave African American Feminists," *Feminist Studies* 27 (Spring 2001): 225–45; Mary Ann Clawson "Looking for Feminism: Racial Dynamics and Generational Investments in the Second Wave," *Feminist Studies* 34 (Fall 2008): 526–54; Becky Thompson, "Multiracial Feminism: Recasting the Chronology of Second Wave Feminism," *Feminist Studies* 28 (Summer 2002): 337–60.

94. Gloria T. Hull, Patricia Bell Scott, and Barbara Smith, eds., *All the Women Are White, All the Blacks Are Men, But Some of Us Are Brave: Black Women's Studies* (Old Westbury, NY: The Feminist Press, 1982). The "Black Liberation Movement" was an umbrella term for the civil rights movement, the Black Panthers, black nationalism, SNCC, and other smaller groups.

95. Jo Freeman, "The Women's Liberation Movement: Its Origins, Structures, and Ideas," 1971, http://library.duke.edu/rubenstein/scriptorium/wlm/womlib/.

96. Frances M. Beal, "Double Jeopardy: To Be Black and Female," in Morgan, *Sisterhood Is Powerful*, 340–53.

97. Hull, Scott, and Smith, *All the Women Are White*.

98. Barbara J. Love, ed., *Feminists Who Changed America, 1963–1975* (Urbana: University of Illinois Press, 2006), 250.

99. *Black Woman's Manifesto* (New York: Third World Women's Alliance, n.d.), http://library.duke.edu/rubenstein/scriptorium/wlm/blkmanif/; Love, *Feminists Who Changed America*, 340.

100. Reprinted in Baxandall and Gordon, *Dear Sisters*, 37–38.

101. Susan Brownmiller, *In Our Time: Memoir of a Revolution* (New York: Dial Press, 1999), 212–14; Michele Wallace, "On the National Black Feminist Organization," in Redstocking of the Women's Liberation Movement, *Feminist Revolution* (New York: Random House, 1978), 174–75, http://scriptorium.lib.duke.edu/wlm/fem/wallace.html.

102. Brownmiller, *In Our Time*, 214–15.

103. Wallace, "On the National Black Feminist Organization," 174–75.

104. The National Black Feminist Organization's Statement of Purpose, 1973, http://www-personal.umd.umich.edu/~ppenock/doc-BlackFeminist.htm.

105. Wallace, "On the National Black Feminist Organization," 174–75.

106. Brownmiller, *In Our Time*, 215–16.

107. Author's telephone interview with Demita Frazier, former member of Combahee River Collective, June 20, 2014.

108. Quoted in Yamissette Westerbrand, "Lesbian Feminism," http://sitemaker.umich.edu/lesbian.history/lesbian_feminism.

109. Westerbrand, "Lesbian Feminism."

110. Karla Hammond, "An Interview with Audre Lorde," *American Poetry Review*, March/April 1980: 18–21, http://www.english.illinois.edu/maps/poets/g_l/lorde/feminist.htm.

111. Jo Freeman, *The Politics of Women's Liberation*, 99.

112. Radicalesbians, "The Woman-Identified Woman," in Baxandall and Gordon, *Dear Sisters*, 107–9.

113. Anonymous Realesbians, "Politicalesbians and the Women's Liberation Movement," in Baxandall and Gordon, *Dear Sisters*, 109–10.

114. Taylor and Whittier, "Collective Identity," 114.

115. Lee Schwing, "On Separatism," in Baxandall and Gordon, *Dear Sisters*, 111.

116. Taylor and Whittier, "Collective Identity," 104–29. Author's interview with Joan E. Biren, April 15, 2010, Washington, DC.

117. Charlotte Bunch, "Lesbians in Revolt," *The Furies: Lesbian/Feminist Monthly* 1 (January 1972): 8–9, http://library.duke.edu/rubenstein/scriptorium/wlm/Furies/.

118. Rita Mae Brown, *Rita Will: Memoir of a Literary Rabble-Rouser* (New York: Bantam, 1997), 267, 271. The rowhouse on 11th Street SE has been nominated for inclusion in the National Register of Historic Places. Joan Biren, e-mail message to author, July 21, 2015.

119. Ariel Levy, "Lesbian Nation," *New Yorker*, March 2, 2009, 30–37.

120. Yolanda Retter, "Lesbian Spaces in Los Angeles, 1970–90," in *Queers in Space: Communities, Public Spaces, Sites of Resistance*, ed. Gordon Brent Ingram, Anne-Marie Bouthillette, and Yoland Retter (Seattle: Bay Press, 1997), 325–37.

121. Pamela Allen, *Free Space: A Perspective on the Small Group in Women's Liberation* (New York: Times Change Press, 1970).

122. Taylor and Whittier, "Collective Identity," 112

123. Enke, *Finding the Movement*, 10–18.

124. Sandler, "Title IX," 473–89; Marcia D. Greenberger and Neena K. Chaudhry, "Worth Fighting For: 35 Years of Title IX Advocacy in the Courts, Congress, and the Federal Agencies," *Cleveland State Law Review* 55 (2007): 491–501.

2. Women's Centers

1. Munson Hall, Special Collections, University of Massachusetts library, http://www.library.umass.edu/spcoll/youmass/doku.php?id=m:munson_hall.

2. Staff of the Everywoman's Center, "Evolution of an Alternative Everywoman's Center: The First Three Years: A Herstory," Amherst: University of Massachusetts (1975): 33. Available on request from the University of Massachusetts, Amherst, Center for Women and Community.

3. Richard H. Schein, "The Place of Landscape: A Conceptual Framework for Interpreting An American Scene," *Annals of Association of American Geographers* 87 (1997): 660–68

4. Staff of the Everywoman's Center, "Evolution," 6.

5. Ray Oldenburg, *The Great Good Place: Cafes, Coffee Shops, Bookstores, Bars, Hair Salons and Other Hangouts at the Heart of a Community* (New York: Marlowe, 1999), chap. 12.

6. Anne Enke, *Finding the Movement: Sexuality, Contested Space, and Feminist Activism* (Durham, NC: Duke University Press, 2007).

7. Carol Shapiro, "How to Organize a Child Care Center" (New York: Women's Action Alliance, 1973), 7–10. Obtained from the library of the Cambridge Women's Center, Cambridge, Massachusetts.

8. Jo Freeman, "The Tyranny of Structurelessness," in *Dear Sisters: Dispatches from the Women's Liberation Movement*, ed. Rosalyn Baxandall and Linda Gordon (New York: Basic Books, 2000), 73–75.

9. New York Radical Feminists, "How to Organize a Small Consciousness-Raising Group," Women's Educational Center, Cambridge, Massachusetts, Records (M47), University Libraries, Archives and Special Collections Department, Northeastern University, Boston, Massachusetts, carton 9, folder 258 (hereafter cited as WEC Archives).

10. Shapiro, "How to Organize a Multi-Service Women's Center," 14, 49–60.

11. La Comisión Femenil Mexicana (CFM) Nacional, established in 1971, had an active Los Angeles chapter whose members determined that employment issues were of primary concern to Chicanas. They won a Department of Labor grant to create the Chicana Service Action Center (CSAC) to provide health care, employment training, and child care for Chicanas. In 1974, CSAC won Department of Education funding for two bilingual/bicultural childcare centers. Called Centro de Niños Child Development Centers, they are still in operation today. Since my focus is on the centers created by radical activists, I have excluded CFM from further discussion. CFM, by accepting federal funding, was working within the existing political system; founders of the Crenshaw and Westside Centers wanted to overthrow that system. "Herstory of Comisión Femenil Mexicana Nacional, Inc., n.d., University of California Chicano Studies Research Center, CFLA papers, collection 65, carton 1, folder 1; author's interview with Sandra Serrano-Sewell, executive director, Centro de Niños, Inc., Los Angeles, February 23, 2010.

12. Teryl Springstead of the California Feminist Federal Credit Union introduced me to the term "Joanie Appleseed." Telephone interview, February 24, 2010. Ann Herschfang adopted ForFreedom as her movement name. Susan Brownmiller, *In Our Time: Memoir of a Revolution* (New York: Dial Press, 1999), 77.

13. Joan Robins interview 1A with Dara Robinson, February 11, 1984.

14. Michelle Moravec, *In Their Own Time: Voices From the Los Angeles Feminist Movement, 1967 to 1976* (B.A. honors thesis, University of California Los Angeles, 1989), 31. In 1970 there were no legal restrictions on abortion prior to viability of the fetus in New York, nor in Alaska, Hawaii, or Washington. US Department of Health, Education, and Welfare, "Abortion Surveillance Report Annual Summary 1970," table 21.

15. Joan Robins interview 1A with Dara Robinson, February 11, 1984.

16. "The Women's Center: The Beginning," n.d., p. 3., Southern California Library, Los Angeles, Los Angeles Women's Liberation Collection 1970–1976, (Barbara Smith), MSS 023, carton 1, folder 3 (hereafter cited as Los Angeles Women's Liberation Collection).

17. Sylvia Hartman, "Women's Center Planned," n.d., Los Angeles Women's Liberation Collection, MSS 023, carton 1, folder 3.

18. Moravec, *In Their Own Time*, 127.

19. "The Women's Center: The Beginning," n.d., pp. 2–3, Los Angeles Women's Liberation Collection, (Barbara Smith), MSS 023, carton 1, folder 3.

20. Hartman, "Women's Center Planned," 2; Moravec, *In Their Own Time*, 32.

21. Hartman, "Women's Center Planned," 1.

22. Ibid., 2.

23. "The Women's Center: The Beginning," 3. UCLA had a Women's Resource Center in the "dismal Powell Library basement" that sponsored events and offered counseling. "A Place of Our Own," unsigned, *Sister*, March 1974, June Mazer Lesbian

Archives, Los Angeles. Robins and others wanted to reach women beyond the campus.

24. Joan Robins interview 1A with Dara Robinson, February 11, 1984.

25. Moravec, *In Their Own Time*, 32; Joan Robins interview 1A with Dara Robinson, February 11, 1984.

26. NOW Archives, Schlesinger Library, Radcliffe Institute, Harvard University, collection MC 496, carton 169, folder 37 (hereafter cited as NOW Archives); Carol Downer, e-mail message to author, June 6, 2014; Simone Wallace, e-mail message to author, June 17, 2014.

27. Pierce F. Lewis, "Axioms for Reading the Landscape: Some Guides to the American Scene" in *The Interpretation of Ordinary Landscapes: Geographical Essays*, ed. D. W. Meinig (Oxford: Oxford University Press, 1979), 12.

28. Carol Downer, e-mail message to author, June 6, 2014.

29. Schein, "The Place of Landscape," 660–80; Simone Wallace, e-mail message to author, June 17, 2014.

30. "The Women's Center Has a Home," untitled, 1969, NOW Archives, collection MC 496, carton 169, folder 37.

31. Simone Wallace, e-mail message to author, June 17, 2014.

32. Abigail A. Van Slyck, *Free to All: Carnegie Libraries and American Culture, 1890–1920* (Chicago: University of Chicago Press, 1995), xxi–xxii.

33. "The Women's Center: The Beginning," 4.

34. Jean Murphy, "Clearing House for L. A. Women's Lib," *Los Angeles Times*, May 24, 1970, p. D1, ProQuest Historical Newspapers: *Los Angeles Times* (1881–1989).

35. "The Women's Center: The Beginning," 4–5; Murphy, "Clearing House."

36. Simone Wallace, e-mail message to author, June 17, 2014.

37. Maria Chardon, "The State of the Movement," *Sister*, March 1974: 1–6, June Mazer Lesbian Archives, Los Angeles.

38. Author's interview with Jeanne Córdova, Los Angeles, March 17, 2010; Barbara Love, ed., *Feminists Who Changed America, 1963–1975* (Urbana: University of Illinois Press, 2006), 64.

39. In 1970 legal abortion was available in California if a physician determined the woman's or child's mental or physical health was at risk, and in cases of rape or incest. US Department of Health, Education, and Welfare, "Abortion Surveillance Report Annual Summary 1970," table 21.

40. Wes Joe, unpublished submission to Los Angeles Cultural Heritage Commission for historic designation of Sisterhood Bookstore, 2010, p. 3. Courtesy of Simone Wallace.

41. Lillian Faderman and Stuart Timmons, *Gay L.A.: A History of Sexual Outlaws, Power Politics, and Lipstick Lesbians* (New York: Basic Books, 2006), 173.

42. "The Women's Center: The Beginning," 5–6.

43. Jean Murphy, "Legal Team Will Offer Help for Woman's Lib Court Cases," *Los Angeles Times*, February 9, 1971, ProQuest Historical Newspapers: *Los Angeles Times* (1881–1986).

44. "Women's Center Will Launch Study Series," *Los Angeles Times*, January 13, 1971, p. G5, ProQuest Historical Newspapers: *Los Angeles Times* (1881–1986); admission ticket to the "Opening of the New N.O.W. Center for Women's Studies,"

NOW Los Angeles Chapter, NOW Center for Women's Studies, December 12, 1970, NOW Archives, collection MC496, carton 169, folder 37.

45. Los Angeles Chapter *NOW News*, "NOW Opens Center for Women's Studies" 2, no. 8 (November 1970): 1–7, Los Angeles Women's Liberation Collection, MSS 023, carton 1, folder 10.

46. Los Angeles Chapter *NOW News*, "NOW Center Opens," 2.

47. Chardon, "The State of the Movement."

48. Moravec, *In Their Own Time*, 32–34.

49. Nancy A. Matthews, *Confronting Rape: The Feminist Anti-Rape Movement and the State* (London: Routledge, 1994), 22.

50. Author's interview with Sherna Berger Gluck, Los Angeles, February 1, 2010.

51. "Westside Women's Center Makes a Dream Come True," *Los Angeles Times*, April 30, 1972: WS12, ProQuest Historical Newspapers: *Los Angeles Times* (1881–1986).

52. Author's interview with Sherna Berger Gluck, Los Angeles, February 1, 2010. Some tensions emerged at the Westside Center between straight and lesbian members. Gluck, a self-proclaimed "straight woman who is woman-identified," lamented straight women's inability to accept "sisters" with different sexual orientations. The center sponsored gay-straight dialogues and hosted lesbian social events, both more heavily attended by lesbian than straight women. In this regard the Westside Center was a microcosm of gay-straight conflicts in the larger women's movement. See Chardon, "The State of the Movement."

53. Moravec, *In Their Own Time*, 34.

54. Chardon, "The State of the Movement"; author's interview with Sherna Berger Gluck, Los Angeles, February 1, 2010.

55. "Women's Liberation School Opens in Los Angeles October 1971," n.d., mimeograph, Los Angeles Women's Liberation Collection, MSS 023, carton 1, folder 6.

56. "Women's Liberation School Opens."

57. "How to Start a Women's Liberation School," n.d., unsigned handwritten memo, Los Angeles Women's Liberation Collection, MSS 023, carton 1, folder 6.

58. "Possible Crenshaw Center Teachers," n.d.; untitled list, "Herstory Seminar." Both are unsigned handwritten memos, Women's Liberation Collection 1970–1976, MSS 023, carton 1, folder 6.

59. Los Angeles Chapter *NOW News* 4, no. 8 (August 1972): 7, Los Angeles Women's Liberation Collection, MSS 023, carton 1, folder 10.

60. "Women's Lib School Lists Class Topics," *Los Angeles Times*, January 16, 1972: E11; "Registration Set for Women's Lib Classes at Center," *Los Angeles Times*, June 1, 1972: 110. Both in ProQuest Historical Newspapers: *Los Angeles Times* (1881–1986). Los Angeles Chapter *NOW News* 4, no. 8 (August 1972): 7; Los Angeles Chapter *NOW News* 4, no. 10 (October 1972). Both in Los Angeles Women's Liberation Collection, MSS 023, carton 1, folder 10.

61. Los Angeles Chapter *NOW News* 4, no. 10 (October 1972), Los Angeles Women's Liberation Collection, MSS 023, carton 1, folder 10.

62. Matthews, *Confronting Rape*, 24.

63. Moravec, *In Their Own Time*, 92; Robinson, interview with Joan Robins.

64. Matthews, *Confronting Rape*, 27.

65. Vicki McNickle Rose, "Rape as a Social Problem: A Byproduct of the Women's Movement," *Social Problems* 25 (October 1977): 75–89.

66. Del Whan, "Gay Women's Service Center in LA, 1971–1972," p. 2, paper presented at "The Early History of Feminist and Lesbian Centers in L.A. (1969–1975)," November 1, 2009, June Mazer Lesbian Archives, Los Angeles.

67. Faderman and Timmons, *Gay L.A.*, 181.

68. Ibid., 185.

69. Whan, "Gay Women's Service Center," 3.

70. Ibid., 5.

71. Ibid.

72. Ibid., 6; see Faderman and Timmons, *Gay L.A.*, for a discussion of the Gay Community Services Center.

73. Joy Novak, "A New Generation of Activism: The Sudden Political Shift in Gay Activism as Seen in Event Announcements from before and after the Stonewall Riots," http://polaris.gseis.ucla.edu/jnovak/289.htm.

74. "The Early History of Feminist and Lesbian Centers in L.A. (1969–1975)," conference outline, November 1, 2009, June Mazer Lesbian Archives, Los Angeles.

75. Author's interview with Jeanne Córdova, Los Angeles, March 17, 2010.

76. Faderman and Timmons, *Gay L.A.*, 189–91.

77. Kirsten Grimstad and Susan Rennie, eds., *The New Woman's Survival Catalog* (New York: Coward, McCann, and Geoghegan, 1973), 33.

78. Faderman and Timmons, *Gay L.A.*, 186–88.

79. Author's interview with Jeanne Córdova, Los Angeles, March 17, 2010.

80. *Lesbian Tide*, October 1973, June Mazer Lesbian Archives, Los Angeles.

81. Feminists in Somerville, a working-class community adjacent to Cambridge, opened the Somerville Women's Educational Center in 1977. See Somerville Women's Educational Center, Inc., Records (M26), University Libraries, Archives and Special Collections Department, Northeastern University, Boston, Massachusetts, carton 4, folder 64.

82. Katharine L. Day and *Crimson* Staff, "Women's Group Seizes Harvard Building," *Harvard Crimson*, March 8, 1971, http://thecrimson.com/article.aspx?ref=355315.

83. "About the Women's Center," *On Our Way: The Women's Center Newsletter* 1, no. 2 (November 8, 1971): 1, http://www.cambridgewomenscenter.org/news/Our%20History_2011.pdf. The 888 Women's History Project is producing a film about the takeover. 888 Women's History Project Inc., "Left on Pearl," http://www.888womenshistory.org.

84. J. Anthony Day, "Graham Denies Alliance," *Harvard Crimson*, March 10, 1971, http://www.thecrimson.com/article.aspx?ref=355353; Judith Freedman and *Crimson* Staff, "Bust Likely at Women's Center," *Harvard Crimson*, March 13, 1971, http://www.thecrimson.com/article.aspx?ref=355393.

85. Weathermen (and women) were members of the radical left-wing Weather Underground Organization, a faction of Students for a Democratic Society (SDS). Formed in 1969 at the University of Michigan, the Weather Underground conducted domestic bombing campaigns in opposition to the US government and especially the war in Vietnam.

86. Author's telephone interview with Marsha Steinberg, February 17, 2010.

87. "About the Women's Center," *On Our Way*, 1, no. 2 (November 8, 1971): 1.

88. Ibid.

89. Katharine L. Day and *Crimson* Staff, "Women's Group Seizes Harvard Building," *Harvard Crimson*, March 8, 1971, http://thecrimson.com/article.aspx?ref=355315.

90. Author's telephone interview with Rochelle Ruthchild, August 16, 2013.

91. Author's telephone interview with Marsha Steinberg, February 17, 2010.

92. Margot R. Hornblower and *Crimson* Staff, "Women Still Hold Harvard Building," *Harvard Crimson*, March 9, 1971, http://www.thecrimson.com/article.aspx?ref=355332; Joyce Heard and *Crimson* Staff, "Harvard Obtains Injunction; Women Brace for Possible Raid," *Harvard Crimson*, March 10, 1971, http://www.thecrimson.com/article.aspx?ref=355349; "About the Women's Center," *On Our Way* 1, no. 2 (November 8, 1971): 1.

93. Mary Eisner and *Crimson* Staff, "Women Still Hold Building: Harvard Issues Statement," *Harvard Crimson*, March 12, 1971, http://www.thecrimson.com/article.aspx?ref=355374.

94. Julie K. Ellison, "Solidarity Builds in Center," *Harvard Crimson*, March 15, 1971, http://www.thecrimson.com/article.aspx?ref=355417.

95. Author's interview with Marie Kennedy, Los Angeles, January 26, 2010.

96. "Cox Gives Final Warning; Women Reiterate Demands," *Harvard Crimson*, March 15, 1971, http://www.thecrimson.com/article.aspx?ref=355416.

97. "About the Women's Center," *On Our Way* 1, no. 2 (November 8, 1971): 1.

98. Carol R. Sternhell, "Chanting Women Vacate Building to Avoid Rumored Bust by Police," *Harvard Crimson*, March 16, 1971, http://www.thecrimson.com/article.aspx?ref=355433; Samuel Z. Goldhaber and Julia T. Reed, "Attorneys Scan Photos for Evidence," *Harvard Crimson*, March 17, 1971, http://www.thecrimson.com/article.aspx?ref=355445; Katharine Day, "Women Continue Work Towards Center," *Harvard Crimson*, March 31, 1971, http://www.thecrimson.com/article.aspx?ref=355670.

99. "Articles of Organization," Women's Educational Center, Inc., WEC Archives, carton 1, folder 46.

100. Author's telephone interview with Rochelle Ruthchild, August 16, 2013; author's telephone interview with Libby Bouvier, August 20, 2013.

101. "Women's Center Projects," October 1972, WEC Archives, carton 10, folder 291.

102. Ibid.

103. Jackie, Tina, Margaret, Judy, and Irene, "Crunch Cronin," in *On Our Way: The Women's Center Newsletter* 1, no. 2. (February 22, 1972): 2, WEC Archives, carton 13, folder 448.

104. Jane de Long, *On Our Way: The Women's Center Newsletter* 1, no. 6. (Jan. 17, 1972): 1, WEC Archives, carton 13, folder 448.

105. Ibid.

106. Amber, "Proposal Number II," *On Our Way: The Women's Center Newsletter* 1, no. 7 (January 29, 1972): 3, WEC Archives, carton 13, folder 448.

107. Jackie, Tina, Margaret, Judy, and Irene, "Organization," *On Our Way: The Women's Center Newsletter* 1, no. 8 (February 22, 1972): 1, WEC Archives, carton 13, folder 448.

108. WEC Archives, carton 1, folder 46.

109. "Women's Center Projects."

110. "Core Notes on Purpose of Women's Center 10/10/74," WEC Archives, carton 3, folder 118.

111. Author's telephone interview with Libby Bouvier, August 20, 2013.

112. Linda, "The Trouble with Kids," *On Our Way: The Women's Center Newsletter* 2, no. 2 (April 10, 1972), WEC Archives, carton 13, folder 448.

113. Staff log, April 18, 1972, WEC Archives, carton 3, folder 125.

114. Author's telephone interview with Libby Bouvier, August 20, 2013.

115. "If you've been by the Women's Center lately . . . ," *On Our Way*, n.d., p. 1, WEC Archives, carton 13, folder 448.

116. "Finding Aid," WEC Archives.

117. Judy Norris, participant in panel "Second Wave Organizations and Their Offspring (The Cambridge Women's Center)" at "A Revolutionary Moment: Women's Liberation in the Late 1960s and Early 1970s" Conference, Boston University, Boston, MA: March 27–29, 2014. Personal notes available from author.

118. Members of Transition House distrusted officers' ability or willingness to keep the address secret.

119. Author's telephone interview with Libby Bouvier, August 20, 2013.

120. Staff log, April 18, 1972.

121. Ibid.

122. Ibid.

123. Author's telephone interview with Libby Bouvier, August 20, 2013.

124. Appendix C: Other Projects at the Center, n.d., WEC Archives, carton 1, folder 47; "Women's Center Projects."

125. "The Women's Center Library," June 17, 1973, WEC Archives, carton 1, folder 47.

126. Ibid.

127. "Affiliated Projects," WEC Archives, carton 10, folder 291; see also "Space," *On Our Way* 1, no. 8 (February 22, 1972): 1, WEC Archives, carton 13, folder 448.

128. Jackie, Tina, Margaret, Judy, and Irene, "Starting March 5—the Women's Center School," *On Our Way* 1, no. 8 (February 22, 1972): 2.

129. "Chicago," *The Women's Center Newsletter* 3, no. 7 (July/August 1973): 5, WEC Archives, carton 13, folder 449.

130. "Fund-Raising Proposal for the Women's School," n.d., WEC Archives, carton 9, folder 251.

131. Ibid.

132. Ibid.

133. "Chicago," *The Women's Center Newsletter* 3, no. 7 (July/August 1973): 5.

134. Appendix C: Other Projects at the Center, n.d., WEC Archives, carton 1, folder 47.

135. Libby Bouvier, comments for the panel "Second Wave Organizations and Their Offspring (The Cambridge Women's Center)" at "A Revolutionary Moment: Women's Liberation in the Late 1960s and Early 1970s" Conference, Boston University, Boston, MA: March 27–29, 2014. Personal notes available from author.

136. Libby Bouvier, "Women's Center Projects, Past and Present," n.d., WEC Archives, carton 10, folder 291.

137. The Women's Center: The Rape Counseling Project," n.d., WEC Archives, carton 1, folder 47.

138. Center Proposals, Rough Drafts, WEC Archives, carton 1, folder 47.

139. "Women's Center Projects, Past and Present," n.d.

140. "Concerts at The Saints," *The Women's Center Newsletter* 3, no. 7 (July/August 1973): 4.

141. Flyer, "Lesbian Mothers' Rap Group," n.d., WEC Archives, carton 10, folder 287.

142. *The Women's Center Newsletter* 3, no. 7 (July/August 1973).

143. "To Lesbian Liberation," letter, Aug. 6, 1973, WEC Archives, carton 10, folder 286.

144. "Dear Sisters," letter, August 24, 1973, WEC Archives, carton 10, folder 286.

145. "To whom it may concern," letter, July 11, 1973, WEC Archives, carton 10, folder 286.

146. "C/O Lesbian Liberation," letter, April 15, 1975, WEC Archives, carton 10, folder 286.

147. Chardon, "The State of the Movement," 1.

148. "Who We Are: Descriptions of Women's Liberation Groups" notes from the Sandy Spring conference, ca. November 1968, Irene Peslikis Papers, David M. Rubenstein Rare Book and Manuscript Library, Duke University, correspondence, box 24, accessed July 9, 2015, http://library.duke.edu/rubenstein/findingaids/peslikisirene/.

149. Deborah Gerson, participant in panel "Comparing City Organizations: Different Approaches to Bringing Women Together" at "A Revolutionary Moment: Women's Liberation in the Late 1960s and Early 1970s" Conference, Boston University, Boston, MA: March 27–29, 2014. Personal notes available from the author.

150. Author's telephone interview with Rochelle Ruthchild, August 16, 2013; author's telephone interview with Libby Bouvier, August 20, 2013.

151. Chardon, "The State of the Movement."

152. Ibid.

153. Schein, "The Place of Landscape," 660–80.

154. Author's telephone interview with Rochelle Ruthchild, August 16, 2013.

155. Author's telephone interview with Marsha Steinberg, February 17, 2010.

3. Feminist Bookstores

1. Junko R. Onosaka, *Feminist Revolution in Literacy: Women's Bookstores in the United States* (New York: Routledge, 2006), 40.

2. Author's interview with Simone Wallace, Los Angeles, February 12, 2010; Wes Joe, unpublished submission to Los Angeles Cultural Heritage Commission for historic designation of Sisterhood Bookstore, 2010, p. 7., courtesy of Adele Wallace, e-mail message to author, February 4, 2010.

3. Anne Braude, "A Short Half-Century: Fifty Years of Women at Harvard Divinity School" (address, Harvard Divinity School convocation, Cambridge, MA, September 19, 2005), accessed October 9, 2012, http://www.hds.harvard.edu/50years/convocation.html.

4. Quoted in Kristen Hogan, "Reading at Feminist Bookstores: Women's Literature, Women's Studies, and the Feminist Bookstore Network," (Ph.D. diss., University of Texas, 2006), 229.

5. Kristen Grimstad and Susan Rennie, *The New Woman's Survival Catalog: A Woman-Made Book* (New York: Coward, McCann, and Geoghegan, 1973), 21–25; Onosaka, *Feminist Revolution in Literacy*, 41.

6. List of feminist bookstores compiled by Womansplace Bookstore, Phoenix, Arizona, January 1982, Records of New Words, Schlesinger Library, Radcliffe Institute, Harvard University, 2002-M130, carton 1 (hereafter cited as Records of New Words).

7. Hogan, "Reading at Feminist Bookstores," 217.

8. Quoted in ibid., 194, 215, 226.

9. Onosaka, *Feminist Revolution in Literacy*, 41.

10. True Colors Bookstore, accessed October 20, 2012, http://www.truecolors bookstore.com.

11. Anne Enke, *Finding the Movement: Sexuality, Contested Space, and Feminist Activism* (Durham, NC: Duke University Press, 2007), 66–70. In 1999 the bookstore collective sued Amazon.com over use of its name. They settled out of court, for an unspecified but generous amount of money, with the understanding that the Minneapolis store would call itself the Amazon Bookstore Cooperative; Amazon.com then licensed the cooperative to use the Amazon name. Clint Bolton, "Amazon.com, Bookstore Settle Suit," InternetNews.com, accessed October 20, 2012, http://www.internetnews.com/ec-news/print.php/232351; author's telephone interview with Carol Seajay, October 2, 2013.

12. Robin Morgan, ed., *Sisterhood Is Powerful: An Anthology of Writings from the Women's Liberation Movement* (New York: Vintage, 1970), 567–83. There was also an annotated "Drop Dead List" of titles hostile to feminism. It included Helen Gurley Brown's *Sex and the Single Girl* (1962), a guide to using sexual assets to one's economic advantage, and Helene Deutsch's *The Psychology of Women* (1944), which postulated that to be an adult, a woman must be narcissistic, masochistic, and passive.

13. Onosaka, *Feminist Revolution in Literacy*, 25.

14. *Off our backs: The Feminist Newsjournal*, accessed October 21, 2012, http://www.offourbacks.org. Publication stopped in 2008 because it was dependent on women who had progressively less time to volunteer for the organization.

15. Onosaka, *Feminist Revolution in Literacy*, 51, 67.

16. Quoted in Hogan, "Reading at Feminist Bookstores," 199.

17. Author's telephone interview with Carol Seajay, October 2, 2013.

18. Quoted in "Reading at Feminist Bookstores," 204, 207–8, 213.

19. Quoted in Onosaka, *Feminist Revolution in Literacy*, 59.

20. Author's telephone interview with Carol Seajay, October 2, 2013.

21. Grimstad and Rennie, *New Woman's Survival Catalog*, 21.

22. Belinda Jack, *The Woman Reader* (New Haven, CT: Yale University Press, 2012), 9.

23. Jack, *Woman Reader*, 1–4.

24. Onosaka, *Feminist Revolution in Literacy*.

25. Ibid., 25–27.

26. Stefanie Weiss, "A Feminist Classic Turns 40," *The Washington Post*, October 4, 2011.

27. Onosaka, *Feminist Revolution in Literacy*, 27–29.

28. Kate Adams, "Built out of Books: Lesbian Energy and Feminist Ideology in Alternative Publishing," *Journal of Homosexuality* 34, nos. 3/4 (1998): 129.

29. Ibid., 128–29.

30. Barbara J. Love, ed., *Feminists Who Changed America, 1963–1975* (Urbana: University of Illinois Press, 2006), 20.

31. Janis Kelly, "Conference of Women in Print," *off our backs* 6 (November 1976): 2.

32. Onosaka, *Feminist Revolution in Literacy*, 31–33.

33. Quoted in Kelly, "Conference of Women in Print," 2.

34. Ibid.

35. Author's telephone interview with Carol Seajay, October 2, 2013.

36. Kelly, "Conference of Women in Print," 2.

37. Ibid., 2.

38. Kristen Hogan, "Women's Studies in Feminist Bookstores: 'All the Women's Studies Women Would Come In,'" *Signs: Journal of Women and Culture in Society* 33, no. 3 (2008): 595–621.

39. Onosaka, *Feminist Revolution in Literacy*, 60–61; author's telephone interview with Carol Seajay, October 2, 2013.

40. Author's telephone interview with Carol Seajay, October 2, 2013.

41. Adams, "Built out of Books," 130–31.

42. *Feminist Bookstores Newsletter*, November 1976, Records of New Words, MS 619, carton 2, folder 1.

43. Ibid.

44. Adams, "Built out of Books," 131–32.

45. Hogan, "Women's Studies in Feminist Bookstores," 595–621.

46. Quoted in Hogan, "Reading at Feminist Bookstores," 186–87.

47. Ibid., 147; National Women's Studies Association website home page, accessed November 12, 2012, http://www.nwsa.org.

48. Hogan, "Reading at Feminist Bookstores," 188.

49. Susan Nestor, "Sisterhood Bookstore," *Sister: Los Angeles Feminist Newspaper* 4, no. 10 (November 1973): 4, June Mazer Lesbian Archives, Los Angeles; supplemented by Simone Wallace's editing of the chapter, August 2013.

50. Wes Joe, unpublished submission to Los Angeles Cultural Heritage Commission, 4.

51. Personal communication from Simone Wallace, March 28, 2014.

52. Reproduced in *Still Here: Celebration of the 25th Anniversary of Sisterhood Bookstore*, program prepared for anniversary event in Skirball Cultural Centers, Los Angeles, November 23, 1997, personal collection of Simone Wallace.

53. Wes Joe, unpublished submission to Los Angeles Cultural Heritage Commission, 4.

54. Author's interview with Simone Wallace, Los Angeles, February 12, 2010.

55. Ibid.; author's interview with Adele Wallace, Los Angeles, January 25, 2010.

56. Author's interview with Adele Wallace, Los Angeles, February 4, 2010. One of Adele Wallace's cousins was a member of the collective.

57. Camilla Snyder, "A Book Store Especially for Ms.," reproduced in *Still Here*, 13.

58. Author's interview with Adele Wallace, January 25, 2010.

59. Adele Wallace, e-mail message to author, March 5, 2012; supplemented by Simone Wallace's editing of the chapter.

60. Nestor, "Sisterhood Bookstore," 4; supplemented by Simone Wallace's editing of the chapter.

61. Wes Joe, unpublished submission to Los Angeles Cultural Heritage Commission, 4.

62. Nestor, "Sisterhood Bookstore," 4; Wes Joe, unpublished submission to Los Angeles Cultural Heritage Commission, 100.

63. Wes Joe, unpublished submission to Los Angeles Cultural Heritage Commission, 100.

64. Quoted in Onosaka, *Feminist Revolution in Literacy*, 57, 58.

65. Author's telephone interview with Simone Wallace, July 31, 2013.

66. Author's interview with Simone Wallace, February 12, 2010; author's interview with Angela Brinskele, Los Angeles, February 26, 2010.

67. Author's interview with Adele Wallace, January 25, 2010.

68. Quoted in Nestor, "Sisterhood Bookstore," p. 4, June Mazer Lesbian Archives, Los Angeles.

69. Author's interview with Simone Wallace, February 12, 2010.

70. Wes Joe, unpublished submission to Los Angeles Cultural Heritage Commission, 5.

71. Adele Wallace, "Sisterhood at the Woman's Building," accessed December 15, 2009, http://www.inkwellweb.com/Sisterhood/Sisterhood%20story.htm. URL no longer active.

72. Author's interview with Simone Wallace, February 12, 2010.

73. Wes Joe, unpublished submission to Los Angeles Cultural Heritage Commission, 5.

74. Irene Wolt, "The Early History of Sisterhood," accessed December 15, 2009, http://www.inkwellweb.com/Sisterhood/Sisterhood%20story.htm. URL no longer active.

75. Carla C., response to "A Call for Voices" in honor of the twenty-fifth anniversary of Sisterhood Bookstore, accessed December 15, 2009, http://www.inkwellweb.com/Sisterhood/Sisterhood.htm. URL no longer active.

76. Author's telephone interview with Simone Wallace, July 31, 2013.

77. Wes Joe, unpublished submission to Los Angeles Cultural Heritage Commission, 6.

78. Author's telephone interview with Simone Wallace, July 31, 2013.

79. Ibid.

80. Ibid.

81. Quoted in Wolt, "Early History of Sisterhood."

82. Author's interview with Simone Wallace, February 12, 2010; author's telephone interview with Simone Wallace, July 31, 2013.

83. http://www.inkwellweb.com/Sisterhood/Sisterhood.htm, accessed December 15, 2009. URL no longer active.

84. Ibid.

85. Ibid.

86. *Still Here.*

87. Wes Joe, unpublished submission to Los Angeles Cultural Heritage Commission, 8. Borders Bookstore closed in January 2011. Carolyn Kellogg, "Westwood's Borders Takes a Bow," *Los Angeles Times*, January 3, 2011.

88. Lynell George, "Beaten by the Big Guys," *Los Angeles Times*, June 15, 1999.

89. Wes Joe, unpublished submission to Los Angeles Cultural Heritage Commission, 1.

90. Simone Wallace, e-mail communication with author, July 16, 2015.

91. Dolores Shelley, "Feminism and Small Business," n.d., New Words Collection, MC619, carton 3, folder 2.

92. Massachusetts Feminist Federal Credit Union account book, 1975–77, New Words Collection, MC619, carton 9, folder 5.

93. Author's telephone interview with Gilda Bruckman, September 18, 2013.

94. Hogan, "Reading at Feminist Bookstores," 232; author's telephone interview with Gilda Bruckman, September 18, 2013.

95. Personal communication with Gilda Bruckman, March 28, 2014.

96. Author's interview with Gilda Bruckman, September 18, 2013.

97. New Words, Inc., First Order to Paperback Booksmith, March 12, 1974, New Words Collection, MC619, carton 5, folder 1.

98. Author's telephone interview with Gilda Bruckman, September 18, 2013.

99. Gilda Bruckman et al., handwritten letter to the editor, *Boston Phoenix*, n.d., New Words Collection, MC619, carton 2, folder 5.

100. Shelley, "Feminism and Small Business," 6.

101. Monique Plante and Corolette Goodwin, "Dear Friends," letter to New Words, October 27, 1976, New Words Collection, MC619, carton 2, folder 5.

102. Gayle Fresan, "Dear Friends," letter, June 11, 1976, New Words Collection, MC619, carton 2, folder 5.

103. Pam Pace, "Dear Sisters," letter, May 1975, New Words Collection, MC619, carton 2, folder 5.

104. "Dear Rita," letter from Paris, June 10, 1975, New Words Collection, MC619, carton 2, folder 5.

105. Suzy McKee Charnas, "Dear Bookwomen," letter to New Words, August 30, 1974, New Words Collection, MC619, carton 2, folder 5.

106. Rita Arditti, Gilda Bruckman, Mary Lowry, and Jean MacRae, "Statement from New Words on Our Second Birthday," April 1976, New Words Collection, MC619, carton 3, folder 2.

107. Rita Arditti, Gilda Bruckman, Mary Lowry, and Jean MacRae, "Statement from New Words on Our Fourth Birthday," April 1978, New Words Collection, MC619, carton 3, folder 2.

108. Ibid.

109. "We opened New Words in 1974," unattributed, n.d., New Words Collection, MC619, carton 3, folder 2.

110. Hogan, "Reading at Feminist Bookstores," 234.

111. "We opened New Words in 1974," unattributed, n.d., New Words Collection, MC619, carton 3, folder 2.

112. Author's telephone interview with Gilda Bruckman, September 18, 2013.

113. Hogan, "Reading at Feminist Bookstores," 240.

114. Jaclyn Friedman, the former Center for New Words program director and founder of Women, Action, and the Media, e-mail message to author, October 31, 2012.

115. Loren King, "Where Did All the Womyn Go?" *Boston Phoenix* (November 2002), accessed October 30, 2012, http://www.bostonphoenix.com/boston/news_features/top/features/documents/02552275.htm.

116. Quoted in Kathleen Liddle, "More Than a Bookstore: The Continuing Relevance of Feminist Bookstores for the Lesbian Community," *Journal of Lesbian Studies* 9, nos. 1/2 (2005), 150.

117. Liddle, "More Than a Bookstore"; Adams, "Built out of Books."

118. Hogan, "Reading at Feminist Bookstores," 63.

119. Onosaka, *Feminist Revolution in Literacy*, 6.

120. Quoted in Hogan, "Reading at Feminist Bookstores," 1.

121. Author's interview with Simone Wallace, February 12, 2010.

4. Feminist Health Clinics

1. David Held, *Political Theory and the Modern State* (Stanford, CA: Stanford University Press, 1989), 201–2.

2. Carol Downer, "Self-Help," *Sister* 4, no. 5 (July 1973), 1, June Mazer Lesbian Archives, Los Angeles.

3. Ibid.

4. Feminist Women's Health Center, *Annual Report 1974*, Women's Community Health Center (WCHC) Records, Schlesinger Library, Radcliffe Institute, Harvard University, collection MC 512, carton 14, folder 9 (hereafter cited as WCHC Records).

5. Catherine DeLory, "Women's Health, Inc.: An Organizational Analysis," pp. 5–6, WCHC Records, collection MC512, carton 1, folder 3.

6. Sheryl Burt Ruzek, *The Women's Health Movement: Feminist Alternatives to Medical Control* (New York: Praeger, 1978), 210–13, 241–65. I estimated the number of service-delivery organizations by counting only those that had Center, Clinic, Collective, or Services in the name in addition to a physical address.

7. Linda Gordon, *Woman's Body, Woman's Right: Birth Control in America*, revised and updated (New York: Penguin Books, 1990), 93–113, 397.

8. Johanna Schoen, "Reconceiving Abortion: Medical Practice, Women's Access, and Feminist Politics before and after Roe v. Wade," *Feminist Studies* 26 (Summer 2000): 349–76.

9. Mary Daly, *The Church and the Second Sex* (New York: Harper and Row, 1968).

10. Calvin Goldsheider and William D. Mosher, "Patterns of Contraceptive Use in the United States: The Importance of Religious Factors," *Studies in Family Planning* 22 (March/April 1991): 102–15.

11. The rhythm method has a failure rate of 25 pregnancies expected per 100 women; use of spermicide alone results in 30 pregnancies per 100 women. Condom use results in an expected 11 to 16 pregnancies per 100 women, diaphragm use in 15, and oral contraceptives in 5. US Department of Health and Human Services, Office of Women's Health, "Birth Control Methods," https://www.womenshealth.gov/publications/our-publications/fact-sheet/birth-control-methods.pdf.

12. Elizabeth Siegel Watkins, *On the Pill: A Social History of Oral Contraceptives, 1950–1970* (Baltimore: Johns Hopkins University Press, 1998), 12.

13. Bernard Asbell, *The Pill: A Biography of the Drug that Changed the World* (New York: Random House, 1995). Sanger turned to Katharine McCormick, daughter-in-law of the inventor of the McCormick reaper, to finance research and development of the Pill.

14. Watkins, *On the Pill*, 141n13.

15. Planned Parenthood Federation of America, "History and Successes," http://plannedparenthood.org/about-us/who-we-are/history-and-successes.htm.

16. Gordon, *Woman's Body*, 209–17; Sheila Rowbotham, *Dreamers of a New Day: Women Who Invented the Twentieth Century* (London: Verso, 2010), 101.

17. Watkins, *On the Pill*, 103–5; Sandra Morgen, *Into Our Own Hands: The Women's Health Movement in the United States, 1969–1990* (New Brunswick, NJ: Rutgers University Press, 2002), 8–9.

18. Watkins, *On the Pill*, 128–31; Morgen, *Into Our Own Hands*, 10.

19. Gordon, *Woman's Body*, 234.

20. Carol Downer insists that Planned Parenthood is not a feminist organization. According to Downer, Planned Parenthood was against abortion until the federal government cut off funding for family planning during the Reagan administration. Planned Parenthood then opened abortion clinics to supplement their revenue stream, putting other providers out of business. Downer also accuses members of the Los Angeles Planned Parenthood facility of cowardice. On the day Operation Rescue staged an anti-abortion demonstration in Redding, California, Planned Parenthood closed its clinic; angry protesters went to the FWHC instead. Author's interview with Carol Downer, February 9, 2010.

21. Gordon, *Woman's Body*, chaps. 12 and 13.

22. *Our Bodies, Ourselves*, "Sterilization Abuse," accessed May 1, 2010, http://ourbodiesourselves.org/book/companion.asp?id=18&compID=55; Gordon, *Woman's Body*, 332–35.

23. Loretta J. Ross, "African-American Women and Abortion," in *Abortion Wars: A Half-Century of Struggle, 1950–2000*, ed. Ricki Solinger (Berkeley: University of California Press, 1998), 161–207.

24. Planned Parenthood, "History and Successes," http://plannedparenthood.org/about-us/who-we-are/history-and-successes.htm.

25. Rev. Martin Luther King Jr., "Family Planning—A Special and Urgent Concern," acceptance speech delivered on receiving the Margaret Sanger Award, Planned Parenthood, accessed April 28, 2010, http://plannedparenthood.org/about-us/who-we-are/reverend-martin-luther-king-jr-4728.

26. Ross, "African-American Women," 180–81.

27. Gordon, *Woman's Body*, 441.

28. Ross, "African-American Women," 183.

29. U.S. Department of Health, Education, and Welfare, "Abortion Surveillance Report Annual Summary 1970," table 21, PDF provided by Lawrence Finer, Guttmacher Institute, June 19, 2009.

30. Morgen, *Into Our Own Hands*, 43.

31. In 1989, Avery was one of twenty-nine people to win the prestigious MacArthur Foundation "genius grant." Byllye Y. Avery, "Breathing Life into Ourselves: The

Evolution of the National Black Women's Health Project," in *The Black Women's Health Book: Speaking for Ourselves*, ed. Evelyn C. White (Seattle: Seal Press, 1990), 4–10; Ross, "African-American Women," 190; Angela Y. Davis, "Sick and Tired of Being Sick and Tired: The Politics of Black Women's Health," in White, *Black Women's Health Book*, 18–26; "Our Story," Black Women's Health Imperative, accessed May 1, 2010, http://blackwomenshealth.org/index.php?submenu=about&submenu=about&src=gendocs&ref=ourstory&category=About%20Us.

32. Del-Em was an acronym for Delivery of the Menses. Carol Downer, e-mail message to author, June 3, 2010.

33. Lorraine Rothman, "Menstrual Extraction," n.d., WCHC Records, collection MC512, carton 15, folder 3.

34. Anna-Kria King, "Dear Gentle Person," letter, n.d., Feminist Women's Health Center, Southern California Library, Los Angeles, Los Angeles Women's Liberation Collection, 1970–76, MSS 023, carton 1, folder 8 (hereafter cited as Los Angeles Women's Liberation Collection).

35. US Department of Health, Education, and Welfare, National Communicable Disease Center, "Abortion Surveillance Report: Hospital Abortions, Annual Summary, 1969," April 1, 1970, appendix A, PDF provided by Lawrence Finer, Guttmacher Institute, June 19, 2009; Gordon, *Woman's Body*, 403.

36. Arlene Carmen and Howard Moody, *Abortion Counseling and Social Change: From Illegal Act to Medical Practice, the Story of the Clergy Consultation Service on Abortion* (Valley Forge, PA: Judson Press, 1973), 69.

37. U.S. Department of Health, Education, and Welfare, "Abortion Surveillance Report Annual Summary 1970," table 21.

38. Laura Kaplan, *The Story of Jane: The Legendary Underground Feminist Abortion Service* (Chicago: University of Chicago Press, 1995). Members of Jane believed that they were allowed to function for so long because they performed abortions for wives, girlfriends, and sisters of police officers. See also Morgen, *Into Our Own Hands*, 35.

39. Chicago Women's Liberation Union, "Jane Abortion Service," accessed May 17, 2010, http://cwluherstory.com/Jane-Abortion-Service.html; "Women Seized in Cut-Rate Clinic: Nab 7 in Abortion Raid," *Chicago Daily News*, May 4, 1972, http://cwluherstory.com/nab-7-abortion-raid.html; "Grand Jury Hears Abortion Case This Month," *Hyde Park Herald*, September 6, 1972, accessed May 17, 2010, http://cwluherstory.com/grand-jury-hears-abortion-case-this-month.html; "Abortion 7 Case Sent to Jury," *Hyde Park Herald*, August 16, 1972, accessed May 17, 2010, http://cwluherstory.com/abortion-7-case-sent-to-grand-jury.html. The August *Hyde Park Herald* article identifies the addresses as 553 Everett and 72 South Shore Drive, while the September article identifies them as 5532 and 7251, respectively.

40. Morgen, *Into Our Own Hands*, 5–7, 31–35.

41. Rickie Solinger, "Extreme Danger: Women Abortionists and the Clients pre Roe v. Wade," in *Not June Cleaver: Women and Gender in Postwar America, 1945–1960*, ed. Joanne Meyerowitz (Philadelphia: Temple University Press, 1994), 335–57; Leslie J. Reagan, *When Abortion Was a Crime: Women, Medicine, and the Law in the United States, 1867–1973* (Berkeley: University of California Press, 1997).

42. National Association for Repeal of Abortion Laws, Executive Director's Report, November 7, 1969, NARAL Papers, Schlesinger Library, Radcliffe Institute, Harvard University. collection MC313, carton 1.

43. US Department of Health, Education, and Welfare, "Abortion Surveillance Report: Hospital Abortions, Annual Summary, 1969," April 1, 1970, table 21, PDF provided by Lawrence Finer, Guttmacher Institute, June 19, 2009.

44. Author's interview with Carol Downer, February 2, 2010.

45. Carmen and Moody, *Abortion Counseling and Social Change*, 31.

46. Ibid., 66.

47. Ibid., 106.

48. NOW, "Stop HLA before It Takes Your Life," 1980, NOW Archives, Schlesinger Library, Radcliffe Institute, Harvard University, collection MC496, carton 210, folder 36.

49. Gordon, *Woman's Body*, 432.

50. Angela Y. Davis, *Women, Race, and Class* (New York: Random House, 1981), 202–21.

51. Ross, "African-American Women," 186.

52. Ibid., 180–81.

53. Alexandra Minna Stern, "Sterilized in the Name of Public Health: Race, Immigration, and Reproductive Control in Modern California," *American Journal of Public Health* 95 (July 2005): 1128–38.

54. Davis, *Women, Race, and Class*, 217.

55. Joyce Wilcox, "The Face of Women's Health: Helen Rodriguez-Trias," *American Journal of Public Health* 92 (April 2002): 566–69.

56. Gordon, *Woman's Body*, 433–34.

57. Mississippi Appendectomy: A Developing Online Archive of Information about Women of Color and Coercive Sterilization, "Fannie Lou Hamer," accessed May 20, 2010 http://mississippiappendectomy.wordpress.com/2007/12/06/fannie-lou-hamer.

58. Stern, "Sterilized," 1128–38.

59. "Synopsis of the Feminist Women's Center Development," n.d., WCHC Records, collection MC 512, carton 12, folder 12; Love, *Feminists Who Changed America*, 123.

60. Author's interview with Carol Downer, February 2, 2010; Collette Price, "The Self-Help Clinic," Feminist Women's Health Center newsletter 1, no. 4 (March–May 1972), WCHC Records, collection MC 512, carton 14, folder 2; *Ms. Magazine*, March/April 1996, 35.

61. See chap. 2 for a full discussion of the Crenshaw Women's Center.

62. Author's interview with Carol Downer, February 2, 2010; Carol Downer's e-mail message to author, August 2, 2010.

63. *Monthly Extract: An Irregular Periodical* 1, no. 2, October–November 1972, Los Angeles Women's Liberation Collection, collection MSS 023, carton 1, folder 8.

64. Author's telephone interview with Carol Downer, July 30, 2013; Carol Downer's e-mail message to author, March 19, 2014.

65. Anna-Kria King, "Dear Gentle Person," letter.

66. Susan Rennie and Kirsten Grimstad, *The New Woman's Survival Catalog* (New York: Coward, McCann, and Geoghegan, 1973), 71.

67. Carolyn Keith, interview with Fran Kaplan, "Owning Our Wellness: L.A. Feminist Women's Health Center: Services, Political Action," *Amazon: A Midwest*

Journal for Women June/July/August 1978, WCHC Records, collection MC 512, carton 15, folder 10.

68. Author's telephone interview with Carol Downer, July 30, 2013.

69. Ibid.

70. Rennie and Grimstad, *New Woman's Survival Catalog*, 71.

71. Author's interview with Carol Downer, February 2, 2010.

72. Author's telephone interview with Carol Downer, July 30, 2013.

73. Keith, "Owning Our Wellness."

74. Francie Hornstein. "Assertiveness in the Doctor's Office," Ames, Iowa, *FWHC Newsletter* 1, no. 4 (September 1975): 4, WCHC Records, collection MC512, carton 14, folder 9.

75. Sandra Morgen, *Into Our Own Hands*, 100.

76. "Come to Self-Help Clinic," pamphlet, n.d., WCHC Records, collection MS512, carton 14, folder 2. Downer and Debi Law visited women's self-help groups in Europe in 1973. "Dear Sisters," letter, unsigned, September 17, 1973, WCHC Records, MC 512, carton 15, folder 3.

77. Author's interview with Carol Downer, February 2, 2010.

78. Carol Downer, e-mail message to author, June 3, 2010.

79. Downer's daughter, Laura Brown, posted their $1,000 bail. Brown was the cofounder of the Oakland FWHC. Carol Downer, e-mail message to author, August 13, 2010.

80. Feminist Women's Health Center, press release, "Big Brother Busts the West Coast Sisters," October 10, 1972; *Monthly Extract: An Irregular Periodical* 1, no. 1-a (September 1972); Feminist Women's Health Center, "Dear Sister" letter from Carol Downer, November 24, 1972, Los Angeles Women's Liberation Collection, MSS 023, carton 1, folder 8.

81. "Medicine: Self-Service Setback" *Time*, October 16, 1972, accessed September 16, 2010, http://time.com/time/printout/0,8816,906600,00.html.

82. Stephanie Caruana, "Great Yogurt Conspiracy," *off our backs* 3, no. 5 (January 1973), June Mazer Lesbian Archives, Los Angeles; Carol Downer, e-mail message to author, August 2, 2010.

83. Feminist Women's Health Center, "Big Brother Busts the West Coast Sisters."

84. The Gynecological Self-Help Clinics of America held its first convention in Iowa City in October 1972 at the suggestion of Carol Downer and Lorraine Rothman. L. & M., "Iowa City," and "Legal Hassling," unattributed, *Monthly Extract: An Irregular Periodical* 1, no. 2 (October–November 1972), Los Angeles Women's Liberation Collection, MSS 023, carton 1, folder 8; "SOS Save our Sisters," *Monthly Extract: An Irregular Periodical* 1, no. 1-a (September 1972), Los Angeles Women's Liberation Collection, MSS 023, carton 1, folder 8.

85. "SOS Save our Sisters."

86. "Legal Hassling," *Monthly Extract: An Irregular Periodical* 1, no. 2 (October–November 1972), Los Angeles Women's Liberation Collection, MSS 023, carton 1, folder 8

87. "Dear Sister" letter from Carol Downer.

88. Caruana, "Great Yogurt Conspiracy."

89. *off our backs* (December 1972), reprinted in Rennie and Grimstad, *New Woman's Survival Catalog*, 71.

90. Memo to Feminist Women's Health Centers from Shelley [no last name given], Re: Investigation by State Health Department, November 5, 1975, WCHC Records, collection MC512, carton 15, folder 1.

91. Letter from Carol Downer to Mr. Bill Wheeler, Board of Medical Quality Assurance, August 12, 1976, WCHC Records, collection MC512, carton 15, folder 1.

92. Women's Community Health Center, *Second Annual Report*, n.d., WCHC Records, collection MC512, carton 1, folder 13.

93. "Department of Consumer Affairs Harass Clinics," Press Release from Los Angeles FWHC, July 27, 1976, WCHC Records, collection MC 512, carton 15, folder 1.

94. "KNX-TV Makes News, Not Reports It [*sic*]," news release, Feminist Women's Health Center, April 26, 1979, WCHC Records, collection MC 512, carton 14, folder 11.

95. Mailgram to John Backe and William Paley from J. Walhandler of the Women's Community Health Center, n.d., WCHC Records, collection MC512, carton 14, folder 11.

96. "Abortion without Pregnancy," *TV Guide*, May 5–11, 1979, WCHC Records, collection MC 512, carton 14, folder 11.

97. Devra Krassner of Boston's Women's Community Health Center, Inc., "Dear . . . ," letter, May 25, 1979, WCHC Records, collection MC512, carton 14, folder 11.

98. Author's interview with Carol Downer, February 9, 2010; Carol Downer's email message to author, June 3, 2010.

99. Author's telephone interview with Carol Downer, July 30, 2013.

100. Downer, "Self-Help."

101. "Come to Self-Help Clinic."

102. *Feminist Women's Health Center Annual Report, 1974*, WCHC Records, collection MC512, carton 14, folder 9.

103. Feminist Women's Health Center newsletter 1, no. 4 (March–May 1972), WCHC Records, collection MC512, carton 14, folder 2; Oakland Feminist Women's Health Center memo, September 5, 1974, WCHC Records, collection MC512, carton 15, folder 4.

104. Feminist Women's Health Center Newsletter 1, no. 4 (March–May 1972).

105. Feminist Women's Health Center/Women's Choice Clinic of Chico, "Dear Sisters," letter, June 28, 1976, WCHC Records, collection MC512, carton 14, folder 6.

106. Author's correspondence with Carol Downer, March 19, 2014.

107. State legislatures, many of them dominated by Republicans, are still trying to use building codes to close down clinics that provide abortions. In 2013 Texas ruled that abortion clinics must meet the same building, equipment, and staffing standards as hospital surgical units, and the Virginia Board of Health voted to require abortion clinics to meet strict, hospital-style codes. In 2014 Arizona legalized the surprise inspection of abortion clinics without a warrant. In 2015, however, the Democratic Attorney General of Virginia reversed the earlier ruling and exempted abortion clinics from hospital standards. And the Supreme Court blocked the Texas restrictions. Laura Vozella, "Va. Board Approves Strict Abortion Clinic Rules," *The Washington Post*, April 12, 2013; Manny Fernandez and Erik Eckholm, "Court Upholds Texas

Limits on Abortions," *The New York Times*, June 9, 2015; Justin Wm. Moyer, "New Abortion Restriction Signed into Arizona Law," *The Washington Post*, April 16, 2014; editorial board, "An Abortion Rights Win in Virginia," *The Washington Post*, May 5, 2015; Reuters, "Supreme Court Temporarily Blocks Texas Abortion Restrictions," *The New York Times*, June 29, 2015.

108. Author's interview with Carol Downer, February 9, 2010.

109. Feminist Women's Health Center, "Dear Sisters" letter; Feminist Women's Health Center, *Annual Report 1974*.

110. Feminist Women's Health Center of Oakland, California, "Dear Sisters," letter, November 9, 1973, Los Angeles Women's Liberation Collection, MSS 023, carton 1, folder 8.

111. *Sister* 4, no. 11 (December 1973): 13, Los Angeles Women's Liberation Collection, MSS 023, carton 1, folder 8.

112. Feminist Women's Health Center/Women's Choice Clinic of Chico, California, "Dear Sisters," letter, June 28, 1976, Los Angeles Women's Liberation Collection, MSS 023, carton 1, folder 8

113. Author's interview with Carol Downer, February 9, 2010.

114. Keith, "Owning Our Wellness."

115. Rennie and Grimstad, *New Woman's Survival Catalog*, 71.

116. *Monthly Extract: An Irregular Periodical* 1, no. 2, (October–November 1972), Los Angeles Women's Liberation Collection, MSS 023, carton 1, folder 8. In *A Room of One's Own*, Virginia Woolf pondered the "safety and prosperity" of one sex compared with the "poverty and insecurity" of the other, concluding that a woman would need five hundred [pounds] a year and a door with a lock on it to become a writer. Virginia Woolf, *A Room of One's Own* (New York: Harcourt Brace, 1929), 2, 109.

117. Z. Budapest, "FWHC Stops Redondo Beach Clinic," *Sister* 4, no. 9 (1973): 10, June Mazer Lesbian Archives, Los Angeles.

118. Ibid.

119. Westside Family Health Center, "About Us," accessed February 17, 2010, http://wwhcenter.org/about.htm.

120. Boston Women's Health Course Collective, *Our Bodies Ourselves: A Course by and for Women* (Boston: New England Free Press, 3rd ed., 1971), 1.

121. Ibid., 61

122. Ibid., 134.

123. "In the Beginning . . . A Herstory of the Women's Community Health Center," WCHC *First Annual Report*, n.d., WCHC Records, collection MC512, carton 1, folder 2. The women organized the conference at the suggestion of Carol Downer, who traveled around the country with a slide presentation to explain the self-help concept to other women. WCHC Records, collection MC512, carton 1, folder 2; carton 14, folder 2.

124. Notes from November 19, 1973, meeting of the founding group, WCHC Records, collection MC512, carton 1, folder 1.

125. Ibid.

126. DeLory, "Women's Health, Inc.," 5, 6.

127. An anonymous "far-sighted sister" donated six hundred dollars, and organizers of the benefit sold a lot of specula.

128. "In the Beginning . . . A Herstory"; untitled minutes of organizing meeting for the WCHC, November 19, 1973, WCHC Records, collection MC512, carton 1, folder 1.

129. WCHC *First Annual Report.*

130. Ibid.

131. The historian Elizabeth Siegel Watkins credits women's concerns about the Pill with sparking the women's health movement of the 1970s. *On the Pill*, 104. In 1970 DES was linked to vaginal cancer in the daughters of mothers who had taken the drug during the first trimester of pregnancy. Since the drug had been prescribed during the height of the baby boom, estimates were that the number of women affected nationally might be three million. WCHC *First Annual Report;* see also Ruzek, *Women's Health Movement,* 38–42.

132. "Brief History of Women's Community Health Licensure: March 1975 to April 1977," WCHC Records, carton 6, folder 7.

133. "Brief History of Women's Community Health Licensure: March 1975 to April 1977"; "Building Department Chronology," n.d.; both in WCHC Records, carton 6, folder 7.

134. Ibid.

135. Ibid.

136. "Clinic Licensure Update, October–November 1977," WCHC Records, carton 6, folder 7.

137. Ray Flynn served as mayor of Boston from 1984 to 1993, WCHC *5th Issue Anniversary Annual Report, 1979,* 10–11, WCHC Records, carton 1, folder 13.

138. Women's Community Health Center, Inc., "For Immediate Release," April 25, 1978, WCHC Records, carton 6, folder 7.

139. "Finding Aid," WCHC Records, accessed June 11, 2009, http://oasis.lib. harvard.edu.

140. Letter to Friends of the Women's Community Health Center, July 22, 1981, WCHC Records, carton 1, folder 10.

141. WATCH: Women Acting Together to Combat Harassment, "Zoning Report—FWHC Board Meeting 7/8/76," WCHC Records, MC512, carton 14, folder 7; Morgen, *Into Our Own Hands,* 102

142. Sandra Morgen, "It Was the Best of Times, It Was the Worst of Times: Emotional Discourse in the Work Culture of Feminist Health Clinics," in *Feminist Organizations: Harvest of the New Women's Movement,* ed. Myra Marx Ferree and Patricia Yancey Martin (Philadelphia: Temple University Press, 1995), 234–39.

143. Ibid.

144. *Monthly Extract: An Irregular Periodical* 1, no. 2 (October–November 1972): 2.

145. Downer, "Self-Help," 1.

146. Author's interview with Carol Downer, Los Angeles, February 2, 2010.

147. Kathryn Kolbert and Andrea Miller, "Legal Strategies for Abortion Rights in the 21st Century," in *Abortion Wars: A Half-Century of Struggle, 1950–2000,* ed. Ricki Solinger (Berkeley: University of California Press, 1998), 99. The Harvard historian Jill Lepore thinks that the gay rights movement achieved its victory with same-sex marriage by couching its argument in terms of equality, whereas the women's movement's fight for reproductive rights has been interpreted as a privacy issue. And, as she observes, equality trumps privacy when it comes to strong legal arguments. Lepore, "To Have and to Hold."

148. "Come to Self-Help Clinic."

149. Baxandall and Gordon, *Dear Sisters*, 123.

150. Amie Newman, "Life Support for Feminist Health Care?" accessed August 18, 2010, http://rhrealitycheck.org/print/1929. When Sandra Morgen conducted interviews in the early 1990s, she contacted forty feminist health clinics (see appendix 2, *Into Our Own Hands*, 241). The discrepancy between forty clinics in the early 1990s and fifteen in 2010 could result from different definitions of "feminist" clinics or the continued decline in feminist clinics from the 1990s to 2010 (or both).

151. The National Women's Health Network, accessed May 1, 2010, http://nwhn.org.

152. Black Women's Health Imperative, "Our Story," accessed May 1, 2010, http://blackwomenshealth.org/index.php?submenu=about&submenu=about&src=gendocs&ref=ourstory&category=About%20Us.

153. *Our Bodies, Ourselves*, "About Us," accessed May 20, 2010, http://ourbodiesourselves.org/about/default.asp

154. Mississippi Appendectomy, Byllye Avery interview excerpt, accessed May 20, 2010, http://mississippiappendectomy.wordpress.com.

155. Women's Health in Women's Hands, accessed July 19, 2015, http://womenshealthinwomenshands.org/.

5. Domestic Violence Shelters

1. Ruth Lister, *Citizenship: Feminist Perspectives*, 2nd ed. (New York: New York University Press, 2003), 113.

2. Donileen R. Loseke, *The Battered Woman and Shelters: The Social Construction of Wife Abuse* (Albany: State University of New York Press, 1992), 21.

3. Sandra Bartky, "Battered Women, Intimidation, and the Law," in *Women and Citizenship*, ed. Marilyn Friedman (New York: Oxford University Press, 2005), 63.

4. R. Emerson Dobash and Russell P. Dobash, *Women, Violence, and Social Change* (London: Routledge, 1992), 60.

5. Mary Marecek, *Say "NO!" to Violence: Voices of Women Who Experience Violence* (Boston: Red Sun Press, 1983), 46. More than six thousand copies of this fifty-page booklet were distributed within a year.

6. Elizabeth Pleck, *Domestic Tyranny: The Making of Social Policy against Family Violence from Colonial Times to the Present* (New York: Oxford University Press, 1987), 18.

7. Linda Gordon, *Heroes of Their Own Lives: The Politics and History of Family Violence* (Urbana: University of Illinois Press, 1988), 2–4, 19–20.

8. Loseke, *The Battered Woman and Shelters*, 20.

9. Betty Friedan, *Life So Far: A Memoir* (New York: Simon and Schuster, 2000), 145, 224.

10. Gordon, *Heroes*, chap. 8. See also Susan Brownmiller, *Against Our Will: Men, Women, and Rape* (New York: Bantam, 1975).

11. Del Martin, *Battered Wives* (Volcano, CA: Volcano Press, 1981), xiii.

12. Lenore E. Walker, *The Battered Woman* (New York: Harper and Row, 1979), xv.

13. Mildred Pagelow, *Woman-Battering: Victims and Their Experiences* (Beverly Hills, CA: Sage, 1981), 33.

14. A comprehensive review essay on family violence published in 1983 found no articles or books on lesbian-couple violence. See Winifred Breines and Linda

Gordon, "The New Scholarship on Family Violence," *Signs: Journal of Women in Culture and Society* 8 (1983): 490–531.

15. Michelle Van Natta, "Constructing the Battered Woman," *Feminist Studies* 31 (Summer 2005): 416–43.

16. Mary Eaton, "Abuse by Any Other Name: Feminism, Difference, and Intra-lesbian Violence," in *The Public Nature of Private Violence: The Discovery of Domestic Abuse*, ed. Martha Albertson Fineman and Roxanne Mykitiuk (New York: Routledge, 1994), 195–223.

17. Martin, *Battered Wives*, 10–14.

18. Most rape crisis work was carried out in existing women's centers (see chap. 2) rather than in separate facilities.

19. Vicki McNickle Rose, "Rape as a Social Problem: A By-Product of the Feminist Movement," *Social Problems* 25 (October 1977): 75–89; Nancy A. Matthews, *Confronting Rape: The Feminist Anti-Rape Movement and the State* (London: Routledge, 1994), 9.

20. Susan Schecter, *Women and Male Violence: The Visions and Struggles of the Battered Women's Movement* (Boston: South End Press, 1982), 34–43.

21. Kirsten Grimstad and Susan Rennie, eds., *The New Woman's Survival Catalog* (New York: Coward, McCann, and Geoghegan, 1973); Grimstad and Rennie, eds., *The New Woman's Survival Sourcebook*, (New York: Alfred A. Knopf, 1975), 214.

22. Kathleen Fojtik, "Wife Beating: How to Develop a Wife Assault Task Force and Project," 1976; Mindy Resnick, "Wife Beating: Counselor Training Manual # 1," 1976; Barbara Cooper, "Wife Beating: Counselor Training Manual # 2," 1976. All in the NOW Archives, Schlesinger Library, Radcliffe College, Harvard University, collection MC496, carton 211, folder 27 (hereafter cited as NOW Archives).

23. Suzanne K. Steinmetz, ed., *National Organization for Women Resource Booklet for Battered Spouses*, NOW Archives, collection MC496, carton 211, folder 11. A coordinator of the national NOW task force and the author of *Battered Wives*, Del Martin was the first American to publicize the problem. See Kathleen J. Tierney, "The Battered Women Movement and the Creation of the Wife-Beating Problem," *Social Problems* 29, no. 3 (February 1982): 208.

24. Brownmiller, *Against Our Will*, 29–30.

25. Betsy Warrior, "History of 'Working on Wife Abuse,' Transition House," n.d., Transition House Records, Northeastern University Libraries, Archives and Special Collections Department, Northeastern University, Boston, Massachusetts, collection M47, carton 10, folder 309 (hereafter cited as Transition House Records).

26. Martin, *Battered Wives*, xi.

27. CETA was the most common source of funding in early shelter work. Federal legislation passed in 1973, CETA was intended to train long-term unemployed people for work in public or nonprofit organizations.

28. Tierney, "The Battered Woman Movement," 209, 213.

29. Breines and Gordon, "The New Scholarship," 490–531.

30. Kimberlé Williams Crenshaw, "Mapping the Margins: Intersectionality, Identity Politics, and Violence against Women of Color," in *The Public Nature of Private Violence: The Discovery of Domestic Abuse*, ed. Martha Albertson Fineman and Roxanne Mykitiuk (New York: Routledge, 1994), 93–118.

31. Barbara Smith, "Introduction," in *Home Girls: A Black Feminist Anthology*, ed. Barbara Smith (New York: Kitchen Table: Women of Color Press, 1983); Alice Walker, *The Color Purple* (New York: Harcourt Brace Jovanovich, 1982).

32. Crenshaw, "Mapping the Margins."

33. Ibid.

34. Ibid.

35. Combahee River Collective, *The Combahee River Collective Statement: Black Feminist Organizing in the Seventies and Eighties* (Albany, NY: Kitchen Table: Women of Color Press, 1986), 14.

36. Author's telephone interview with Demita Frazier, member of the Combahee River Collective, June 20, 2014; Casa Myrna Vazquez website, accessed July 8, 2014, http://www.casamyrna.org/index.php/about-us/history; Inquilinos Boricuas en Acción website, accessed July 8, 2014; http://www.iba-etc.org/about.html.

37. Marecek, *Say "NO!" to Violence*, 44.

38. Jennifer A. Bennice and Patricia A. Resick, "Marital Rape: History, Research, and Practice," *Journal of Trauma, Violence, and Abuse* 4 (July 2003): 228–46.

39. Sue E. Eisenberg and Patricia Micklow, "The Assaulted Wife: 'Catch 22' Revisited," *Women's Rights Law Reporter* nos. 3/4 (Spring/Summer 1977): 138–61.

40. Elizabeth Schneider, "The Violence of Privacy," in *The Public Nature of Private Violence: The Discovery of Domestic Abuse*, ed. Martha Albertson Fineman and Roxanne Mykitiuk (New York: Routledge, 1994), 43.

41. Ibid., 38.

42. Martin, *Battered Wives*, "The Failure of the Legal System," 87–118; see also Sandra Bartky, "Battered Women, Intimidation, and the Law," in Friedman, *Women and Citizenship*, 52–63.

43. Bennice and Resick, "Marital Rape."

44. Jane Maslow Cohen, "Private Violence and Public Obligation: The Fulcrum of Reason," in *The Public Nature of Private Violence: The Discovery of Domestic Abuse*, ed. Martha Albertson Fineman and Roxanne Mykitiuk (New York: Routledge, 1994), 352.

45. Pauline W. Gee, "Ensuring Police Protection for Battered Women: The *Scott v. Hart* Suit," *Signs: Journal of Women in Culture and Society* 8 (1983): 554–67. *Bruno v. Codd* was a similar case brought against the New York City Police Department in 1977.

46. Erin Pizzey, *Scream Quietly or the Neighbors Will Hear* (Short Hills, NJ: Ridley Enslow, 1977), 9–10.

47. Ibid., 11–12.

48. Ibid., 44–45.

49. Ibid., 45.

50. John M. Johnson, "Program Enterprise and Official Cooptation in the Battered Women's Shelter Movement," *American Behavioral Scientist* 24 (July/August 1981): 827–42. Pizzey became a media personality resented by her early coworkers. She left Chiswick Women's Aid to form the National Women's Aid Federation in 1974.

51. Pizzey, *Scream Quietly*, 130–31.

52. Walker, *The Battered Woman*, 193.

53. Pizzey, *Scream Quietly*, 5–7. Two of the earliest shelters in the United States were established for the families of men with drinking problems. Haven House

in Pasadena, California, was opened in 1964 by women from Al-Anon; Rainbow Retreat in Phoenix, Arizona, opened in 1973. Dobash and Dobash, *Women, Violence, and Social Change*, 83–84; Martin, *Battered Wives*, 206–9; Walker, *The Battered Woman*, 202; Schecter, *Women and Male Violence*, 55–56.

54. Schecter, *Women and Male Violence*, 62–65.

55. Secrecy of location was paramount among all shelters during the 1970s. In the twenty-first century a promising new approach to the problem of domestic violence is emerging: The majority of states have passed or introduced laws to allow the use of Global Positioning System (GPS) to track abusers in domestic violence cases. When an offender enters an "exclusion zone" ranging from a few blocks to the entire town, an alert is sent to the police, who issue an arrest warrant. The shelter director testing this approach in Amesbury, Massachusetts, refers to the system as "contain[ing] the offender so the victim doesn't have to be contained." See Rachel Louise Snyder, "A Raised Hand," *New Yorker*, July 22, 2013, 40.

56. Martin, *Battered Wives*, 197–205. The CDBG funding was later withdrawn. Enke, *Finding the Movement*, 181–96. See also Dobash and Dobash, *Women, Violence, and Social Change*, 86, for a description of another activist shelter, Bradley-Angle House in Portland, Oregon.

57. Schecter, *Women and Male Violence*, 65.

58. Tierney, "The Battered Women Movement," 211.

59. The current Department of Health and Human Services (DHHS) was formed after the Department of Education was separated from HEW in 1979.

60. Dobash and Dobash, *Women, Violence, and Social Change*, 66–68.

61. Johnson, "Program Enterprise and Official Cooptation."

62. Pizzey, *Scream Quietly*, 7.

63. Author's interview with early members of RESPOND, Somerville, MA, June 22, 2009.

64. Pauline Dwyer, RESPOND internal memo, October 1989. RESPOND Archives, Somerville, MA. (Hereafter cited as RESPOND Archives. Further information on the location of the archives withheld for reasons of confidentiality.)

65. Varney, "A Women's Crisis Center in Somerville."

66. "Memo to Our Co-Community Workers in Somerville," October 19, 1974, RESPOND Archives.

67. Author's interview with early members of RESPOND, Somerville, MA, June 22, 2009.

68. Maureen Varney, "A Women's Crisis Center in Somerville," 1974, 4, RESPOND Archives.

69. Letter to Mayor S. Lester Ralph from Anne Broussard and Pauline Dwyer, November 12, 1974, RESPOND Archives.

70. "New Program RESPONDs to Women's Crisis Needs," *Somerville Journal*, January 30, 1975, RESPOND Archives.

71. Jean Luce, "Overview" [of early days of RESPOND, with other founders Pauline Dwyer and Marie Siraco, October 1989], n.d., RESPOND Archives.

72. Pauline Dwyer, Letter to Mr. William J. Seretta Jr., December 6, 1974, RESPOND Archives.

73. *RESPOND Annual Report 1974–1984*, RESPOND Archives.

74. Anne Broussard, Letter to Paul Duhamel, December 4, 1974, RESPOND Archives; Author's interview with Marie Siraco and other early members of RESPOND, June 22, 2009.

75. "New Program RESPONDs to Women's Crisis Needs."

76. Varney, "A Women's Crisis Center," 3.

77. *RESPOND Annual Report, 1974–1984.*

78. Luce, "Overview."

79. Newsletter, College of Public and Community Service, University of Massachusetts Boston, n.d., RESPOND Archives.

80. Varney, "A Women's Crisis Center," 1.

81. Ibid., 1, 3.

82. Ibid., 4.

83. Ibid., 25.

84. Ibid., 2.

85. RESPOND Board Minutes, March 4, 1975, RESPOND Archives.

86. Author's interview with early members of RESPOND, Somerville, Massachusetts, June 22, 2009.

87. Varney, "A Women's Crisis Center," 2.

88. RESPOND board minutes, March 4, 1975.

89. Letter from Jean Luce to Lisa Leghorn and Betsy Warrior, May 2, 1975, RESPOND Archives.

90. RESPOND Board minutes, April 1, 1975, RESPOND Archives.

91. Letter from Luce to Leghorn and Warrior.

92. Author's interview with early members of RESPOND, Somerville, Massachusetts, June 22, 2009.

93. Marie Siraco, notes from October 1989, RESPOND Archives.

94. Luce, "Overview."

95. Varney, "A Women's Crisis Center," 3.

96. Maureen Varney, notes from October 1989, RESPOND Archives.

97. Ibid.

98. Author's interview with early members of RESPOND, Somerville, Massachusetts, June 22, 2009.

99. RESPOND Board minutes, April 1, 1975, 1.

100. "New Program RESPONDS to Women's Crisis Needs."

101. RESPOND flyer for Firesticks event, February 8, RESPOND Archives.

102. RESPOND, Inc., Statement of Income and Expenses, January 1, 1975, through June 30, 1975, RESPOND Archives.

103. Author's telephone interview with Jean Marie Luce, September 25, 2009; RESPOND, Inc., Statement of Income and Expenses, January 1, 1975, through December 31, 1975, RESPOND Archives.

104. Ibid.

105. "What Is RESPOND?" n.d., RESPOND Archives.

106. RESPOND, Inc., Financial Report: May 1, 1976–April 30, 1977, RESPOND Archives.

107. Ibid.; *Annual Report 1974–1984*, RESPOND Archives.

108. "Support Group," Report on Support Group and Refuge Participants, 1977 and 1978, unattributed; n.d., RESPOND Archives.

109. Letter from Janet McDonald to Board of Directors, December 22, 1979, RESPOND Archives.

110. "A Plea for Battered Women," *Somerville Journal*, January 3, 1980, RESPOND Archives.

111. Author's interview with early members of RESPOND, Somerville, Massachusetts, June 22, 2009.

112. Ibid. In 2008 the organization opened a new facility that housed twenty women and their children. "Reaching Out" newsletter for RESPOND, Inc., 17, no. 1 (Summer 2008), RESPOND Archives.

113. Brownmiller, *Against Our Will*, 29–30.

114. Lisa Leghorn and Jean Rioux, "Transition House proposal for funding," n.d., p. 5, Transition House Records, collection M47, carton 10, folder 298.

115. Love, *Feminists Who Changed America*, 274–75, 478–79.

116. Leghorn and Rioux, "Transition House proposal."

117. Ibid.

118. Ibid.

119. Ibid.

120. Schecter, *Women and Male Violence*, 65, 66.

121. Leghorn and Rioux, "Transition House proposal."

122. Ibid.

123. Margaret Hunt to Joan Tighe, letter, Boston/Cambridge Ministry in Higher Education, April 18, 1977; "Transition House," n.d., Transition House Records, collection M47, carton 10, folder 297.

124. Margaret Hunt to Joan Tighe, letter.

125. Transition House, List of Proposals Sent Out, April 1976 to October 1977, n.d., Transition House Records, collection M47, carton 10, folder 298.

126. Warrior, "History of 'Working on Wife Abuse.'"

127. Lisa Leghorn to "Dear Friends," letter, April 28, 1977, to Area 3 Planning Team, Transition House Records, collection M47, carton 10, folder 297.

128. Margaret Hunt to Joan Tighe, letter.

129. Lisa Leghorn to "Dear Friends," letter.

130. Walker, *The Battered Woman*, 199–203.

131. Dobash and Dobash, *Women, Violence, and Social Change*, 60.

132. RESPOND, accessed December 13, 2012, http://www.respondinc.org/Home.aspx; Transition House, accessed December 13, 2012, http://www.transitionhouse.org/; Casa Myrna, accessed December 13, 2012, http://www.casamyrna.org.

133. See Lori A. Brown, *Contested Spaces: Abortion Clinics, Women's Shelters, and Hospitals* (London: Ashgate, 2013).

134. RESPOND, http://www.respondinc.org/Home.aspx; Transition House, accessed December 13, 2012, http://www.transitionhouse.org/; Casa Myrna, accessed December 13, 2012, http://www.casamyrna.org.

135. Jean Luce, "Dear . . . ," letter, May 7, 1976, Transition House Records, collection M47, carton 10, folder 297.

136. Robert A. Woods and Albert J. Kennedy, eds., *Handbook of Settlements* (New York: Russell Sage Foundation, 1911), 53, 193, reprinted by Arno Press, New York, 1970.

137. Vida Scudder, *On Journey* (New York: E. P. Dutton, 1937), 135, 150.

138. Walker, *The Battered Woman*, 198.

139. Loseke, *The Battered Woman and Shelters*, 29.

6. After the Second Wave

1. Daphne Spain, *Gendered Spaces* (Chapel Hill: University of North Carolina Press, 1992).

2. The controversy associated with trying to change one's skin color was thrown into the national spotlight in 2015 when Rachel Dolezal, a civil rights activist who gained a following as a black woman, had to step down as director of the Spokane, Washington, chapter of the NAACP when it was revealed that she is white. Leah Sottile and Abby Phillip, "How Rachel Dolezal Created a New Image and Made a Black Community Believe," *The Washington Post*, June 15, 2015.

3. Michelle Goldberg, "What Is a Woman?" *New Yorker*, August 4, 2014, 24–28. For an academic approach to this issue, see Petra Doan, "The Tyranny of Gendered Spaces—Reflections from beyond the Gender Dichotomy," *Gender, Place, and Culture* 17 (2010): 635–54.

4. Monica Jaeckel, "Mother Centers Germany: All About Us," accessed June 29, 2012, http://monikajaeckel.com/wordpress/wp-content/uploads/2009/08/mc21_all_about_us.pdf.

5. Mother Centers International Network for Empowerment, "MINE background," accessed July 1, 2012, http://www.mine.cc/node/17.

6. Walter Simons, *Cities of Ladies: Beguine Communities in the Medieval Low Countries, 1200–1565* (Philadelphia: University of Pennsylvania Press, 2001).

7. Gerda Wekerle and Sylvia Novac, "Developing Two Women's Housing Cooperatives," in *New Households, New Housing*, ed. Karen Franck and Sherry Ahrentzen (New York: Van Nostrand Reinhold), 223–42.

8. Ibid., 236–37.

9. "First All-Woman Police Station in Thrissur," *Times of India*, February 25, 2012, accessed July 5, 2012, http://articles.timesofindia.indiatimes.com/2012–02–25/kochi/31100261_1_police-station-respective-stations-new-station. In South America, Brazil, Colombia, Ecuador, Peru, and Uruguay have all established women-only police stations. See Sarah Hautzinger, *Violence in the City of Women: Police and Batterers in Bahia, Brazil* (Berkeley: University of California Press, 2007), 182.

10. Prafulla Marapakwar, "Maharashtra only state without a single all-women police station," *Times of India*, March 5, 2015, accessed July 9, 2015, http://timesofindia.indiatimes.com/India/Maharashtra-only-state-without-a-single-all-women-police-station/articleshow/46462551.cms.

11. J. Yardley, "Indian Women Find New Peace in Rail Commute, *New York Times*, September 16, 2009, accessed June 29, 2012, http://www.nytimes.com/2009/09/16/world/asia/16ladies.html.

12. Jyoti Puri, *Woman, Body, Desire in Post-Colonial India: Narratives of Gender and Sexuality*. (New York: Routledge, 1999), 87.

13. Yardley, "Indian Women Find New Peace." Although women-only railway cars are attributed to contemporary demands, Gloria Steinem recounts riding

in them in the 1960s; she considered them a legacy of British colonialism. Gloria Steinem, *My Life on the Road* (New York: Random House, 2015).

14. S. Umachandran, "All-Women Taxis Roll Out in Chennai," *Times of India*, September 11, 2009, accessed July 1, 2012, http://articles.timesofindia.indiatimes.com/2009–09–11/chennai/28111834_1_women-drivers-cabs-taxi-service.

15. A. D'Mello, "Women Taxi Drivers Give Mumbai the Thumbs-Up." *Times of India*, May 28, 2009, accessed July 1, 2012, http://articles.timesofindia.indiatimes.com/2009–05–28/mumbai/28189927_1_women-taxi-drivers-priyadarshini-taxi-service-revathi-roy.

16. "Pink Taxis Worldwide," *Radio Netherlands Worldwide*, August 31, 2010, accessed July 3, 2012, http://www.rnw.nl/english/article/women-only-taxis-introduced-mexico-city.

17. D. Duncan, "Girl Taxi' Service Offers Haven to Beirut's Women," *Wall Street Journal*, July 25, 2009, accessed July 1, 2012, http://online.wsj.com/article/SB124847696096780319.html.

18. "Amani Ya Juu History," accessed July 23, 2014, http://www.amaniafrica.org/history.

19. "What's New at Amani!" accessed July 23, 2014, http://amaniyajuunews.wordpress.com/tag/amani-uganda/. There are also Amani centers in Chattanooga, Tennessee, and Washington, DC.

20. Faranjis Najibullah, "Iran: Tehran Opens Controversial Women-Only Park," Radio Free Europe, February 17, 2008, accessed May 24, 2012, http://www.wluml.org/node/4652. In 2012 there were plans for women-only restaurants and sex-segregated telephone booths. "Tehran to Open Women-Only Restaurants," *Tehran Times*, May 20, 2012, accessed May 24, 2012, http://www.tehrantimes.com/component/content/article/98027; National Council of Resistance of Iran, "New Plan to Gender Segregate Telephone Booths," February 19, 2008, accessed May 24, 2012; S. Davis, "Kabul Women-Only Park Reopens Thanks to USAID," *USA Today*, January 3, 2011, accessed May 24, 2012, http://www.usatoday.com/news/world/afghanistan/2011–01–02-kabul-womens-park_N.htm.

21. L. Nasseri, "Miniskirts, Headscarves Don't Mix at New Tehran Park," *Bloomberg News*, November 12, 2008, accessed May 24, 2012, http://www.bloomberg.com/apps/news?pid=newsarchive&sid=aqMF7_gsnjMI&refer=home. Women-only parks are also in Isfahan, Mashad, and Shiraz.

22. Nasseri, "Miniskirts, Headscarves."

23. "Headscarves Off in Tehran's First Female-Only Park," *Agence France-Presse* (*AFP*), June 17, 2008, accessed May 24, 2012, http://afp.google.com/article/ALeqM5i3ULRnBikyjztV35v-2JF3ncgdaQ.

24. Najibullah, "Iran: Tehran Opens Controversial Women-Only Park."

25. Charlotte Perkins Gilman, *Herland*, with an introduction by Ann J. Lane (New York: Pantheon Books, 1979), 18–19. See also Frances Bartowski, *Feminist Utopias* (Lincoln: University of Nebraska Press, 1989).

26. Georgina Hickey, "Barred from the Barroom: Second Wave Feminists and Public Accommodations in U.S. Cities" *Feminist Studies* 34, no. 3 (Fall 2008), 382; as of this writing, twenty-five golf clubs exclude women, including the prestigious Augusta National Golf Course in Georgia. See Peggy Kusinski and Katy Smyser,

"Four Chicago-Area Golf Courses Ban Women," accessed June 28, 2014, http://www.nbcchicago.com/investigations/men-only-golf-clubs-chicago-162984136.html.

27. Katherine Peter and Laura Horn, "Gender Differences in Participation and Completion of Undergraduate Education and How They Have Changed Over Time," National Center for Education Statistics, accessed July 17, 2015, http://nces.ed.gov/das/epubs/2005169/.

28. Bernice Resnick Sandler, "Title IX: How We Got It and What a Difference It Made," *Cleveland State Law Review* 55 (2007): 473–89.

29. Lisa N. Sacco, "The Violence Against Women Act: Overview, Legislation, and Federal Funding," Congressional Research Service (May 26, 2015), accessed July 17, 2015, http://www.crs.gov. The VAWA was reauthorized in 2013.

30. Nancy Folbre and Julie A. Nelson, "For Love or Money—or Both?" *Journal of Economic Perspectives* 14, no. 4 (Fall 2000): 123–40.

31. Pierrette Hondagneu-Sotelo, "The International Division of Caring and Cleaning Work," in *Care Work: Gender, Labor, and the Welfare State*, ed. Madonna Harrington Meyer (New York: Routledge, 2000), 149–62; Barbara Ehrenreich and Arlie Russell Hochschild, *Global Woman: Nannies, Maids, and Sex Workers in the New Economy* (New York: Henry Holt, 2002); Cameron Lynne MacDonald and Carmen Sirianni, eds., *Working in the Service Society* (Philadelphia: Temple University Press, 1996).

32. Joya Misra, "Caring *about* Care," *Feminist Studies* 29, no. 2 (Summer 2003): 387–401.

33. Mary Daly and Katherine Rake, *Gender and the Welfare State: Care, Work, and Welfare in Europe and the USA* (London: Polity Press, 2003), 149. More than two decades of neoliberal policies at the federal and local levels have reduced funding for caregiving services, placing the burden on families—i.e., women. See Lisa Duggan, *The Twilight of Equality? Neoliberalism, Cultural Politics, and the Attack on Democracy* (Boston: Beacon Press, 2003).

34. Dolores Hayden, *Redesigning the American Dream: The Future of Housing, Work, and Family Life*, (New York: W. W. Norton, 1984), 3–6; Howard Dratch, "The Politics of Child Care in the 1940s," *Science and Society* 38 (Summer 1974): 167–204.

35. D'Vera Cohn, Gretchen Livingston, and Wendy Wang, "After Decades of Decline, a Rise in Stay-at-Home Mothers," accessed July 1, 2014, http://www.pewsocialtrends.org/2014/04/08/after-decades-of-decline-a-rise-in-stay-at-home-mothers/.

36. Marcia Angell, "The Women at the Top," *New York Review of Books* 61, no. 5 (March 20, 2014): 18, 20–21.

37. David Cotter, Joan M. Hermsen, and Reeve Vanneman, "The End of the Gender Revolution? Gender Role Attitudes from 1977 to 2008," *American Journal of Sociology* 117, no. 1 (July 2011): 259–89.

38. Robert Barnes, "Court Strikes Mandate on Contraceptives," *Washington Post*, June 30, 2014, accessed July 1, 2014, http://www.washingtonpost.com/national/supreme-court-sides-with-employers-over-birth-control-mandate/2014/06/30/852e5c84-fc61–11e3-b1f4–8e77c632c07b_story.html.

39. Ruth Marcus, "Judging from Experience: It's No Coincidence That the Women Dissented," *Washington Post*, July 2, 2014.

40. Jess Bidgood and John Schwartz, "After Buffer Zone Ruling, Abortion Rivals Prepare to Square Off Anew," *New York Times*, June 27, 2014, accessed July 1, 2014, http://www.nytimes.com/2014/06/28/us/supreme-court-abortion-clinic-massachusetts-buffer-zone-ruling.html?_r=0.

41. George Will, "Colleges Become the Victims of Progressivism," *Washington Post*, June 6, 2014, accessed July 22, 2014, http://www.washingtonpost.com/opinions/george-will-college-become-the-victims-of-progressivism/2014/06/06/e90e73b4-eb50–11e3–9f5c-9075d5508f0a_story.html.

42. Nick Anderson and Scott Clement, "1 in 5 Women Say They Were Violated: Survey's Results Probably Understate Scope of Crisis," *The Washington Post*, June 14, 2015, A1, 10.

43. Rick Bower, "Mormon Church Excommunicates Women's Group Founder," *Washington Post*, June 22, 2014, accessed July 20, 2014, http://www.washingtonpost.com/national/mormon-woman-facing-excommunication-holds-vigil/2014/06/22/04c13560-fa6a-11e3-b836-a372189b76a6_story.html.

44. Shelby Sebens, "Oregon Opts to Dramatically Expand Women's Birth Control Access," *Reuters*, July 7, 2015, accessed July 8, 2015, http://mobile.reuters.com; Barbara Feder Ostrov, "California, Oregon to Allow Hormonal Contraceptives Without a Doctor's Prescription," *Washington Post*, July 15, 2015.

45. Editorial Board, "An Abortion Rights Win in Virginia," *Washington Post*, May 5, 2015.

46. Quoted in Connie Schultz, "Abortion as a Mother's Practical, Moral Decision," *Washington Post*, November 23, 2014.

47. Wendy Davis, *Forgetting to be Afraid: A Memoir* (New York: Blue Rider Press, 2014).

48. Quoted in Jill Filipovic, "Reclaiming Abortion," *Washington Post*, June 14, 2015.

49. Jessica Valenti, "SlutWalks and the Future of Feminism," *Washington Post*, June 3, 2011.

50. Rebecca Walker, "Becoming the Third Wave," *Ms.* 39 (January–February 1992): 39–41. Walker is the Yale-educated daughter of Alice Walker and goddaughter of Gloria Steinem. See R. Claire Snyder, "What Is Third-Wave Feminism? A New Directions Essay," *Signs: Journal of Women in Culture and Society* 34 (Autumn 2008): 181.

51. In *The Morning After: Sex, Fear, and Feminism on Campus* (Boston: Little, Brown, 1993), Roiphe challenged women's claims of date rape on campus, arguing that the sex was often consensual. Paglia's *Sexual Personae: Art and Decadence from Nefertiti to Emily Dickinson* (New Haven: Yale University Press, 1990) was a best-seller but considered neoconservative by many feminists. See Molly Ivins, "I Am the Cosmos," *Mother Jones*, September/October 1991, 8–10.

52. Rebecca Walker, "Being Real: An Introduction" in *To Be Real: Telling the Truth and Changing the Face of Feminism* (New York: Anchor, 1995).

53. Tamara Straus, "A Manifesto for Third Wave Feminism," *AlterNet*, October 24, 2000, accessed July 20, 2014, http://www.alternet.org/story/9986/a_manifesto_for_third_wave_feminism.

54. See also Leslie Heywood and Jennifer Drake, eds., *Third Wave Agenda: Being Feminist, Doing Feminism* (Minneapolis: University of Minnesota Press, 1997); Jennifer

Baumgardner and Amy Richards, *Manifesta: Young Women, Feminism, and the Future* (New York: Farrar, Straus and Giroux, 2000); and Stacy Gillis, Gillian Howie, and Rebecca Munford, eds., *Third Wave Feminism: A Critical Exploration* (New York: Palgrave, 2007).

55. Riot Grrrl was an underground feminist movement of the early 1990s, closely tied to punk music and radical activist politics. Riot grrrls self-published magazines called "grrrl zines" to reach their audience.

56. Snyder, "What Is Third-Wave Feminism?" 177.

57. Nick Anderson, "Student Activist Turned her Pain into a Movement," *Washington Post*, June 17, 2015.

58. Ibid.

59. Anjali Enjeti, "The Last 13 Feminist Bookstores in the U.S. and Canada," *Paste*, May 9, 2014, http://www.pastemagazine.com/blogs/lists/2014/05/the-last-13-feminist-bookstores-in-the-us-and-canada.html.

60. "The American Gay Rights Movement: A Timeline," *Infoplease*, n.d., http://www.infoplease.com/ipa/A0761909.html.

61. Eun Kyung Kim, "Is Feminism Still Relevant? Some Women Posting Why They Don't Need It," TODAY.com, July 30, 2014, http://www.today.com/news/feminism-still-relevant-some-women-saying-they-dont-need-it-1D79996867. See also http://womenagainstfeminism.tumblr.com/.

62. Nina Burleigh, "Women against Womyn: First Wave, Second Wave, Third Wave, and Now Three Steps Back," *New York Observer* 28 (August 4, 2014): 4–5.

63. Monica Hesse, "Men's Rights Activists Gathering to Discuss all the Ways Society has Done Them Wrong," *Washington Post*, June 30, 2014, http://www.washingtonpost.com/lifestyle/style/mens-rights-activists-gathering-to-discuss-all-the-ways-society-has-done-them-wrong/2014/06/30/a9310d96-005f-11e4-8fd0-3a663dfa68ac_story.html.

64. "Get the Facts," National Museum of Women in the Arts, accessed July 15, 2012, http://www.nmwa.org/advocate/get-facts.

65. "Our History," National Museum of Women in the Arts, accessed July 15, 2012, http://www.nmwa.org/about/our-history. For the museum's twentieth anniversary, a group of "feminist masked avengers" calling themselves the Guerilla Girls created a special tabloid-style poster. The huge banner headline read "HORROR ON THE NATIONAL MALL! Thousands of women locked in the basements of D.C. museums. Why does macho art world keep female artists out of sight?" Guerilla Girls, accessed July 15, 2012, http://www.guerrillagirls.com/index.shtml. None of the founders of Guerilla Girls was active in the Woman's Building, although one displayed her work in an exhibition there in its later years. "Kathe Kollwitz," e-mail message to author, July 17, 2012.

Index

Page numbers in italics refer to figures.

www.ingramcontent.com/pod-product-compliance
Ingram Content Group UK Ltd.
Pitfield, Milton Keynes, MK11 3LW, UK
UKHW041832260225
455625UK00006B/71